STATE AND RELIGION IN THE SUDAN

STATE AND RELIGION IN THE SUDAN
Sudanese Thinkers

Mahgoub El-Tigani Mahmoud

African Studies
Volume 71

The Edwin Mellen Press
Lewiston•Queenston•Lampeter

Library of Congress Cataloging-in-Publication Data

Mahmoud, Mahgoub El-Tigani.
    State and religion in the Sudan : Sudanese thinkers / Mahgoub El-Tigani Mahmoud.
       p. cm. -- (African studies ; v. 71)
    Includes bibliographical references (p.) and index.
    ISBN 0-7734-6748-3 (hc.)
    1. Sudan--Politics and government--1985- 2. Islam and politics--Sudan. 3. Religion and
state--Sudan. I. Title. II. African studies (Lewiston, N.Y.) ; v. 71.

DT157.66.M34 2003
322'.1'09624--dc21

                                                          2003044538

This is volume 71 in the continuing series
African Studies
Volume 71 ISBN 0-7734-6748-3
AS Series ISBN 0-88946-175-9

A CIP catalog record for this book is available from the British Library

The Edwin Mellen Press
Box 450
Lewiston, New York
USA 14092-0450

The Edwin Mellen Press
Box 67
Queenston, Ontario
CANADA L0S 1L0

The Edwin Mellen Press, Ltd.
Lampeter, Ceredigion, Wales
UNITED KINGDOM SA48 8LT

Printed in the United States of America

DEDICATION

To Kareem

TABLE OF CONTENTS

FOREWORD

Carolyn Fluehr-Lobban

Professor of Anthropology, Rhode Island College (Providence)

INTRODUCTION

It is my pleasure to introduce to an English speaking audience this work by one of Sudan's new generation of scholars. Mahgoub el-Tigani is one who has been steeled by the events in the country, especially since 1985, and he is one who is critical of the old paradigms and the old order. Indeed, this work was originally written underground in Khartoum in 1989 after the Omer al-Bashir coup d'etat that brought the National Islamic Front to power, and this work was denied publication by the University of Khartoum Press that had already become fearful of reprisals from the new regime before its first year of rule was completed. The manuscript was later smuggled out of Sudan to Cairo when the author had to seek political refuge from the NIF regime in 1990.

Mahgoub el-Tigani may hesitate to see himself as part of this new generation of scholars, since his scholarly-activist time in the Sudan dates back to the Nimeiri years, but the dedication of his book "to the Sudanese, free and independent thinker" reveals the essential quality of his text that is meant to stimulate and provoke thought among Sudanese and Sudanists, especially those concerned with Islam, Islamism, and Sudanese identity. The great advantage of translation of scholarly works from Arabic to English is the opening to the West of indigenous thought and especially sources, which are not available or known outside of the region. This is a trend which I fervently hope will continue, for there is much original thought occurring in the Sudan and in other African countries where the language of discourse may not be English.

HISTORICAL BACKGROUND TO INDIGENOUS
SUDANESE THOUGHT

El-Tigani begins with the early separation of religion and the state during the Funj in the 16th century, which establishes an original model relationship between the two that is "natural" for the Sudan. Religion here is witnessed in the form of the religious brotherhoods, the *turuq*, and the early religious sheikhs who displayed an original thought over matters of religion and society, such as the discussion recorded in <u>Tabaqat Wad Daif Allah</u> over the use of "*tunbak*", Sudanese tobacco. El-Tigani reflects his own Sudanese roots with the deep respect, which he holds for the learned sheikhs of the popular Sufi *tariqa*.

This relatively freer style ended with the advent of Turco-Egyptian rule, which had the effect of alienating people from the official religion of the state. Into this context was born Muhammad Ahmad al-Mahdi, also rooted in the Sufi "path of disciples" whose successful religious-political revolution ousted imperialist rule from 1884 until the British reconquest in 1898. With the birth of the Mahdist state certain tensions developed between the `ulama who rejected Mahdism and the religious *turuq* who were weakened temporarily by the strength of the Mahdist state. The Mahdist state, contrary to a popular belief in its conservative, static nature, was actually innovative of necessity due to the challenges of the time and the multicultural new Sudanese population it served.

As an early form of the state and Sudanese nationalism, the Mahdist state was not without its weaknesses, especially in regard to the consideration of non-

Muslims, but this can be explained, according to el-Tigani, because the Islamic movement became directed against both foreign colonialism and Egyptian Muslim thought, rather than directing its energies toward the process of internal nation building. In this light el-Tigani recalls the contributions of Mohammed 'Abdu and Ahmed Lutfi al-Sayed, including also liberal humanists like Taha Hussein.

MUSLIM REVIVALISM IN SUDAN

El-Tigani begins with a consideration of the writings of Hassan al-Turabi (Tagdid Usul al-fiqh al-Islami), whom he sees as having a vision of progress, but one that is restricted to a Muslim world view emphasizing renewal (*tagdid*) and the [renewed] call to Islam (*Da'wa*) with its new mission. Such renewal can take place with a reinvigorated study of Qur'an and Sunna together with the scientific advances of the day for a unified approach to religion in contemporary life. However, Turabi fails (as does much of "modern" Muslim thought) to offer a theoretical program for the modernization of Islamic jurisprudence, a new science of Islamic jurisprudence. One of the most serious problems is the barrier to the free expression of thought and ideas in most Muslim countries today, including the Sudan. Most reformist Sudanese Muslim thinkers are in exile, like Mahgoub el-Tigani himself. Indeed, he sees self-styled "innovators", such as Turabi, actually as traditionalists who reflect the bewilderment of their elite class and speak, in a contradictory way of modernity while practicing traditionalism.

Interestingly, the next major thinker that el-Tigani discusses is the communist leader and theoretician, 'Abd al-Khaliq Mahgoub, who was executed by Nimeiri in 1971 for his alleged role in the successful three day coup against his May regime. It is not usual for Turabi and 'Abd al-Khaliq to be compared in this way, and this is certainly one of the strengths of el-Tigani's book. Of course, 'Abd al-Khaliq separated political life from religion, in the process of building a society free of exploitation from religious falsification. In such a society the right of the human mind to the free exercise of independent thought and rationality prevents the real "*Jahiliya*" (the time of ignorance in pre-Islamic Arabia) from returning.

Adding to the Sudanese contribution to Muslim thought el-Tigani considers the thinking of Sadiq al-Mahdi and Mahmoud Mohammed Taha. He differentiates the pragmatism of al-Mahdi with the uncompromising mission of Turabi to Islamize state and society. Sadig al-Mahdi has more of a populist approach with a consistent concern for popular participation of the masses in governance, while Turabi expresses little such concern. Al-Mahdi rejects the extremism of right wing groups and the secularism of left wing parties, making his approach closer to that of Turabi than that of 'Abd al-Khalig Mahgoub. Although al-Mahdi would not revise the *hadd* punishment of death for apostasy, he would like to find a way to ameliorate this penalty, but he is not specific in providing an alternative. International human rights standards respecting freedom of religious thought challenge this position. *Shura* [consultation], human experience and reason are the foremost premises for any Islamic model of rule, and al-Mahdi notes positive aspects of the world order, such as the United Nations.

By contrast, Turabi expresses some satisfaction with the lack of popular involvement of Sudanese Muslims writing in Tagdid (1980:40), "It is our good fortune in the Sudan that we are living in a weak country regarding inherited Islamic history and culture ... it is an advantage in some respect since there would be no vigorous resistance anticipated to stop the advancement of a renewed Islam." Likewise, he would have little consideration for international human rights standards since they have been conceived in a western, non-Islamic context, and may even be anti-Islamic in their application.

Moving to the complex thought of Mahmoud Mohammed Taha, Tigani explores its Marxian dialectical roots, displaying Taha's strong belief that Islam excludes from its web of existence no system of thought. Indeed the evaluation of Marxism by Taha is mixed, but he acknowledges the role that material interests play in human existence. The Marxian dialectic permits Taha to develop an evolutionary view of Islam in his well-known view of the change in Islamic teachings and practice based upon the separate revelations at Mecca and Medina. Throughout, Taha remained committed to a socialist model of societal development, although he was openly critical of the socialist states of China and the former Soviet Union. Contrary to the socialist experience Taha placed a high premium on individualism and free thinking. In this he emphasizes both individual freedom and social justice based upon: 1) economic equality - i.e., socialism, 2) political equality - i.e. parliamentary democracy that develops into direct democracy, and 3) Social equality - especially full equality between women and men. El-Tigani makes it appear as though the Republican Brotherhood [and Sisterhood] developed without Taha's intervention or assistance, although it is true that the Republican movement eschewed direct political involvement, and it is true that they actively agitated with the Sudanese masses. By contrast, 'Abd al-Khalig disputed the value of the democracy of parliaments which are made up of elite class members with narrowly based class rather than national interests.

Taha's "Second Message of Islam" is indeed the most sensitive part of his thought, but it is his effort to reconcile the traditional Shari`a with the needs of the present age. The redeeming mission of Islam begins with the Second Message that completed the Prophecy of Muhammad, a more advanced stage of Islam having its own practice, prayers and interpretations. However, the emphasis of Taha's thought on "the knowledgeable individual and his own [personal] vision" (p.102) is for el-Tigani an unauthorized superimposition of a Prophetic privilege, a special miracle upon the ordinary Muslim.

Beyond this fundamental critique, el-Tigani sees a strong comparison between the thinking of Taha and that of Sayed Qutb who sees the current period of the 20th century, with its entire decline, as a second time of "*Jahiliya*" (ignorance). One of the best things about el-Tigani's analysis here is that he often surprises the reader with his comparisons; in this case he treats Sadiq al-Mahdi, Hassan al-Turabi and 'Abd al-Khaliq Mahgoub together in the same group as not accepting this sharp condemnation of the 20th century. All see material progress, and the development of the rational sciences as the antithesis of ignorance. Ironically, it was a type of "*jahiliya*", or ignorance, that was implemented in the executions of two of these important thinkers, Mahmoud Taha and 'Abd al-Khaliq Mahgoub, by the Nimeiri military regime.

And el-Tigani sees each of these thinkers in his own right as a Muslim revivalist; this is not the usual thinking in the West about Islamic theoreticians, and may well suggest that indigenous conceptions of ideological orientation may be quite different from those developed in the West. In this regard, Sadig al-Mahdi and Hasan al-Turabi may be regarded in the West as "revivalists", while 'Abd al-Khaliq Mahgoub would be simply dismissed as a communist, and Mahmoud Mohammed Taha as a "reformer" or, in light of a recent work by one of his disciples, 'Abdullahi An-Na'im, as one advocating an Islamic Reformation. By treating these indigenous Sudanese thinkers together, el-Tigani has offered a fresh perspective that may help, in a practical way, to find the common ground among the "modernist" Muslims in the Sudan.

THE CONSTITUTIONAL DEBATE

The constitutional debate is central to the future of the Sudan after the necessary and inevitable end of the civil war, which has been waged between non-Muslims and Muslims chronically since 1955, and most recently since 1983. Although the struggle is most fundamentally about political and economic equity, the just representation of all Sudanese in constitutional theory and in practice is at the crux of the hostilities and deep mistrust that exist between Southerner and Northerner, between non-Muslim and Muslim. Of critical concern is the status of non-Muslims in an Islamic state and their constitutional protection in a predominantly Muslim country where Islam has been perceived historically as playing a hegemonic and coercive role in religious-state affairs.

Sadiq al-Mahdi mentions that according to the "modern system of Islam," there can be no denial of political, economic or social rights that create citizens of a lower grade. He further states that it is the right of Sudanese non-Muslims to oppose any Islamic orientation that raises the banner of "*jihad*" against them.

The issue of Shari`a is central to the debate; for al-Mahdi making Shari`a the state law in force in the Sudan is inappropriate. Rather Shari`a rule should be incorporated into state legislation. This method seeks the persuasion of the Sudanese people to freely adopt his Shari`a program by the process of fair national elections.

Turabi, on the other hand, rejects the secular, western state model inherent in al-Mahdi's thinking because it is a product of western colonialism favoring instead an Islamic constitution and an Islamic state. El-Tigani shows how Turabi and the Muslim Brotherhood/NIF coopted the Islamist movement making themselves the sole voice for an Islamic model of government with all of the others being branded as "secularists." When the time came for the NIF to make its political move by seizing state power in 1989, they had already prepared the way ideologically for their monopoly. When the Islamist "transformation" of government was put into place, el-Tigani shows, it was not done through Shari`a and its `ulama (legal scholars) but through temporary presidential decrees, even though the People's Assembly was available to provide at least the veneer of a democratic method of Islamization. Clearly, there was not constitutional basis for this Islamization.

For Mahmoud Taha the issue of Shari`a is resolved by a distinction between the classical Shari`a of the First Message of Islam and the new Shari`a of the Second Message. In the Second Message, emphasizing the Meddinan texts, there exist solutions to the modern constitutional issues of the rights of women and of non-Muslims in an Islamic state. Therefore, all verses in the Meccan texts that stipulate male guardianship over women are abrogated by the later verse, "And women shall have rights similar to the rights against them, according to what is equitable; but men have an advantage over them" (Sura II:228), and "Remind, you are only a reminder. You are not mastering them" (Sura II:69-70). When Taha strongly rebuked the state's 1983 Islamization move with the September laws and the renewal of war against the South, the Nimeiri regime moved against him, exercising pressure on the state-appointed judicial officials to have him declared an apostate, and finally executing him "extra-judicially" in January 1985 (p.106).

'Abd al-Khaliq Mahgoub was never anti-Islamic in his writing or speaking, although as a communist he was widely accused of being anti-religious. On the contrary, according to el-Tigani, he saw Islam as promoting reason and contemplation so that Muslims may conceive of and seek the good life. Further,

Islam encourages *ijtihad*, or freedom of interpretation, to establish the good life. However, quite distinctly from other Sudanese thinkers who employ an Islamic framework, 'Abd al-Khaliq does not see Islam as canceling out disparities of class and social position, despite its egalitarian admonitions. The real conflict is not about religion, of course, but between revolutionary and anti-revolutionary forces, embedded in class realities.

INTELLECTUALS AND WOMEN

Thanks to Mahgoub el-Tigani, Sudanese women are considered seriously for the first time in a major translated work as having a role in political-religious philosophy, not simply as activists in campaigns for social equality. He begins this serious treatment of women with the Sudan's preeminent women's leader, its first woman parliamentarian, Fatima Ahmed Ibrahim. For those who may not be familiar with Fatima Ibrahim, briefly, she was a founder of the Sudanese Women's Union in the late 1940's that was a significant part of the nationalist movement; she was the driving force behind <u>Sawt al-Mara</u> (Voice of Women), the most significant theoretical and practical journal of the women's movement in the 1950's and 1960's; she was the first woman elected to Parliament during the first period of Sudanese democracy in 1965; she fought alongside her trade union leader husband, Shafie Ahmed al-Sheikh, in the broad democratic movement; and she, along with other Sudanese democrats, men and increasing numbers of women, has had to seek political refuge outside of Sudan after 1989. Like 'Abd al-Khaliq Mahgoub, Fatima is a socialist thinker, who sees the need for a national democratic revolution in order to emancipate women. Women are likewise held back by old customs, superstitions, and sectarianism, which they, unfortunately, absorb from their families and the influence of men over them.

All of the other thinkers considered by el-Tigani might be classified as liberal on the question of women's rights rather than revolutionary, like Fatima Ibrahim. What is significant here is that a strong conservative tradition, such as that prevailing among some sheikhs at Cairo's Al-Azhar Islamic University, which might seek to have women withdraw from public life altogether, is not to be found among Sudan's intellectuals.

Sadiq al-Mahdi explains that the Islamic Call is built on the basis of equity between males and females, however, as el-Tigani queries, would Sadiq accept women as state officials and leaders? And would he accede if a feminist consensus (*ijma`*) were to supersede the prior patriarchal interpretations? These are very good questions, indeed, that el-Tigani raises.

Other theoreticians, such as female scholar Zakiya Ahmed Satti, support the rights of women protected by Islam, such as security in marriage, but she also does not address the sensitive questions of the day, such as the right of women to work, to hold political and judicial office, and to hold power within the high echelons of the state, including head of state.

The donning of the veil, which has elicited so much attention in the East and West as a symbol of religious revival, is given some attention by Sudanese Muslim modernists. While modesty is enjoined, the prescriptive use of full head and body covering is a matter of individual choice. Likewise, the instructive example of the Prophet's wives is viewed by 'Abd al-Halim Abu Shiqqa as a private attitude; indeed the wives of the Prophet's Companions conducted public lives without complexity or sensitivity. Nothing restricted the movement of women in society or their meetings with men, however Abu Shiqqa ends with a more traditional view of women as having their primary role within marriage and the family. This is markedly different from the views of Fatima Ibrahim.

Haja Kashif Badri and others have documented the history of the highly successful Sudanese women's movement, especially through the activities of the Women's Union, which was opposed by the Muslim Brotherhood, members of the al-Mahdi family and Imams of the many local mosques. What is significant is that the struggle to improve women's rights has not focused on the modernizing of the Shari`a, perhaps as el-Tigani suggests, because organizational matters and disputes preoccupied the Women's Union. It is my understanding from my research on the Shari`a that certain aspects of Islamic law were modified due to pressure from the Women's Union, especially in the family law matters of female consent in marriage and a liberalized rights to judicial divorce for women. It is an unquestioned fact of post-independence Sudanese history that the Women's Union was an important part of the popular democratic forces in the 1950's through the late 1960's. Mahgoub el-Tigani pays great respect to this movement, its many leaders, its intellectual and political debates, as well as rivalries that are too often overlooked in the usual treatments of Sudanese history. He does note that the movement remained based primarily in the north without much orientation or success in the rural Sudan or in the South. He also admonishes Sudanese men to adopt a less conservative, less monopolistic attitude towards women in public and familial affairs, thus allowing women to pursue their own political agenda, which has a proven track record in Sudan independent of male intervention.

DEMOCRATIC LIBERALISM INEVITABLE

The liberal trend is obvious, as well as inevitable, in el-Tigani's view. Even the neo-conservatives, such as Turabi, and those representing the older paradigms, such as Sadig al-Mahdi, demonstrate a certain liberal attitude towards such issues as engagement with modern ideas and technology, the greater involvement rather than isolation of women, and the need for some new "*ijtihad*," some fresh interpretations for modern conditions.

As a faithful Sudanese Muslim Mahgoub el-Tigani pays great respect also to the powerful and significant Sufi traditions that permeate Sudanese Islamic expression. Five centuries of Sufi presence, from the earliest days of the introduction of Islam to the present continued popularity of the Sufi Brotherhoods, have imprinted a mystical, transcendent character to Sudanese Islam, one that has little to do with official interpretations, or the seizing of state power. Indeed, the mystical orders have eschewed such worldly entanglements. This has infused the Sudanese Muslim character with a romantic, emotional, non-materialistic and unscientific view of life. They have not been popular with official Islam, which tolerates their presence but has not moved against them due to their indigenous and popular character. I recall being discouraged by one of the Shari`a High Court judges whom I knew about the "dangers" of attending a popular Sufi "*dhikr*" outside of Omdurman. "*Ghayr Islam*," he said, "this is not Islam," because of their singing and dancing in remembrance of God. Despite many attempts to suppress the Sufi orders, from the time of the Mahdi until the present moment, their influence and embeddedness in rural Sudanese Islam has remained unchanged. The deeply personal relationship with God together with the decentralized organization of the Sufi orders reflects a fundamental democratic and egalitarian attitude of the mass of Sudanese Muslims.

This natural historical attachment to egalitarian Islam together with a proud history of resistance to foreign invasion marks the best of the Sudanese character as demonstrating attributes of dignity and nobility. This analysis shows el-Tigani's love of his country and its people. I would like to add a personal note that it is this Sudanese Muslim whom I most admire and respect, however it is lamentable that the best values reinforced by Islam have not witnessed a more compassionate treatment of non-Muslim Sudanese, especially since the NIF seized power. That the civil war rages on four decades after its first shots were fired in 1955 is unforgivable and is not reflective of the liberal thought or egalitarian traditions many espouse, especially in the thought of 'Abd al-Khaliq Mahgoub and Mahmoud Mohammed Taha. This work begins a critical treatment of Muslim thought in the Sudan. Its range covers a great landscape, from the ideal of an egalitarian, tolerant Islam in the Sudan, to indigenous ideas about a reformed Islam, to the triumph of an extremist, politicized Islamic movement dominated by the NIF. It is a critical matter toward the creation of a new Sudanese politics to understand this religious-political spectrum among northern Muslim intellectuals. The critical review this work helps to begin is essential to the building of new Sudanese persona, along with the new paradigms of politics. This is where Islam and progressive Islamic thought can be used to help build a unified nation where all of Sudan's people, women and men; persons from all regions and all religions are first class citizens.

PREFACE

Anthony Blasi

Professor of Sociology, Tennessee State University (Nashville)

President, Sociology for Religion Association, USA

At the very moment my colleague Mahgoub El-Tigani Mahmoud told me that he was ready to bring forth his English translation of his book on the state and religion in the Sudan, I was pondering three bronze medallions. They were found in a box of mementos that had belonged to a family member born ninety years ago and whom I had been called upon to eulogize. In order to understand my relative's life, I was looking to the pre-World War I world from which she came. That world, borne in the consciousness, life ways, and enthusiasms of her Italian parents, was recapitulated in the medallions, which were objects favored by her father. One of them marked the first anniversary in 1901 of the burial of King Umberto. The second, bearing no date, commemorates the liberators of Rome. The third celebrates free thought. The movement for the creation of a united nation of Italy set up a secular state in the form of a constitutional monarchy modeled after that of Britain. The nascent national government sought to liberate itself from the past by taking Rome from the pope and making the city the new capital. That same government could only hope to unify the new nation by guaranteeing cultural freedom for the disparate regional groups who had overthrown foreign powers and feudal tradition. Despite the hopes enshrined in the three pieces of bronze, the story did not turn out happily. The king, a would-be imperialist conqueror, had been assassinated by an anarchist in 1900. The pope who lost Rome in 1870 resisted modernity for eight years more, as did another pope from 1903 to 1914. A Fascist reaction against Communism and disorder suppressed cultural freedom from 1922 to 1943. This sad sequence of events, well known to students of European history, has remarkable parallels with the history of Sudan, as well as some differences.

The first medallion, commemorating the slain king, raises the issue of the state as a governing authority. A constitutional monarch is a multivalent symbol, embracing both democratic and feudal orderings of sovereign legitimacy. Sudan too has competing claims to the right to govern. As our author points out, most serious intellectuals in modern Sudan favor democracy; all accept consensus as a foundation for the nation's modern politics. One thinker, Hassan al-Turabi, accepts consensus while rejecting parliamentarism as non-Islamic. All four thinkers studied by our author grapple with the problem of linking a present consensus with an Islamic heritage. The dialectic of continuity and change that inheres in history creates the multivalent nature of the symbols and procedures of sovereign rule. Even regimes that come into being through revolution adopt multivalent symbols; the American government, for example, surrounded itself with "federal architecture" early on, an eighteenth century imitation of ancient Greek styles that seeks to speak architecturally from timelessness. The first French revolutionary government failed to invoke tradition and found itself transformed into a pseudo-medieval empire under Napoleon Bonaparte. While the Sudanese intellectuals have settled upon consensus, usually under a democratic form, within an Islamic framework that respects religious and ethnic minorities, the exact formulation has not been settled upon. Multivalent symbols do not come easily. Meanwhile, a sad story of political violence unfolds.

XVI

The second medallion, commemorating the 1870 liberators of Rome, calls to mind the liberation of Khartoum fifteen years later by the Mahdi. The Mahdi was a spiritual leader as well as a nationalist one. The very prospect of a religious figure establishing a national government in a national capital raises the issue of respect for religious and ethnic minorities under the Sudanese regime. The Mahdi died within a year of his victory; the issue of religion and national unity remains unsettled in Sudan to this day. The liberation of Rome had consolidated a secular regime in Italy, leaving the problem of religion to be solved through negotiation about sixty years later. The liberation of Khartoum was too temporary, however; the Mahdi's successor waged a war of conquest against Egypt, only to lose the Sudan. Real negotiations have yet to begin, though there have been attempts.

The third medallion celebrates free thought; Giordano Bruno[1] is depicted standing behind a large open book, one page reading "libero" and the other "pensiero." Before the book, as if to invite the reader by providing light, stands the torch of freedom. Unlike the two commemorated events, free thought requires "cultural space," as it was, permanence. People express their free thoughts in time through the to-and-fro of discussion. Different people with different concerns come to appreciate one another's points of view where free speech and free publication thrive. Only in that kind of environment can the needs of the diverse parties of a complex society be satisfied. The kind of consensus meant by the intellectuals whom Mahgoub El-Tigani Mahmoud introduces, is a noisy and dynamic process that elicits assent as a contract elicits assent, but unlike a contract it is ever under a continuing negotiation. Such a consensus cannot come without pluralism and freedom; our author notes that respect for plurality and freedom is a genuine Islamic and Sudanese tradition.

[1] Giordano Bruno was burned at the stake in 1600 for his deviant ideas. While some of his ideas seem fanciful from today's perspective, the notion that set the authorities against him was that the earth traveled in an orbit around the sun.

As historians of culture know, Western European intellectual tradition emerged in the thirteenth century in a dialogue with the Arab world. The most influential Christian philosopher of the era, Thomas Aquinas, adopted a concept of *tradition* that is very close to the Islamic idea of consensus that is so important for contemporary Sudan. Aquinas held that creation reflected the mind of the Creator, and that humans were endowed by the Creator with powers of observation and with intellect so that they could grasp onto if not entirely comprehend truths that emanate from the divine mind. Because the created reality was so variable and vast and ever in flux, a legislative act could never be articulated in a way that would be suited to every day and age. But in tradition thousands upon thousands of intellects ponder what their owners have observed and arrive at practical conclusions. Indeed, tradition becomes the best interpreter of the law and can even repeal a law.

Magoub El-Tigani Mahmoud presents us with four Sudanese intellectuals grappling with the workings and problems of tradition. Thus Hassan al-Turabi holds that Islamic consensus needs to be freed from classical Islamic jurisprudential tradition in order to meet the requirements of contemporary times; however, he insists that the consensus must be an Islamic one. Mahmoud Mohamed Taha stresses Islam's original principles and sees the need for a second communication, or second message, of Islam. Sadiq al-Mahdi holds that the earliest Islamic thought was the most enlightened and that a proper interpretation of it would satisfy contemporary requirements. 'Abd al-Khaliq Mahgoub finds religion operative as a motive in people's lives, not a substantive content to be enacted as law. These thinkers confront us with important questions. Can Islam, or for that matter any religion, retain its identity and coherence as the process of tradition or consensus goes on? Should a religion be articulated in the language of general principles and be re-communicated in an updated form? Can an original religious inspiration adapt through interpretation? Should a religion be principally an inspiration? Arguments over such questions appear throughout the contemporary world, not only in Islamic discourse. Observing how the four thinkers described in this book address these questions can be instructive for Moslem and non-Moslem alike.

Underlying the entire presentation one senses the author's anxiety. He is clearly distressed by the prospect of a disintegrated homeland. The standpoints of the leading national intellectuals betray more fractiousness than consensus. Can that intellectual life contain so much conflict and absorb so much disagreement? Can it promote a respectful ethos for living together on the basis of human rights? Or is Sudan falling headlong into catastrophe, cut off from the wise use of science, fighting its way into permanent national poverty? Our author points to the failure of the present government to allow for, much less promote, a peaceful dialogue among the differing schools of thought. Mahmoud Mohamed Taha was assassinated after a mock trial. Hassan al-Turabi was detained until he agreed to collaborate with the regime. Sadiq al-Mahdi had to live in exile, was once condemned to death *in absentia*, and has been imprisoned and tortured several times. 'Abd al-Khaliq Mahgoub was imprisoned, exiled, imprisoned again, and assassinated after a mock trial. "God be with you, oh people of Sudan!" our author exclaims. "It is only with parliamentary democracies that the people of Sudan manage to resolve ideological and political conflicts."

ACKNOWLEDGMENTS

Many friends have encouraged me to write about Sudanese thinkers. The acknowledgments of the Arabic version of this book (Cairo, 1995) are due Dr. Ali Osman Salih and Mr. al-Bashir Sahal Juma' of the National Committee for the Commemoration of the Sudanese writer Dr. Jamal Mohamed Ahmed. To Mr. al-Daw Suliman I owe a tremendous appreciation for the great risk he has willingly taken to smuggle the Arabic manuscript outside the Sudan that has been suffering confiscation of thought since the 30th of June, 1989, under a notorious banning of the freedom of expression and publication up to this day.

Special thanks and regards are extended to Ustadh Hilmi Sha'rawi, Director of the Arab Research Center who sincerely encouraged the publication of this work. To Ustadh Amir Salim, the LRLC Director, Dr. Marlyn Tadros, Dr. 'Ala Ghanam, Mr. Mohamed Ramadan, and all members of the Legal Research and Resource Center (LRRC), the enlightening human rights institution at the beautiful city of Cairo which published the Arabic book, I express my great appreciation.

In this English edition, I wish to acknowledge with immense gratitude the continuous encouragement of my friends in the United States, Professor Richard Lobban, Jr., Professor Levi Jones, and Mr. Dave Peterson to translate the Arabic version of Sudanese Thinkers. I am grateful to Mr. Ralph Cook who has generously provided me with a computer typewriter when, in May 1996, I came as a political refugee to Nashville, the Music City of the United States.

XX

Special thanks and regards are due Professor Carolyn Fluehr-Lobban, the distinguished American scholar of Sudanic studies who made a thorough reading followed by thoughtful remarks on the manuscript. I am honored to have her foreword placed on the front part of this work. I wish to acknowledge further the preface by Professor Anthony Blasi that portrayed a sociological dimension of the Sudanese thought in the light of a comparative profile of the Italian experience.

In addition to the critical reading of Professor Fluehr-Lobban and the Commentary Preface by Professor Blasi, the English manuscript has been rigorously read by the Africana Studies Professor Mayibuye Monanabela to whom I express my heartfelt appreciation. I am greatly indebted to Professor Johnanna Grimes at the Tennessee State University's Writing Center for her careful revision and exacting of the English text that advanced the presentation of the *Mufaakiroun Sudaniyoun* to the English reader. The full responsibility of the text, however, remains my sole responsibility.

In the Arabic version, I have dedicated my love to my wife Zeinab, the mother of Rasha and Angie as they hold together with determination to support the right of free expression for the People of Sudan. My small family, including our late mothers Fatima and Aisha, has always contributed with unrelenting support to allow the completion of this translation. It is for the free Sudanese thinkers and the independent Sudanese women, as it is for my family and my grandson Kareem, the son of Nasir who has kindly helped formatting the transcript for publication, that I dedicate this work.

M.E.M.
TSU, Nashville
January 2003

INTRODUCTION

SUDANESE DIVERSITY OF CULTURES AND THOUGHT

The Sudan is a country gifted with a great diversity of cultures and social structures. This diversity involves a complicated mixture of population groups. Many ethnic groups exercise different languages, customs, and living styles. They coexist in a vast country with an overwhelming rural structure; even the small urban sector of the country is largely rural.

The Sudanese ethnic origins have been known since ancient history. Comprised of tribal groups, they included the Nubians, Beja, Arabs, and Nilotics in addition to the other African sections of the population. A multiplicity of languages and dialects expressive of this multiethnic affiliation prevails in the daily life of people. Every single person carries a multiplicity of social relations based on these identifications. Kinship relations influence an individual's precepts as individuals relate to ethnicity and blood ties. One way or another, all Sudanese people are actually related to each other.

Unresolved Conflicts
Despite the general existence of this multiethnic behavior in the workaday life, power relations always manipulated the Sudanese social and ethnic domains. Many political alliances have proliferated around the domains of ethnicity and culture since old times up to the modern history of the country. Two main

antagonistic approaches came into play. At one extreme, Sudan is viewed as a society whose social and cultural fabric is greatly interwoven into a large ethnic and linguistic majority of the population, irrespective of the diversity and multiplicity of the country's cultures and social structures. The other extreme views the diversity of Sudanese society as a potential for a great unity that should be established on the basis of liberal policies and pluralist practices. Both approaches touch heavily upon the nation state, constitutional law, administration, and political organization with due consideration to regional and international relations.

Francis Deng (1987:69) describes succinctly the cultural diversity of Sudan in these words: ""There is no doubt that the people of the Sudan are inherently religious and God-fearing, and have a profound sense of right and wrong that goes far deeper than the outward manifestation of formal doctrine. This applies alike to Muslims, Christians, and the so-called animists. In the face of religious diversities ad potentials for conflict, the Founding Fathers of the post-colonial Sudan wisely choose to accept the principles of mutual respect, tolerance, and understanding represented by the slogan of "Religion to God and the Nation to all." The need for a secular state is as pertinent today as it was then."

Because of all these societal dimensions of the Sudanese social life, the diversity of Sudanese society is regarded a sensitive political issue by scholars and politicians. The Sudanese masses have earlier captured this fact for they developed over time an increasing concern for a collective national identity that would respect the diverse heritage and ethnic identifications of the whole country.

Religious and Ethnic Polarization

In the Sudanese contemporary political and power relations, nonetheless, cultural diversity continues to stimulate intellectual disputes between different political parties. The disputes most recently included a new wave of political extremists who advocate violence to settle disputes by force. This writer is deeply concerned with this particular advocacy because it negatively affects the nation formation and nation building of Sudan as a multicultural society.

It is a recognizable right in international norms for a people to maintain and develop their own culture. As a multi-cultural nation, the Sudanese cultures must be equally maintained and preserved against acts of falsification, disfigurement, or eradication. The Sudanese intellectuals, in particular, have a significant role to play as agents of change, monuments of knowledge, and symbols of culture. Many Sudanese scholars, thinkers, and politicians attempted to explain the Sudan's problems of cultural diversity and political change according to their own ideologies or philosophical orientation. These contributions helped to accumulate a wealth of ideas on the issues of rethinking religion, the impact of culture, and the economic and political progression of the State.

This book presents a critical discussion on some of these Sudanese intellectual contributions that mirrored the diversity of Sudanese cultures and social structures as a central fact about the nation of Sudan with respect to the process of nation building. The aim of the writer is to show that the ideas or political commitments assuming the existence of one culture, religion, or language in Sudan constitute a national threat to the well being of the Sudanese people and land.

This work endeavors to highlight concrete aspects of the Sudan's cultural diversity using a sociological analysis of the main ideas of a few contemporary

Sudanese thinkers whose writings reflected a substantial part of the North Sudan Muslim ideologies and political thought. This writer contends that, seen in the light of a careful examination of their ideas, many convergent strains exist among the Sudanese schools of thought regardless of the conflict that underlies their dialogue.

"O mankind! We created you from a single (pair) of a male and female, and made into you nations and tribes, that ye may know each other (not that ye may despise each other)." (The Holy Qur'an, S. XLIX:13).

BEGINNINGS AND EVOLUTION

AL-TABAQAT: SEPARATION OF STATE AND RELIGION

The Sudanese society maintains a great respect for religion in general and Islam in particular. The penetration of Islam into Sudan came with mercy and forgiveness. Islam recognized the freedom of trade and assured the right to religious beliefs. The forefront of the early Muslims who lived in the country included disciples of the Prophet, scholars, traders, discoverers, and warriors. They intermarried with the indigenous groups who as descendants of ancient civilizations also established many Christian kingdoms before they finally accepted the virtues of Islam. In a short while, Islamic kingdoms succeeded the old political system. Spiritual orders flourished all over the country under the banner of Sufi leaders. A new blend of folklore augmented the original cultures and arts that continued to characterize the diverse society of the Sudan.

Al-Shaikh Mohamed Daif-Allah, a Sudanese medieval historian, reported this peaceful transition with the newly established norms and practices. Daif-Allah said in his famous book, Al-Tabaqat: "Until the beginning of the 10th century of the *Hijrah* [the Muslim calendar] in the year 900 ... no school of jurisprudence existed to interpret the *Qur'an* [the holy book of Islam]. A man would be divorcing a wife who might be married to another man in the same day of marriage without applying the Islamic rule of *'idda* [the time of seclusion for a divorced woman before she could be married again]."

Daif-Allah noted: "Soon, however, al-Shaikh Mohamed al-Arrakki of the *Qasir* [village] came from Egypt and taught the people about the *'idda* ... then came al-Shaikh Ibrahim al-Boulad from Egypt ... After a short period of time al-Shaikh Taj al-Deen al-Buhari arrived from Baghdad ... and al-Shaikh al-Talmassani came from Al-Maghrib [Morocco]." Thereafter, an influx of jurists and leaders of *truruq* (Sufi orders, singular *tariqa*) occurred *and Tariq Al-Qoam* (the Path of the Disciples) spread about in the areas of Al-Gezira and Dar Al-Funj region. Both king of the Funj *Sultanate* (kingdom) in Sennar the capital of the Sultanate and the *Manjuluk* (Shaikh of the 'Abdallab Dynasty) in his capital Qarry encouraged the Sufi establishment. The *turuq* apparently did not take part in the governance of the country although the Sufi leaders have ever since influenced the northern Sudanese cultures and social structures up to this day.

It is worthy of notice to mention that the Sudanese Sufi orders always acted as independent groups from the ruling entities of the country. This attitude was probably originated in the medieval ages or even the earlier times when the authority of the state was separated from the ruling Shaikh of the 'Abdallab as well the Sultan of Sennar. Al-Shaikh 'Ageeb *al-Manjuluk* (the only leader glorified by the others) was the elder son of 'Abd-Allah Jama' who destroyed in alliance with Imara Dungus the founder of the Sennar Sultanate the last Christian kingdom of northern Sudan in Soba. Shaikh 'Ageeb assumed the role of the political leader of the 'Abdallab.

'Ageeb recognized the influence of the Sufi orders, however, in the social and religious affairs of the dynasty although he was personally known as a pious leader. The *Manjuluk* did not take responsibility of religious affairs besides his political duties as a leader of the 'Abdallab. Many jurists came to his kingdom from Egypt, Baghdad, and al-Maghrib to teach *al-Fiqh* (jurisprudence) of whom none participated in the military, administrative, or financial functions of the dynasty.

Such ingenious separation of the state from the *turuq* as symbols and institutions of Islamic practice and leadership characterized the experience of Sudanese Muslims from the very beginning. God-fearing, spiritually inspired, and popular, the Shaikhs leading the *turuq* exerted substantial influence in society. They equally advised the political leaders of the time in different occasions on worldly affairs.

Daif-Allah mentioned some of these instances in <u>Al-Tabaqat</u>. He wrote: "Idris Wad al-Arbaba, Shaikh al-Islam, the pious and the one following the path of all the great men of Islam, issued a legal interpretation that the use of *tunbak* [Sudanese tobacco] was *haram* [illegal]. He paid a visit to al-Shaikh 'Ageeb Al-Manjuluk to assure his legal *fatwa* [interpretation]. He said that the Sultan of Istanbul [the Ottoman Caliph] in addition to the *Madzhab* [school of Islamic jurisprudence] of the Imam Malik prohibited the use of *tunbak*. The obedience of the Sultan was obligatory whenever a legal text of the *Shari'a* [Islamic law] was not available. Al-Shaikh Arbab further informed 'Ageeb that the Prophet on whom God bestowed prayers and peace relayed to Arbab the illegality of the *tunbak*. Al-Shaikh Mohamed al-Hamim and al-Shaikh Hassan wad Hassona both witnessed the meeting with the Prophet."

Shaikh Idris sent an additional correspondence to al-Shaikh 'Ali al-Ajhorri who was a distinguished scholar of Islam in Egypt through his student Hamad wad Abu-'Agrab. The <u>Tabaqat</u> goes on to report the dialogue that took place at a mosque between al-Ajhorri and al-Shaikh Ibrahim al-Laggani on the illegality of *tunbak* in Egypt. Ajhorri recognized the correct *fatwa* of Idris wad al-Arbaba (al-Tabaqat, undated: 9-10).

Another important example on the relation between political rulers and the leaders of the Sufi orders is also mentioned in Al-Tabaqat. The example referred to al-Shaikh Khogali Ibn 'Abd al-Rahman Abu al-Jaz "whose glory was so high that it was said the greatest *'ulama* [jurists] or *sultan* [king] felt like children when they would be sitting with him" (Ibid. 75).

Shaikh Khogali resembled the independence of the *'ulama* who practiced faith and jurisprudence apart from any involvement in the political affairs of the state. Daif-Allah informed readers about the manners of al-Shaikh Khogali: "He would never write to the Sultan in any worldly affair. Nor would he ever ask the Sultan to serve his own disciples although he was considerate of the needy. Because Khogali was highly esteemed person, the Sultan would never have rejected his request. Even when someone would ask al-Shaikh Khogali a favor from the Sultan, the Shaikh would reply, 'I will not send with you my disciples or any of my children. God be with you! You can take this clay [for blessing]. And yet, if you are patient, I will petition your case before that unjust Sultan or send a petition through one of his entourage should they come to visit me. No offender, however, shall ask me a favor'" (Ibid: 76).

Such was the dignity of the men of Islam, their high esteem over kings, and their principled stance at the same time to announce their own interpretations or jurisprudence, as in the case of the *tunbak*.

MEDIEVAL INTELLECTUALITY AND FREEDOM OF THOUGHT

The Tabaqat was a unique register on the conditions of central and northern Sudan after the emergence of Islamic kingdoms in the medieval ages until the time of their demise by the Ottoman Egyptian conquest. The Tabaqat reported the existence of cultural diversity, which was largely reflected by the Sufi orders and the mixture of Islamic knowledge and the indigenous beliefs that constituted their uniqueness. The story of al-Shaikh Isma'il, player of the *rababa* (a local musical instrument) presented a clear picture of that mixture.

Isma'il, the master of the *rababa*, said Wad Daif-Allah, "was a prominent Shaikh that had been taught the Qur'an by the jurist Mohamed Wad Manofali, the successor of his father [in the *tariqa*]. Isma'il learned both Islamic fiqh and theology … He himself taught the *Hadith* [deeds and sayings of the Prophet], theology, and the Qur'an. Also, he was a poet who wrote poetry on praise of the Prophet, with words depicting features of the *Awliya* [holy men]" (Ibid. 27).

In the meantime, al-Shaikh Isma'il was leading a life equally of entertainment, humor, and singing. "His disciple, al-Noor al-Rayashi, informed me [i.e., Daif-Allah] that whenever al-Shaikh Isma'il would be motivated by a mode of entertainment, he would walk about in his courtyard and would bring girls, brides, and grooms for dancing. He would play the *rababa* with tones so touching that an insane person would recover while sane persons would be in ecstasy" (Ibid: 28).

To conclude: "This man belonged to the *Malamatiya* [the sect of the blamed ones] who were members of a group of Sufi persons that apparently committed wrongful acts so that they would be reprimanded in order to humiliate themselves. Some of them would involve in such practices so that they would abrogate them as soon as they would be criticized for such acts by people," explained Daif-Allah (Ibid: 29).

In some of his ceremonies, al-Shaikh Isam'il "would be mounting his horse with many poor people surrounding him with their arrows – so numerous that the horse would not be seen. They would be cheering and singing loudly beautiful songs. All the inhabitants, women and men, would be rallying around him, repeating his songs" (Ibid: 29). Daif-Allah also mentioned that al-Shaikh Isma'il, player of the *rababa*, was fond of beautiful women.

The personality of al-Shaikh Isma'il as one of the *Malamatiya* sect exemplified a unique blend of religious knowledge, Sufi tradition, and jurisprudence coupled with a strong commitment to share with the poor the popular lifestyle of that time

What was the relationship of the spiritual leader Isma'il with the rulers of the country? Daif-Allah mentioned that al-Shaikh Isma'il "came before Sultan Dekain who asked him whether or not he had made a song that included verses [unacceptable] to the king. Isma'il answered the king by saying, 'Did the Satan in your mind suggest that to you?' The king said he would have Isma'il killed for that answer. But the king's uncles advised him by saying, 'would you kill the son of our Shaikh because he is drunk and proud of himself? We would be destroyed for his blood.' The king then complained to Wad Manofali, the religious mentor of Isma'il, who replied that he could not control Isma'il since he had already learned the Qur'an and was living his youth" (Ibid: 29).

A few lessons might be heavily drawn from this particular story: the religious leaders of medieval Sudan maintained a prestigious position before political leaders, including sultans. The Shaikhs were not answerable to kings, but rather to their own mentors. Society at large was tolerant of and quite agreeable to different modes of behavior within the life of Sufi groups.

It might appear that these major features of medieval heritage evolved on the separation of secular powers from that of the sacred sects and the men of Islam. The Tabaqat did not inform readers about other details on these experiences. The book made the point, nonetheless, that the Sudanese people of central Sudan enjoyed living a free life in a free land for centuries. This freedom came to an end with the advent of the Turkish-Egyptian rule of the country (1821-1885). Run by foreigners, Central Sudan suffered the brunt of foreign rule because it was detrimental to the psycho-political, economic, religious, and socio-cultural life of the population. It estranged them, stripped them of their political systems, and distorted their social values. Equally important, the other regions of Sudan suffered the atrocities of slavery, economic backwardness, and cultural deprivation throughout the 60 years of the Turco-Egyptian rule.

The alienating administration of the Ottoman-Egyptian rule of the Sudan never understood the social fabric or political structure of the country. Nor did the Turkish rulers ever appreciate the cultural diversity of the nation that had been based on egalitarianism and ethno-tribal alliances since ancient times. The brutal genocide of Sudanese people in the beginning of the Ottoman rule fueled the country with hatred and a strong determination to resist the strangers-in-power.

The natives of Sudan, however, continued to preserve their integrity, cultural pride, and adherence to Sufi leaders and sects as social and religious practices. Most important, the ever-growing generations continued to struggle relentlessly for a complete restoration of freedom.

Deeply entrenched as they were in the spiritual life of people, the position of Imams (jurist religious leaders) and Shaikhs of the *turuq* was greatly strengthened. This very reason enabled Mohamed Ahmed al-Mahdi, a young revolutionary Shaikh, to rally support increasingly around his leadership. A learned jurist and a devout Sufi, al-Mahdi lived closely with the poor and the needy while crossing "the path of disciples," in accordance with Sufi traditions and a renowned piousness and self-respect. To this day, al-Mahdi's successful leadership of the Sudanese nation is highly remembered. His *ratib* (collection of verses from the Qur'an) is daily recited by the *Ansar* (followers of al-Mahdi).

Under the newly established independent state of the *Mahdiya* (era and system of the Mahdist state, 1885-1899), the *'ulama* retained a significant status in the social life. For example, al-Shaikh Mohamed al-Mekki, the older son of al-Shaikh Isma'il al-Wali, maintained a close position with the Imam al-Mahdi and his successor al-Khalifa Abdullah. "Strongly confident in him, al-Khalifa entrusted al-Shaikh al-Mekki with the task of bringing up Ahmed, son of the middle Mohamed Osman al-Mirghani (leader of the *Khatmiya* Sufi group, which did not support the *Mahdiya* as ideology or state). Moreover, showing a sign of appreciating al-Mekki's influential position in the *Mahdiya*, al-Khalifa presented to al-Mekki the mule of King John of Abyssinia, the saddle, and all of the other belongings on it that had been captured in the battle of Galabat" (al-Kordofani, Sa'adat al-Mustahdi, 1972: 12).

Looked upon by al-Mahdi and his followers, the *Ansar*, the *'ulama* who rejected Mahdism as an Islamic salvation movement "did not recognize many aspects of al-Mahdi's mission because it was not complying with their own beliefs. The *'ulama* were convinced that Mahdism contradicted their own school of jurisprudence" (Abu Salim, al-Haraka al-Fikriya, 1989: 54). The substance of the matter, however, was not solely centered on a conflict of beliefs and jurisprudence. In fact, al-Mahdi explained in a correspondence between him and al-Shaikh al-Amin Mohamed al-Dareer, a prominent jurist of the Khartoum *'ulama*, that "his [i.e., al-Mahdi's] young age and humble knowledge compared to the great knowledge of al-Shaikh al-Amin should not preclude him from being a Mahdi [a savior of redeemer]. The Mahdi subsequently accused the *'ulama* of rejecting his Mahdism for worldly involvement. He devoted a large part of his speech to delineating the humility of this world, the glory of the other world, and the dangers of involving one's self in the pleasures of worldly affairs, status, and material life" (Ibid: 55).

Mohamed Saeed al-Gaddal (1981) summed up the position of the *'ulama* in the conflict that broke out between them and al-Mahdi with reference to the analysis written by 'Abd-Allah Ali Ibrahim on <u>Al-Sura' baina al-Mahdi wa al-'Ulama</u> (The Conflict between The Mahdi and the Scholars). In the words of al-Gaddal "[Ibrahim] puts the cause of religion in the Mahdist revolution within its historical framework. The religious leaders in the days of the Funj exercised a great influence in the state while still not occupying any formal position. The Turkish rulers dominated the religious institutions. They installed governmental religious establishments under a direct control of the state. The religious institutions were thus divided into two parts: a "governmental" division, so to speak, and another division that existed outside the power of the state."

Gaddal then made a point that, "In this climate of intense Sufi religious beliefs that were embodied in many factions [of the Muslim community], the Imam Mohamed Ahmed [al-Mahdi] took the initiative and gave the people an idea of a redeemer, as acceptable at that particular time. The Mahdi criticized all those religious leaders who had been overwhelmed in his view by the pleasures of a worldly life. He saw their opposition to his movement, the *Mahdiya* - a "natural" stance that has always been practiced in every revolution" (al-Gaddal, al-Siyasa al-Iqtisadiya, 1981: 40).

Scrutinizing many theories on the cause of the Mahdist Revolution, al-Gaddal summarized the impact of major factors that might have generated a correlation between the atrocities and injustices of the Turkish rule of the Sudan and the strong resistance on part of the people to that rule. This resistance culminated finally in the outburst of the Mahdist Revolution. Other factors pertained to the impact of religion, as well as the role played by al-Mahdi, the charismatic leader of the instigation and advancement of the movement.

Gaddal referred to the theoretical perspective of Professor Holt, namely that certain factors constituted a presupposition to the emergence and growth of a successful movement. Social change, according to al-Gaddal, is not a spontaneous event. Rather, there is a continuity of thought to bridge the ideologies that prevail in a preceding epoch with those that penetrate in a new time. Revolutions voice the ideas that are expressive of the interests of all sections of a society.

Gaddal illuminated the issue of consciousness in the 19th century Sudan. "The rise of social consciousness to a high stage of maturity came about as a result of the contradictions occurring between the Turkish-Egyptian reign and the beneficiaries of the system, in the words of Holt. This consciousness crystallized within a framework of a Sudanese society that had already developed its own special characteristics. It was enunciated in the Islamic Sufi heritage, the personality of al-Mahdi, and tribal traditions" (Ibid: 38-47).

Many studies have been written on al-Mahdi of which al-Gaddal authored Laoha li Thaiyer Suddani [A Postulate of a Sudanese Revolutionary) (1986). There is near consensus among most of these studies that Islam had a great impact on the life, ideological orientation, and leadership of the Mahdi, as well as his perceptions of politics, social life, and administration. The short life of forty years that the Imam lived does not allow a possible evaluation of performance of the state under his patronage. This is to be compared with the relatively long period of his successor's rule that extended to 13 consecutive years, and provided researchers with substantial information on the Mahdist State under his leadership. The Mahdi united the Sudanese people at that particular time in one nation, including many groups in the remote areas of the South, notably the Shuluk, and the Eastern and Western parts of the country.

The Grand Imam al-Mahdi led the Sudanese nation to a remarkable victory over the ruling strangers of the Ottoman-Turkish Empire and the Europeans employed in the Sudan to consolidate the imperial rule of the *Khedive* [the viceroy of Egypt] in Cairo. He set up the first Sudanese State at the turn of the century with an Islamic insight, and advanced through the state machinery nationalism and a religious revivalism. The *Mahdiya* perpetuated the cultural heritage of many tribal groups that became a dominant source of political allegiance and social support to the new state.

In the area of political economy of the state, al-Mahdi imposed a wide range of state interventions in the traditional system of land ownership. "In so doing," wrote al-Gaddal, "the Mahdi relied heavily upon his spiritual authority to implement a policy of land ownership consonant with the philosophy of Islam. *Allah* [God] is the only owner of land and He has placed it under the guardianship of mankind to dispose of it. Land would not be a privilege in itself or a personal property for the appropriator. Land is strictly used as a social functionary and a ruler is entitled to regulate its utility" (Ibid. 57).

A tradition characteristic of al-Mahdi is his exercising a harsh discipline of austerity through cohabitation with the poor in order to appreciate their economic and social distress. As his son, 'Abd al-Rahman, later recalled, "I and my brothers never complained when we were short of food for a day or so. We were tempered to be patient and to curb our desires. I remembered how many sympathizers whispered at the hunger and deprivation of the sons of al-Mahdi. But we were not touched by their comments. The Khalifa knew about that. On his part, he was convinced that living in such conditions would free our minds from thinking about al-Mahdi as a king or a Sultan, but that al-Mahdi was a Redeemer to purify human souls and to strengthen their relation with Almighty Allah" (al-Mahdi, Jihad, undated: 3-4).

Another tradition of al-Mahdi is that he showed great respect to the 'ulama and the other intellectuals who were assembled in Maglis Al-Shura (the advisory council of the State). Although the influence of the turuq such as the powerful Samaniya Tariqa was largely weakened by the Mahdist ideology of the state, "thus speeding up the cancellation of Sufi groups as a whole" (Abu Salim, al-Haraka al-Fikriya, 1989: 35), al-Khalifa advocated a principled way of al-Mahdi's tradition. This included the establishment of an advisory council for the state. The council was composed of the 'ulama and religious scholars, although the Khalifa himself "was not a scholar. He wouldn't have ascended to the high position he had been occupying hadn't he been a disciple and a sincere friend of al-Mahdi," explained Abu Salim (Ibid. 42).

Notwithstanding, it is this writer's viewpoint that al-Khalifa was actually a brilliant politician as well as a competent administrator to have been able to build up the State of the *Mahdiya* – a task that al-Mahdi had already conferred on him in full confidence before his death. The Khalifa faced many national, regional, and international opponents of the Mahdist State of whom the empires of the day (British, French, Italian, etc.) were directly involved in antagonistic military operations to destroy the nationalist movement of the Sudan. It should be acknowledged that al-Khalifa 'Abdullah did play a prominent role to survive that "nationalist" state of Islamic *Jihad* (holy war) for 13 years in accordance with the *Mahdiya* doctrine. However, this commitment generated costly sacrifices of which both Khalifa and his enemies in and out the country massively victimized the Bedouin population of Sudan.

The ideals of the Mahdist State, primarily those of al-Mahdi and the Khalifa, guided performance of the State on the basis of cultural diversity and religious revivalism. Chief among these ideals is the fact that the Mahdist State was not monopolized by a power structure of a single group. In fact, al-Mahdi had essentially initiated that tradition because he did not allow any member of his own family or even clan or geographical affiliation to act as a favorite group in the movement. al-Mahdi selected as his successor al-Khalifa 'Abdullah who belonged to an ethnic group from Western Sudan that was uniquely sincere to the *Mahdiya* as a movement of Islamic *Jihad*.

The Mahdi's selectivity of al-Khalifa is attributable to his keen knowledge of the social groups of the country. Shown by the actual discourse of events, al-Khalifa, the political and administrative leader of the State, proved his competence although many *Ansar* resisted his authority. Inasmuch as history is concerned, such resistance was not directed towards any consolidation of the *Mahdiya* or its ideological state.

When the State was firmly stabilized, an admixture of Sudanese ethno-regional groups had already existed in Omdurman, the capital city of the *Mahdiya*. This large assembly of Sudanese people, irrespective of their cultural diversity, could be noted as one of the greatest legacies of Imam al-Mahdi and his successor, the Khalifa. Spreading from all over the country in great armies across the frontiers for the war of *Jihad*, the Sudanese nationals joined together to form a cohesive group of the *Ansar* to extend support for the *Mahdiya* indoctrination. Thus, the State evolved on the Mahdist ideology that required an overall commitment of all members of society in spite of their differences in economic, political, cultural, and social activities. Moreover, some of these differences were partially removed in legal and practical terms through a strict application of laws of the land, army leadership, Shari'a teachings, etc.

A tragic impact of the *Mahdiya* doctrine on people was clearly witnessed in the collective activities of Jihad, especially the decisive battle of Karari when tens of thousands of the *Ansar* were killed by the imperialist army of Egypt and Britain. Those killed were martyrs of *Al-Shihada* (dying for Allah in a holy war). Needless to say their heroism and the honor attached to the Jihad were not confined to a specific group but rather acquired by all of the *Ansar* across the country.

Throughout the *Mahdiya* movement and state policies and practices, rethinking Islam was a rule, not an exception, to meet the needs of the revolution and to unite the *Ansar* for the Jihad under the firm leadership of al-Mahdi and his successor, the Khalifa. The Mahdist Revolution attracted many nationals of the neighboring countries to join the armies of *Jihad* through its principal teachings and struggles.

In conclusion, the revolution comprised a unique chapter of the Sudanese national striving for independence and freedom. The State helped a great deal to maintain cultural diversity by preserving the tribal and ethno-regional affiliations of the country under the *Mahdiya* doctrine as a predominant religious ideology of the state. Although the Mahdist doctrine aspired to mold all Sufi sects into the *Ansar* group as one national body, the *turuq* continued to influence their own following.

True, the *turuq* were definitely weakened by the limitations or prohibitions made on them, particularly in the early days of establishing the new state. The *Jihad* absorbed energies of the population at the expense of education, free association, etc. "It is not correct, however, to say that the *'ulama* did not play any role in the state or that they were decisively usurped. In actual fact, the Khalifa always consulted with them in the religious affairs [of the state and society] with due respect to their views. Also, they voiced their opinions in the disputes occurring in all aspects of the social life" (Abu Salim, al-Haraka al-Fikriya, 1989: 191).

Take, for instance, this statement, "The Khalifa always consulted with them in the religious affairs [of the state and society]." This statement implies that the *Mahdiya*, similar to the medieval traditions of the country, continued to separate jurisdictions of different branches of the state from the direct influence of jurists. The *emirs* (leaders of the army) were responsible for military activities and leaderships, and accountants were positioned in *Bait al-Mal* (the state treasury) as employed administrators. The Khalifa acted as leader of the state and successor of the Grand Imam by executing the Jihad and consulting with the *'ulama* who were not, whatsoever, authorized to rule the State.

Up to this point, we have almost approached the colonial era under the Condominium Rule of the Sudan by Egypt and Britain beginning in 1899. This era started after Kitchner and his army ravaged the Mahdist State at the battle of Karari with savage violations committed against the human rights of all captives of the war. For the people of Sudan, Kitchner and his soldiers passed away in the course of history, but the *Mahdiya* heritage and national ideals continued to live to play a significant role in the Sudanese modern history and national sentiments.

By the same token, Sudanese Sufi *turuq* were never buried beneath the memory of time. The *turuq* flourished along the liberal attitude of new rulers towards Islam and the cultural diversity of Sudanese masses: "Spiritual life is immortal, as Allah wishes," Muslims believe.

Was there any relation between witchcraft and Sufi beliefs in the Sudanese society at these days, including the pre-Mahdist Sudan? Richard Hill speaks On the Frontiers of Islam (1970) about the values and social customs of Sudanese people during the years 1845-1848 of the Ottoman-Egyptian rule. Based on stories told by an Italian author at that time, Hill mentions that, "The Sudanese were noted for their belief in witchcraft, especially the existence of witches in Sennar and the lands beyond that area" (Hill, Tukhum, 1987: 153). Thereafter, many reports of British administrators (1899-1955) mentioned that large sections of the Sudanese populace believed in sorcery and/or witchcraft. Some crimes, including murder, were reported to have been committed in response to that belief (Mahmoud, Tatawur, 1984).

No doubt that some stories of the Tabaqat might have been reflective, to some extent, of Sudanese beliefs in sorcery or witchcraft (i.e., the artificial power of perception beyond the actual ability of the human mind). This, however, might have equally intermixed with religious belief in the supernatural deeds of Sufi leaders by virtue of their spiritual dedication and piousness. Mindful that sorcery or witchcraft are based on deception and bad faith in the first place, whereas Sufi tradition is a pure spiritual life of God-fearing practices, it should be recalled that sorcery is sometimes exercised in many parts of the country using Sufi symbols to "deceive" a victim. At any rate, it is extremely important for analytical purposes to draw a clear distinction between the two systems of Sudanese beliefs, as was earlier explained.

The ideas and points of philosophers, thinkers, writers, and the other layers of intellectuals on issues of religious belief developed an intriguing expression of the very distinctive characteristics of Sudanese society in the context of the social life. These characteristics include the Sudan's cultural diversity, different milieu of thought and action, and religious multiplicity that includes a plethora of Sufi *turuq* and liberal political practices.

CONTEMPORARY PROBLEMS: THE EGYPTIAN REVIVALIST

Except perhaps for a few poets, who depicted certain aspects of sorcery or witchcraft in some parts of the Sudan, a majority of Sudanese writers have stressed in their writings a concern for Islam. Many writers center their attention on the relations existing between religion and the socio-political and ideological evolution of the country, the way religion influences the direction of evolution, and the impact exerted by the forces of society to determine the direction of change. To understand the contributions of some of these thinkers, a brief analysis is useful on the experience of Egyptian intelligence with respect to nationalism, traditionalism, and modernity since it has been dealing with problems similar to those of the contemporary Sudanese society.

Rethinking religion is not a new phenomenon in the countries neighboring Sudan. The Intellectual Origins of Egyptian Nationalism, a book written in 1960 at Oxford by the Sudanese writer Jamal Mohamed Ahmed, a founder of modern Sudanese-African diplomacy, is an interesting study on the emergence and development of Egyptian nationalism.

Jamal traces the origins of Egyptian nationalist thought in the early beginnings of modernity at the start of the 20th century. He notes that a violent resistance was effectively waged against the penetrating forces of modernity by the old systems of traditionalism under the leadership of notable religious Shaikhs. Some of the Shaikhs, nonetheless, aligned themselves with the invading and/or new powers, for example, Napoleon Bonaparte, the Ottoman Sultan, and Mohamed 'Ali, the cunning viceroy of Egypt.

Despite the fact that many Shaikhs were educated in the Azhar University of traditional Islamic education, they became pioneers of modernity since they closely touched upon European styles of life and secular schools of thought. These innovative spheres of action and thought enlightened their minds with experimental sciences and the new values emanating thereof. According to their perception, modernity provided a tool with which Western powers managed to defeat the Muslim East, that had to be liberalized to keep pace with the changing world of the time.

These enlightened Shaikhs were motivated to struggle against foreign forces' domination, as well as the local forces of traditionalism. The liberal Shaikhs resisted the foreign powers because they considered them illegitimate rulers who exploited Egypt and restricted the national advancement of its people. Equally important, these modernist Shaikhs antagonized their own colleagues who failed to see the ongoing transformation of the whole world from traditional systems to modernity. They were deeply concerned with the task of identifying appropriate ways to adapt the declining civilization of the East to Western modernity. The challenge was that such adaptation should not be enforced at the expense of faith or the other ideals of Oriental life.

This intellectual conflict was greatly increased beyond any conceivable thought. Led by al-Tahtawi, 'Abdu, and al-Afghani, Egyptian thought developed into distinguished schools of religious revivalism. From these sprang the idea of "Islamic universality," which would give birth to a new Caliphate exemplifying the 'Abbasite great Caliph Haroun al-Rasheed in the old days of the Islamic Empire. In essence, wrote 'Abdu, "I struggle to learn, to study faith and the real ethics of Islam from its original sources. I have tried to show that religion is revealed to the human kind as a light of guidance against the faculty of the mind. If well preserved, the mind is competent to test the validity of a religion's facts. The mind, indeed, should undertake that task" (Ahmed, Usul, 1960:43).

Here, Jamal Mohamed Ahmed comments that Imam 'Abdu was moved in his search to find a valid synthesis of both religious faith and modern rationality by taking an intellectual stance that generated immense hostility against him. And yet, since his own disciples were not able to adopt this complexity of views and attitudes along with the traditional doctrines of the old times, they defaulted in understanding the origins of his thought. In the end, many groups accused him of being an atheist, a *Mo'tazila* [modern Islamic thinker], and a *physiocrat* [secularist]" (Ibid).

Despite these controversies, a liberal school of Islamic thought emanated from these origins. This was eventually translated inside the Al-Azhar University in the form of books, magazines, and associations of which prominent examples were Al-'Urwa al-Wothqa, A'lam al-Muslimeen, and Al-Rowad associations. Shaikh 'Abd al-Raziq authored Al-Islam wa Usul al-Hukm (Islam and the Rules of Governance) in which he explained negative aspects of the monopolizing power of the Caliphate, as well as that of the monarchism, over and above Muslims. Qasim Amin shone as a pioneer of women's liberation for he projected a viable way to revitalize the Muslim society by advancing the women's status. So many other ideas and actions ensued, albeit they were addressed to the issue of achieving national independence rather than religious revivalism. Thereafter, concludes Jamal, Khalid Mohamed Khalid reiterated with other writers a comprehensive discussion of the impact of religion and politics on the Muslim world.

It appears as if Jamal Mohamed Ahmed, who wrote perceptively on the origins of intellectual thought in Egypt, creatively surpassed his time to envision a conflicting development of intellectual and national thought in the Sudan. A writer with a grace of vision, Jamal also prepared another visionary article on "Confederacy of the United States of the Nile," in which he made an attempt to restructure the existing political borders of Africa as a whole.

The Sudanese society differs in several ways from the Egyptian society both theoretically and practically. Each society maintains a social identity and a distinguished national entity although they have been uniquely related over time in close ancient and modern relationships. Historical development, however, never evolved in the same way in the two countries. The structure of each society is different in psychological and political development.

The Sudan's vital corridor to Africa and the Arab countries never suffered the greedy scramble of European powers to rule it, as Egypt did. The Sudan never experienced a reign of feudalism or a deeply rooted capitalism that enslaved the peasantry, as Egypt had. Nor has Egypt witnessed a society with a multitude of languages and dialects as Sudan had and still has. Moreover, Egypt has not practiced the admixture of cultural diversity in the issues of faith and religious beliefs that Sudan always had, according to the Al-Tabaqat. Certainly, Egypt has been deeply Islamic. It is a country of the ancient pharaoh's magic and lethargy, as well as religious practices that are repeatedly mentioned in the Qur'an.

Apart from the societal differences that exist between the Sudan and Egypt, it is possible to find common characteristics in the evolution and development of religious revivalism in both countries. Previously observed, there were many immigrant religious leaders who chose Sudan a permanent homeland. The Sudanese people have maintained, in turn, the popularity of religious sects that once included a popular musician whose followers equally revered as a holy man. Another religious leader, Imam al-Mahdi, promoted Sudanese nationalism through a holy war of Islamic faith. This type of leadership has not been clearly experienced in the Egyptian society. True, Ahmed 'Urabi led Egypt in a rebellion against the viceroy and colonialism. But 'Urabi, unlike al-Mahdi did not fight his cause for an Islamic *Jihad*.

Many other Islamic thinkers came about with new ideas to modernize Muslim societies. Of these thinkers, the Imam Mohamed 'Abdu and his disciples have been highly recognized prominent revivalists. Thereafter, their activities bifurcated in varying degrees: Ahmed Lutfi al-Sayed (a modernist philosopher) adopted Western liberalism; Taha Hussain (a scholar and writer) had been concerned for the East, yet he intensified his interest in Western literature and methodologies. Another vanguard group of writers and thinkers pursued a search for a formula that would combine, without contradiction, fundamentals of faith with those of scientific empirical research. Egypt, after all, was subsequently ruled by Jamal 'Abd al-Nasser, a salient leader of a nationalist stature in the Arab and Third World Countries.

Nasser had earlier shown up in a dim light before his flames of patriotism erupted all over the Third World Countries. He defied the Western colonialism, nationalized the Suez Canal, constructed the High Dam of Aswan, achieved rearmament of the Egyptian army, and expanded heavy industry in Egypt by direct relations with the Soviet Union and the other socialist states. The days of Nasser's reign witnessed a newly born experience of state socialism based on the corporate of the public sector and popular cooperatives. But the state did not strengthen the necessary alliance needed with the organized groups' beneficiaries of the socialist transformation of the state. Opportunists and other renegades penetrated the system, prepared the collapse of 1967, and thereon remained in the succeeding changes of the Egyptian polity.

NEW EVOLUTIONARY THINKERS

On recalling the rooted traditions of the Sudanese egalitarianism of faith and culture, it is disheartening to consider the difficulties the Sudanese have been recently facing under a fascist rule that is disjunctive from that heritage. We have seen how King Dekain refrained from killing Shaikh Isma'il, the master of the *rababa*. We also saw how strongly Shaikh Khugali Abu al-Jaz confronted the Sultan, and how Shaikh al-Dareer criticized loudly the "disobedience of Mohamed Ahmed [the Grand Mahdi] to the leaders [of religious status]," then how the State of the *Mahdiya* removed from the leaders of Sufi orders much of their prerogatives.

Throughout the medieval ages of Sudan, many rulers did not exercise violence to humiliate people to satisfy government concern. Most governments of the post-independence Sudan (1956 to the present time), however, grossly violated the traditions of the medieval heritage. Contradicting the tolerant traditions of the nation, they committed the atrocious acts of civil war and other anti-democratic practices humiliating the populace. Some governments were so intolerant that they banned the freedom of expression. Many scholars were incarcerated for no crime but their thought. Ironically, prison employees and executioners have emphatically sympathized with victims under the gallows more than their killer rulers did.

Of these victims, we still focus closely upon Mahmoud Mohamed Taha, a religious revivalist executed at 71 years of age by a tyrannical regime, and 'Abd al-Khaliq Mahgoub, a socialist thinker who had been executed at his early 40's by the same regime in 1971. Also discussed in this book, the ideas of Sadiq al-Mahdi, an Islamic statesman, and Hassan al-Turabi, a leader of a politico-religious group, will be critically examined. The thinkers in consideration have been disseminating different views on religious revivalism in relation to intellectual and political schools of thought throughout succeeding decades of the post-independence Sudan.

A substantial part of this book is meant to elucidate a fundamental fact, namely, that irrespective of the ideological and political struggles between the thinkers in question, many convergent aspects underlie their Muslim ideas. Although they address themselves to Islamic issues, directly or indirectly, their thoughts have invariably exerted an important impact on Sudanese people, especially those maintaining a strong faith in Abraham, the other messengers of God, and

Muhammad, peace be upon them. It is of interest to investigate with a rigorous review of their ideas many facts concerning the national heritage of the country, which comprises deeply rooted social and historical exigencies of the society at large.

It is true the thinkers have been strongly associated with their local communities whose cultural and religious backgrounds helped to shape their own life preferences and value-orientations. But these particular aspects of the thinkers will not be elaborately discussed in this work. It is assumed, furthermore, that serious national problems have consistently influenced the thought of these leaders, each on his/her own right. The complexities involved in these problems are closely correlated with religion and the political stands of the thinkers towards the State. In this book, only Mahmoud Mohamed Taha, 'Abd al-Khaliq Mahgoub, Sadiq al-Mahdi, and Hassan Turabi will be intensively cited accompanied by this author's commentary, as is appropriate.

The writer hopes that another work would pay attention in the near future to important contributions by the other Sudanese thinkers, namely Jamal Mohamed Ahmed, Francis Deng, Mohamed Omer Bashir, and a few others who have all enriched the Sudanese intellectual life with thought and deep insights. Rethinking religion, in particular, is a topic firmly dealt with and adequately scrutinized by the four thinkers about whom this work is mainly prepared. Unfortunately, the thinkers have not frequently enjoyed the freedom of expression to pursue their thought freely. Earlier mentioned, Taha and Mahgoub were extra-judicially killed, and the other thinkers, Sadiq and Turabi who are brothers-in-law, were subjected to arbitrary detention many times.

What is more is that Turabi collaborated with a group of officers to overthrow the democratic rule of the former in coup de'etat on June 30th, 1989. Turabi has since became an accomplice with the military tyranny to exclude Sadiq and all of the other Sudanese thinkers and politicians from national decision-making, save the National Islamic Front (NIF) – his own political party. Notwithstanding, the Sudanese brave and faithful people continue to appreciate the contributions of thinkers, and to highly value their relevancy to the nation building and to the good life. It is not usually the state that evaluates a thinker.

In this critique, we refer to the works of the thinkers, in addition to the works of their adherents. This very analysis, however, deals with the individual views of the writers more than any political views by their supporters or foes. We are interested in the extent of their commitment to the rights of people to enjoy the essential freedoms and human rights, particularly religious beliefs and the freedom of thought.

THINKERS AND PHILOSOPHERS

RETHINKING THE CLASSICAL JURISPRUDENCE

Sudanese thinkers have always involved themselves in the cause of developing society by rethinking religion as a vital component of the Sudanese daily life. They pragmatically used their intellectual skill to serve the interests of their own groups with a view to serve society as a whole. They were aware that society would fall into a state of rigidity if it were to forgo the freedom of expression.

The Sudanese thinkers struggled to preserve the right to express views freely to insure the respect of disagreement in the face of repressive authorities. This important aspect of Sudanese intellectuality will be analyzed with reference to the original works of the thinkers more than to secondary sources of information. An assessment will subsequently explore the similarities and differences in their views.

Hassan al-Turabi writes in his book <u>Tagdid Usul al-Fiqh al-Islami</u> (Renewal of the Origins of Islamic Jurisprudence) on the need to connect jurisprudence consistently with the reality of contemporary life: "People have already acquiesced or were content with generalities. They were now claiming *al-Do'at* [religious scholars or missionaries] to provide for practical methods to rule society, administer the economy, and organize the public life to guide the behavior of the individual Muslim in modern society" (al-Turabi, <u>Tagdid</u>, 1980: 7).

By originating the problem in the "acquiescence and content" of the Islamic world to "generalities," it can be immediately noted that Turabi addresses himself to a society of Muslims with a common faith. He does not mention the presence, let alone the rights, of non-Muslims as sections of that society. Nor does he refer to the social, cultural, and political implications of his idea. Since he projected society as an all-Muslim entity from the very start, it was unnecessary for him to talk about any problems anticipated in the existence of the Muslim and non-Muslim citizens of the same society. He did not care to assess the urgent necessity to insure a fair and just settlement for such problems in the actual reality.

Turabi further assumes that the "Islamic society [which Tagdid does not clearly identify] has already attained a certain stage of "progression": The movement of Islam passed over the theoretical generalizations of the early *Da'wa* [Mission of Islam]. These were laid out from the start to remind people of the origins and fundamental premises of religion [lest they might be lately denied or ignored]. From the time the movement of religion stepped forward in great length into the stage of the *Da'wa*, the Movement has been required to handle problems of jurisprudence that involved the substance and branches [elaboration] of the *Ahkam* [rules] in detail. The reason is that the development of jurisprudence could only take place in our contemporary society through a perfectionist version of jurisprudence for the religion of Allah, the Al-Mighty God" (Ibid.).

The Turabi web of thought is clearly shown in the previous statement. We might rearrange his ideas as follows: (1) the start of Islamic *Da'wa* was initiated by "theoretical generalizations" to stabilize the origins and fundamental premises of religion. This task has not been adequately apprehended by the perception of society at that time. (2) The Movement of Islam was subsequently advanced to employ "branches" of the emerging jurisprudence in order to find practical solutions for the changing realities of life. (3) The contemporary modern society appears well prepared by virtue of the detailed [sophisticated] life it actually acquired to allow the establishment of a perfectionist version of jurisprudence congruent with the lifestyles of its modern life.

There are many problems, however, that arose from the theorization of Turabi to the Movement of Islam, past and present. One problem related to his thesis that the Movement of Islam (during the Prophet's time and the succeeding Caliphates of the Guided Companions) comprised a "Stage of generalizations." The stage passed away as the Movement advanced to "new realities." Was that "advancement" of the Movement transcended over the Prophet's time without any ensuing residual for the next stages? If the answer is no, what common characteristics combined the Prophet's time with "the new realities" of our times today?

Other questions also arise, as well, on the stage of "progress" that the Movement of Islam "theoretically" experienced along the passage of time. With what authenticated criteria did the Movement deal with the post-Caliphate times? What "new realities" came about? Did the stage in question entail a linear line of progression, i.e., it lent itself to a quantitative statistical form whereby the value of (x) increased mutually with an increase in the value of (y) over time, or was it something else?

More questions pertain to the Turabi thesis on the "stages" of the Movement regarding the concept of "detailed jurisprudence". What conditions were established, thereof, to determine the handling of "each jurisprudence" (pertinent to each stage of progression)? What means of "a perfectionist version of jurisprudence were used, in accordance with the religion of Allah"? Was Turabi calling for an individual jurist or a group of jurists to deal with these problematical tasks?

On the other side, how would the "perfectionist version of Islamic jurisprudence" be applied or rather adapted to the "advanced realities" of the Eastern, as well as Western, societies of the age? These societies, on their turn, attempt to match up complex settings of the social life with the high-level technological achievements their societies maintain.

These questions are probably originated in the sharp divergence or the possible convergence between Islamic jurisprudence and the other universal movements of secularization and human rights norms. They place the Movement of Islam in the midst of a conflict that is pervading the modern social life of the whole world on all national, regional, and international levels of interaction. It is expedient to assess the answers of the thinker Hassan al-Turabi to these questions as they provide a broad basis of comparison with the other views of the Sudanese thinkers in this book.

There is no special ranking for these questions or any specific replies that might corroborate them in the Tagdid. There are, however, important indications. First, a complete rehabilitation of Islamic jurisprudence is at the top of the agenda for the Movement. The reason is that, "the kind of jurisprudence that the Movement possessed is not substantial for the needs of the Da'wa or those beholding it whatsoever induction or deduction they might creatively reach on its basis" (al-Turabi, Tagdid, 1980: 7-8).

The factors most influential in this situation, Turabi explains, included "the material development which led to the emergence of large sections of life ... that exhibited articulations of a new texture that has never been met by the traditional jurisprudence" (al-Turabi, Tagdid, Ibid.). The heart of the matter then is contained in that material development and the new relations it has produced. These are manifestations that transcended, according to him, the objectives and rules of the traditional jurisprudence of Islam.

Turabi makes the strongest point of his departure from traditional jurisprudence in this statement: "The relationships of the social life and the statuses [that regulate them] have been exclusively changed. Some postulates of the rules that once represented the concept of righteousness in accordance with the criteria of religion a thousand years ago are no more fulfilling to the domain of religion today. They would not accomplish the objectives in demand because the means have also changed and the prerequisites of life have been largely developed. Hence, the results that ensue in the application of a certain rule in its earlier form [in modern time] are completely out of context" (Ibid.).

Having seen the need for a revision of the inherited jurisprudence, how would Turabi furnish the Muslim society with a viable alternative to carry out the "new mission" of the Movement at the present time?

In the Tagdid, Turabi mentions that the alternative is "to make a new discipline that shall amalgamate the spiritual knowledge received in written or literal forms [i.e., the Holy Qur'an and the revealed Sunna] with the human sciences that are daily innovated and integrated by both experimentation and vision. With this united science, we would be renewing our knowledge on religion and the requirements it conferred upon our recent life, stage by stage" (Ibid.).

Despite this open invitation to amalgamate scriptural knowledge with the sciences and experiences of the human mind, it is not clear what proportions or forms the proposed amalgam would take. Equally important, it is not apparent that Turabi is calling for a superimposition of any of the two components of the holy knowledge and the human science over one another. Actually Turabi assumes the existence of an Islamic society without defining its features or conditions.

"[The Islamic society]," Turabi says, "is held together by fixations of unity and collective methods of decision making. These are safeguards that guarantee any differences in jurisprudence, whatsoever, would not lead to a practical disagreement in the final analysis. These unifying methods are attributed to the Principle of *Shura* [consultation] that gathers together the partners in conflict as well as the Principle of *Ijma'* [consensus] that represents the authority of the Muslim public" (Ibid. 10).

Turabi sets up a theoretical model on the classic traditions of jurisprudence based on fundamental principles of the Shari'a, the *Shura* and *Ijma'* principles as techniques of collective consultation and consensus. He explains that, "*Ijma'* stands as a real expression of the vast majority of Muslims. It becomes a compulsory judgment upon all Muslims who must surrender to it in practice, in spite of any earlier differences that might have made of it only relatively authentic" (Ibid.).

Turabi further explains, "The *Ijma'* comes about after a [general] round of counseling would have been exercised [by Muslims of a society]. The points of view on which a vast majority would be rallying [their support] would represent an *Ijma'* that should be exceptionally advocated" (Ibid.). He does not, however, explain in <u>Tagdid</u> how the *Shura* [consultation] would be managed on a national level. Nor does he specify the proceedings envisaged in the process of *Shura* or that of *Ijma'*. He doesn't show whether these principles conform or not to the modern parliamentary systems of representation.

Although Turabi has emphasized in the introduction of <u>Tagdid</u> the need to implement his "religious" model, he refers to human sciences as domains through which a huge heritage has been procured in almost all aspects of the social life. These domains included politics, economics, culture, technology, etc. He points out a possibility of intertwining human sciences with scriptural knowledge.

The task of making "a new amalgamated science" of the two distinct forms of knowledge, however, cannot be simply reduced to "a careful revision" of the jurisprudence heritage of the Islamic scriptural knowledge alone, as Turabi seems to suggest. The texts of the scriptural knowledge, in actual fact, are fixed fundamental principles of faith. The jurisprudence heritage, on its part, might entail a greater possibility of exercising consultation and consensus at a larger scale within any meaningful process of jurisprudence revision.

Likewise, the proposed "amalgamated science" requires a qualified caliber to derive from all these sources of knowledge the points of agreement between the classical jurisprudence, the scriptural knowledge, and the human sciences that is most concerned with the requisites of the contemporary life. This colossal task essentially tables democracy and human rights as inevitable preconditions for the implementation of a global project. This is not a local or regional endeavor as is repeatedly initiated by other Muslim scholars.

The declaration issued by the International Institute of Islamic Thought in Washington D.C. (1986) on <u>Islamiyat al-M'arifa, al-Mabadi al-'Ama, Khitat al-</u>

'Amal, al-Ingazat (The Islamization of Knowledge, General Principles, Work Plan, Achievements) is an example of such initiatives. The Institute characterizes the existing crisis of the Muslim World as "a crisis of thought. The remedy of that crisis must necessarily realize this fact. To sustain the efforts of salvation and reformation, the cause of thought and the methodology of thought must be placed at the top of the agenda" (International Institute, Islamiyat al-M'arifa, 1986: 16).

Does the High Institute of Islamic Thought in Washington, where the metropolis of global capitalism of the day is situated on a basis of economic and political power, technology, and modern sciences, offer a practical solution to the crisis? Does the Institute handle the problem of amalgamating the Islamic classical jurisprudence and scriptural knowledge with human sciences in a united framework of good faith and humanity?

The Institute theorizes the crisis of thought with regard to two major dimensions: (1) "The cultural invasion and the alteration that is impelling the minds of the Islamic *Umma* [nation] in the sphere of human and social sciences [in general]. The result is that the Islamic thought and heritage, in particular, is either surpassed or they are studied as an extinguished phenomenology that allegedly ceased to have any bearing in the contemporary life and epistemology; and (2) "Breaking off the ties that link up this *Umma* with the Islamic heritage by converting that heritage into a mere source of commendable historical inheritance. The issue of making this heritage a basis for construction and lively interaction [with modernity] by keeping up the useful, developing the advantageous, and revivifying the good things, nonetheless, has been an irreconcilable point of rejection. The Institute, therefore, seriously undertakes the task of alerting the Islamic *Umma* about the significance of Islamic heritage. The Institute reminds the Muslims that the role to be played by their *Umma* has not been exhausted yet" (Ibid. 17-18).

The Institute undertakes another important methodological step. It consigned (the late) Professor Isma'il al-Farouqi to a mission of "preparing and editing an elaborated plan as a guideline in the areas of Islamic knowledge for the services of thought, intellectuals, and the Muslim students of science." In this respect, the Institute is critical of the fact that a Muslim today "learns ... in universities all over the world about knowledge from books, accomplishments, global outlooks, problems and ideals through a non-Islamic perspective."

"Today, the Muslim scholars," the Institute affirms, "teach the Muslim youth in Islamic universities the western culture and ideas that turn the youth away from their cultural origins and religious roots. This situation needs to be changed. It is the responsibility of educators and the learners of whom many are professor members of the Muslim teaching group to master the origins of the modern branches of knowledge. They have to grasp thoroughly the sciences offered by all these branches."

"This task is a top priority [for the Muslim scholars] to achieve a high level of efficiency. Additionally, the Muslim educators must incorporate the modern branches of knowledge into the infrastructure of the Islamic heritage. The incorporation must come subsequent to a rigorous scrutiny of the modern branches of knowledge. The process would have to eliminate certain elements while the remaining knowledge would be remodeled or reinterpreted compatibly with an international Islamic perspective, including all the values and concepts that might be required by Islam."

The Institute lays out other tasks upon the Muslim educators and learners to promote the model they ought to exhibit as pioneers of this task. For example, "they have to innovate a new method that could possibly guide the branches of knowledge after they would be reformulated to serve the high Islamic ideals. They must teach the new generations of Muslim and non-Muslim educators how to follow the Islamic track to expand the fields and context of the human knowledge. They must explore new discoveries on the mysteries of creation, besides the effort to form new conceptions of goal-achievement to please God" (Ibid. 51).

It is important to recall that both the Institute and Hassan Turabi stress the need to establish "a new amalgamated science" to end the crisis of thought of the Muslim World today. Still, this writer spells out significant differences between their views. The Institute sets out a plan based on a clear recognition of "the origins of the modern branches of knowledge." By so doing, the Institute realizes at once the necessity of "mastering" the knowledge of these branches as a precondition to a further process of scrutinizing them to be compatible with the perspective of Islam.

The Institute, however, does not give any concrete solution or even a detailed conceptualization of the standards or "perspectives of Islam." On his part, Turabi has earlier criticized "the limitations of the scientific base of Muslims during the times of classical jurisprudence." These two conflicting evaluations of the origins of Islamic knowledge and the classical jurisprudence are not prejudiced to the remarkable consensus between the Institute and Turabi on the significance and relevance of modern human sciences to the Muslim World of the day.

A sharp contrast, however, is evident between the two references with respect to the extent to which the origins of Islamic knowledge and the classical jurisprudence comply with modernity. Another contrast is pertinent to the implications thereof regarding the adoption of "an amalgamated science" that is required to advance the Islamic knowledge in the present time.

The Institute seems to be quite confident that the Islamic heritage continues to play an effective role in life because "it has not been exhausted yet. One reason is that the Islamic heritage embodies a foundation of intellectual construction with a lively interaction [with modernity]." In other words, the Institute is much more convinced of the validity of classical jurisprudence [that is firmly grounded on the origins of Islam, the Holy Qur'an and the Sunna] than Turabi is.

The Institute fails, nonetheless, as Turabi does, to elucidate its own organization of the Shari'a in any modern terms. True, the Institute proclaims the merits of Islamic heritage that allowed Muslim societies over the centuries to "keep up the useful, develop the advantageous, and revivify the good things." The question, however, is: How would these merits be maintained in compatibility with modernity in the light of the continuous change and the discontinuity of culture and the social structure of Muslim societies in the contemporary life? What methodology would the Institute use to establish the "new amalgamated science"? In what way would it be possible for the Institute to modernize the classical jurisprudence while still preserving the "origins" of Islam?

These questions have been raised within the complex patterns and forms of the public life and its material development, as well as their direct or indirect impact on the private life of the Muslim individuals and groups. It is certain that the material development of the public life is not only confined to the impact of technology. Rather, the effect of the public life pervades the whole social life in terms of governance, public administration, bureaucratic and/or democratic organizations, the political economy and its ramifications, etc.

Eventually, the need is felt to find the right interpretation of the origins of Islam towards the establishment of the "new scheme," the one science that brings about a logical harmony between complexities of the public life, preferences of the private life, and the high orientations of Islam. The laying out of major ideas about this one "new science," the emphasis on clarity of its context and scope, and the recognition of the worth and originality of Islamic sources of knowledge as a foundation of the new science are valuable to the establishment of the modern Islamic knowledge.

Substantive answers to the issues thus far discussed, especially those related to the status and role of classical jurisprudence in "the new science" in consideration remain to be seen. To conclude, the idea of rethinking the Islamic classical jurisprudence has consistently been raised by the folk Muslim peoples all over the world. Many official Muslims, including Shari'a judicial and/or academic authorities, disapproved the idea.

This situation most likely occurred because it has not added any thrust to clarify the generalizations made by Islamic thinkers or institutes of thought. After all, faith is more assuring to a Muslim's spirituality than these ambiguous disputes that have not resolved in any enduring plan of action or betterment of the public life. The introduction of workable programs to promote the social, economic, and political conditions of Muslim societies is a necessary precondition to imbue the Muslim mind with intellectual precepts of religious revivalism together with the other needs of life.

A CRITIQUE OF THE MODERNIST MODELS

Jamal Mohamed Ahmed, the renowned Sudanese writer, points out the occurrence of a similar conflict in Egypt since the advent of the 20th century. The conflict involved the Muslim innovators who were led by the *Imam* (religious leader) Mohamed 'Abdu and al-Shaikh 'Ali 'Abd al-Raziq on one side and the other *'ulama* (scholars) of the Al-Azhar University, the eminent institution of Islamic education, that never perceived the need for a renewal of Islamic thought. The latter, unlike 'Abdu and his companions, never thought of adopting any movement to renew religion far from the prevailing traditions of classical jurisprudence. The galvanization of this conflict of thought and the way it developed took place within a greater conflict in the political life.

The ongoing conflict encountered the struggle between the Ottoman Caliphate and the European colonial powers to control the Middle East. Because the nature of the conflict was overwhelmingly national, it largely reduced the opportunity of the concerned Azhar scholars to decide upon the ongoing debate on the classical jurisprudence. Jamal concludes in book, The Intellectual Origins of Egyptian Nationalism, by saying that the conflict emanated from a scholastic dispute between learned *'ulama* and resulted in a remarkable development of Egyptian nationalism (see, The Intellectual Origins for more details).

Up to this day, the striving for politics and power struggles does not overlap with thought and intellectual dialogues in Muslim societies. Whereas the activities of political economy are practically restricted to a few desirable objectives that are forcefully pursued for material gain, the practice of thought, on the other end, is a wide venture that encompasses a high degree of persuasion. Because thought only thrives in a liberal democracy, thinkers are often victimized for the exercise of this liberality in non-democratic societies. In the absence of liberal freedoms and human rights, the Muslim countries continue to suffer the crisis of thought under investigation.

The crisis of thought that continues to plague the public life of Muslims with confusion is based on the notorious barriers by the public authorities to curtail the exchange and dissemination of ideas. Amazingly, the early Muslims faced the same curtailment of thought in the opening decades of Islam. The Prophet Muhammad, for example, spent 13 years of his life arguing with the unbelievers for the new religion. He suffered grievous hurt for the sake of the new ideas of Islam.

Today, after the passage of long centuries since the emergence of Islam in Mecca, many systems of rule in Muslim nations largely use the authority of the State to persecute intellectual activities. Numerous Muslim societies are systematically thwarted by ruling groups that impose harsh measures on all aspects of the social life to curb the freedom of thought. The confiscation of the Press, restrictions on the right to hold opinions without interference, as well as the freedom of expression are daily violated in contempt of human rights. The Arab organization for Human Rights and the Arab Lawyers Union, among many other human rights organizations, documented gross human rights violations by Sudan Government, as well as the other warring parties in the civil war of Sudan. (See, for example, the Sudanese Human Rights Quarterly publication SHRO-Cairo, the Sudan Human Rights Organization in Cairo.)

Article 19 of the International Declaration of Human Rights that guarantees the freedom to seek, receive and impart information and ideas of all kinds, regardless of frontiers is virtually outlawed by many Muslim authorities. No surprise that the "High Institute of Islamic Thought" with the knowledgeable elite it represents has sought refuge in a non-Islamic nation, i.e., the United States of America, to carry out intellectual activities. The reason is self-evident. It is namely that the Institute would not find in Muslim countries the liberties that are so indispensable for thought, as available in the U.S.

The anomaly takes us back to the serious question of what conditions are necessary for the achievement of an Islamic thought that would capture the increasing level of "material advancement and the scientific progression" of the 21st century. The achievement of this important goal, however, encounters another bewilderment. A righteous form of adaptation must be fully attained between scriptural knowledge and jurisprudence on the one hand and the contemporary endeavors to reestablish the role of scriptural knowledge in the public affairs and the social life on the other. Otherwise, the crisis would continue unabated in the new century.

This situation takes us further to the discussion Turabi makes in Tagdid on the conditions of exercising "the new amalgamated science" as a viable solution to the crisis in question. One of the conditions is to "try to settle the dispute [among Muslim scholars on Islamic revival and the new amalgamated science] or to get the parties involved to be more appreciative of the problem. The aim is not to end up having a single viewpoint" (al-Turabi, Tagdid, 1980: 10). Another condition pertains to the "obligation conferred upon the early jurists towards *Ijtihad* [scholarly work] and *Madzahib* [schools of jurisprudence] to develop Islamic opinions and *fatawi* [legal decisions] with respect to the fundamental particulars [of Islam]."

The idea is that, "Life is not a stagnant reality. Nor is the religiosity or the kind of problems dealt with by the early jurists the only form of Islam," affirms Turabi.

"The Lord has destined for eternity the challenges entailed in the needs of people and the difficulties of satisfying them. The Muslims must change their [present] forms of life to handle these challenges with the origins of Muslim beliefs and the Shari'a Law as the sole Muslim law" (Ibid. 10-11).

These conditions, however, would not rule out the enormous differences between the transformations that occurred in Muslim societies since the Prophet's early time and the succeeding times of the Wise Caliphs of the Meddina State. These changes were made by the incorporation of the non-Arab peoples and cultures into the enlarging Islamic Empire, and the unprecedented material development of mankind in the present time.

Many Muslim thinkers believe that Islam is possessive of a great potential to absorb these massive discrepancies. The question, however, relates to the extent and limits of that potential and its absorption capacity. Turabi and the Institute of Islamic Thought have already persuaded Muslims to accept the critique of classical jurisprudence and the necessity to build up a new version of Islamic thought. The new version is sought to adapt the classical jurisprudence to modernity to face the challenges of social change. And yet, the theoretical framework of Turabi, in principle, stimulates more problems than it could possibly solve.

A major problem remains unsolved regarding the "most appropriate form of Islamic life" that the thinker postulates. It is true the challenges of the present life for Muslims are quite known, almost by heart. Neither the answers nor the alternatives, however, are practical or convincing. Moreover, "the form of religiosity" as adhered to by the early Muslims and the problems they experienced

47

in the social life might be correctly seen as only changeable in form, not in context or nature as Turabi and the Institute seem to suggest.

To overcome this perplexity, a few thinkers made an attempt to conceptualize "new interpretations" for the "origins" of religion. Other thinkers simply tried to escape the problem by avoiding the whole dispute in toto. Many others further held that "the form of religiosity" is virtually unchangeable for it is intrinsically founded on the '*Ibadat* [worship practices] that are fundamental fixations of the religious faith.

Turabi mentions that, "The expansion and proliferation of judicial judgments and the availability of a large amount of a 'secondary jurisprudence' made it possible to consolidate the 'fundamentalist jurisprudence.' The Imam al-Shafi'e, for example, handled 'the origins of jurisprudence' with a comprehensive scientific methodology that was conducive to rule making and a systematization of jurisprudence" (Ibid.).

We have already seen that the High Institute of Islamic Thought in Washington, D. C., concentrated on "the significance of mastering the origins" and "their modern branches" in the process of revitalizing Islamic thought. At this point, Turabi draws attention to the risks involved in the "rigidity of the early jurisprudence." He affirms that the science of studying the origins of jurisprudence "became an abstractive perspective that developed, as the whole jurisprudence has been developing, into useful exaggerations, bifurcation, and other complexities" (Ibid. 12).

Turabi assures us that "the science of the classical origins through which we seek to find guidance is no more suitable to satisfy our contemporary needs on a full scale. The reason is that it is a science influenced by the impact of the historical circumstances in which it had grown up, even more so by the nature of the jurist problems as encountered in the jurisprudence of that time" (Ibid.).

Descending from these heights of theoretical evaluation, Turabi touches upon one of the substantive realities of Islamic jurisprudence. "The jurists were not tackling, for the most part, problems of the public life. Thus the public life evolved away from them, except when only those interested in a *fatwa* [judicial decision] would be approaching them. These were individuals concerned with individual cases mainly. Therefore, the fundamentals of jurisprudence moved to a concern with rituals, marriage, and divorce."

"The questions of *al-Siyasa al-Shari'ya al-Kuliya*, i.e., the comprehensive legal policy or how a society's life would be run as a whole, were issues the *Awliya al-Umur* [responsible leaders] were not interested in. These included the processes of production, distribution, importation, exportation, and the treatment of a high cost of living or depressing it. Nor did the leaders seek the advice of jurists to provide them with the necessary jurisprudence on these matters. Likewise, the questions of the public economy and political conditions were equally ignored" (Ibid. 14-15).

This writer recalls at this point that the Imam Mohamed 'Abdu (1900) succinctly summed up the criticisms under consideration. Al-Shaikh Hussain al-Mursifi, another enlightened scholar of the Al-Azhar, criticized the backwardness of the "men of religion" who failed to address themselves to the contemporary issues of the time. Al-Mursifi, however, did not generalize his evaluation as Turabi loosely did.

Al-Mursifi attacks in specific terms the individuals whom he considered as enemies of progression. These were "the men of religion, government officials, and the feudal lords." Mursifi affirms that, "The worst elements in society are the demagogues, the leaders of the mob who exploit religion to their own ends. The first symptom of the decay of the Islamic civilization came in correspondence with the unrestricted life of extravagance the leaders lived. They were owners of land who gained the largest profits from agriculture as they only paid to the workers what was adequate to keep up a spirit in a body. The ensuing result was crime and poverty" (Ahmed, Usul, 1960: 22).

The learned 'Abdu and al-Mursifi exposed the problems of the Muslim society in actual reality. With factual analysis, they helped to raise awareness in the public life without resort to any alteration of facts or beautification or exaggeration of the issues in question. The Imam 'Abdu criticized, for instance, the jurists of the late Islamic Caliphate. He praised the Sufi leaders who engulfed Islam with a moral support that "gave it an order of thought and behavior much higher than that attributed to it by the jurists and the sophisticated ones" as he said. The Sufi influence, nonetheless, was lost in the succeeding times to the jurists. In the process, the vision of the intrinsic ethos of faith was virtually replaced. The jurists exercised an idle leadership devoid of ambition in the service of Caliphs and Emirs [princes]. Superstition and lethargy subsequently prevailed as the superstitious and the lethargist took over" (Ibid. 43).

Indeed, the strong criticisms and *Ijtihad* that 'Abdu persistently pursued to modernize Al-Azhar through the innovating *fatawi* and reform policies he introduced into the system are well known. An example in Sudan is perhaps related to the Grand Mahdi who, as earlier mentioned, flatly attacked jurists of the Khartoum Turkish-Egyptian administration. Al-Mahdi further condemned the jurists' opposition to his movement to revive Islam in Sudan as "an evil practice for worldly delights and the acceptance of rulers' hedonism" (al-Gaddal, al-Siyasa al-Iqtisadiya, 1981: 40-141). From thereon, al-Mahdi led a social revolution to replace the regime with a state of Islamic *Jihad*.

Turabi asserts that, "When Islam was embracing the whole life [in early Muslim communities], the public economic and political practices were committed to religion. This [public commitment] activated the fundamental rules that were suitable to that peculiar life" (al-Turabi, Tagdid, 1980: 15). This statement invokes some dispute for it may be contradictory to statements already emphasized by the same thinker.

The dispute is precisely centered on the historical stage at which "Islam was overwhelmingly influential." Is this stage relevant to the State of Meddina, that of the Prophet with the light of revelations overshadowing the Muslim community for generations, or does the period in question contain some other succeeding times, irrespective of the State of Meddina? What then are the characteristics of such a period?

At this important juncture, one recalls the assessment of Turabi that the early Muslim society was transcendental because the "relationships of the social life and the statuses [regulating them] have been exclusively changed. Some provisions of the rules that once represented righteousness, in accordance with the standards of religion a thousand years ago, are no more fulfilling to the domains of religion today... The traditional science of Islamic rules that used to guide us is not any more suitable to fulfill our contemporary needs" (Ibid. 8-12).

If these contradictory statements are not tautological as well, where is the determining variable, which alone, or in interaction with other influential factors, ensures a whole embracing of an Islamic life – one activated by "suitable" fundamental rules yet consonant with modernity? Where and how would Muslims set the limits to sort out the kind of jurisprudence Turabi theorizes for their private and public life? Equally important, who are the jurists entrusted with scholastic authority to decide upon these assertions when Turabi claims that the most authenticated version of Islamic jurisprudence is "redundant" in some ways and "inadequate" for the present time?

The alternative suggested by Turabi to classical jurisprudence is tautological since it has adopted the same major elements of that jurisprudence, albeit an ambiguous reference is made to "a life commitment that wholly embraces Islam." However, he has not explained the nature of that commitment or the legal, social, and political obligations it bears on Muslims today.

The Turabi model seems to be a return to the transitional parameters of Islamic jurisprudence, rather than an ambitious review of the forerunners. Otherwise, the model is simply a confused alternative to the early jurisprudence. I am more confident that the good pioneers of Islamic jurisprudence are much more consistent in their views than the modernists, including Turabi, who exemplify the bewilderment of their elite group and its lack of coherency of thought. Earlier, the Prophet said, "The best of you are put unto my time, followed by those who would succeed you, then those who would succeed them," or so he spoke.

This critique does not mean that the idea of establishing a new Islamic thought is not important. On the contrary, it is an idea that echoes many of the preceding claims of Islamic revivalists, including Imam al-Mahdi and Imam 'Abdu, each in his own right.

As earlier analyzed, 'Abdu presented a clear correlation in his writings between the modern needs of the Muslim society and the revisions required on the Islamic heritage to achieve its objectives. These namely include, "the emancipation of society from ignorance and recklessness." The Imam al-Mahdi called for the Mahdist thought as a way to rally support for the Sudanese people against foreign domination. The High Institute of Islamic Thought has been calling for an educational rehabilitation of the prevailing Muslim systems as a strategic plan of action to keep pace with the modern life. The fact that the Turabi model is ill defined and so largely inflated renders its denouncement in practical terms, unless it would somehow revalidate itself with appropriate delineation.

Perhaps it is now suitable to highlight the works of the other Sudanese thinkers who have provided important details or new approaches to modernize Muslim societies with respect to Islamic jurisprudence, past and present. As will be immediately discussed, many agreements, as well as distinct disagreements, are focused upon among these authors concerning religious revivalism. For that purpose, a comparison of their ideas is briefly discussed in the subsequent section.

The comparison begins with 'Abd al-Khaliq Mahgoub, a Sudanese socialist thinker, who lends his attention to the impact of the inherited jurisprudence on contemporary life, in contrast with the Turabi model. The interest in this contrast springs up from a deep political conflict that has consistently differentiated their opinions from each other.

In theoretical terms, however, both of these thinkers ascertain the role to be played by religion in the nation building of the Sudanese diverse society, although their ideological and political priorities are quite different. Turabi envisages an all-encompassing commitment to Islamic jurisprudence in the Sudanese society (on the assumption that all citizens are Muslims, regardless of the existence of non-Muslim citizens in the same society). 'Abd al-Khaliq views the status and role of religious beliefs within the framework of a secular political life that separates political activities from religion.

The conceptualization of 'Abd al-Khaliq is based on an obligation of his party "to develop [socialist] political propaganda on the cause of Islamic religion and its relation to their movement of social progression in the country. [The party] made many attempts intermittently. But they were lacking in the deep insights and philosophical knowledge required for a successful endeavor ... The significance of this refined propaganda is not only needed as a response to the attacks launched by reactionary propagandists. It goes beyond that point to make of Islamic religion a factor in the service of the basic interests of people, not an instrument in the hands of the exploitative reactionary forces. These are forces not associated at all with the earth of this land or the interests and aspirations of its people."

Mahgoub contends, "We are in need of this line of thought on the philosophical level because there are strenuous attempts made in the educational system to abandon secular life. These attempts aim to bring up a generation by means of falsifying Islamic ideals to use them against social progression and socialism. To confront this dangerous activity, our party is obliged to permeate student's life, not as an advocate of political struggle, but as an intellectual power to face out this danger and to place religion in its appropriate setting within the movement of people" (SCP, al-Marxiya, Undated: 169-170).

The vision of 'Abd al-Khaliq is limited to "the role of religion" within a framework of "political struggle and movement of people." He expands that role "in the service of the basic interests of people." This is a stimulating viewpoint for it addresses a direct relationship between Islamic religion and "the basic interests of people", i.e., "the reality of the social life." It contrasts sharply with Turabi's notion of "reality", i.e. "the requirements religion confers upon recent life."

'Abd al-Khaliq is explicitly open in attributing political tasks to religion in the service of the basic interests of people, "the revolutionary classes and strata … the working class, the peasants, students, soldiers, etc." In the area of Islamic jurisprudence and the "boundaries" of its application in the social life, 'Abd al-Khaliq is opposed as a thinker to "the falsification" of Islamic ideas [by political groups]" against "social progression and socialism."

One application of this instance is that Islamic heritage [being an object of falsification and political manipulation] is projected in a modern perspective by a theory of social change. The model of Turabi is centered about an Islamic society established with a vague commitment to an all-encompassing Islam and put under the authority of some modernist jurists who emphasize "material advancement" and technology of the era. Opposite to Turabi, 'Abd al-Khaliq lays out a clear-cut scheme of establishing a society free of exploitation and the forces of falsifying Islam for "material gain." The alternative is fairly defined in terms of "social progression and socialism" in the writings of 'Abd al-Khaliq and the literature attributed to him.

"Social progress" is a national target accomplished through the enforcement of democratic tasks by the Sudanese Revolution – the revolution of the Sudanese people to enjoy socialism and democratic freedoms. These tasks would be materialized as a result of a strict struggle that is launched "against the backward social and production relations. These relations have been restricting the advancement of the country and inhibiting its energies since medieval times or even before, and the social formations that have no place in the world today other than museums" (Ibid.).

Turabi fails to present a detailed program for the social and religious change anticipated in Sudan by his theological model while 'Abd al-Khaliq furnishes his party with a calculated plan of action. This is an elaborated program of agrarian reform for a country that is predominated by a traditional rain-fed agriculture and is dependent on the government-controlled irrigated schemes in the modern sector of the labor market.

'Abd al-Khaliq calls for the engagement of Sudanese people in a popular political struggle "to foster agrarian reform in the modern sector and the rate of its growth, and to attract the old (traditional] sector to the modern life via necessary economic proceedings. This also means liberalization of the masses from the suffocating tribal formations that obstruct the forces of production, which are topped by the repressive strata that exploit the public. [All these measures must be] accompanied by a democratic reformation of the state apparatus and legislation" (Ibid.).

The role to be played by religion is recognized by 'Abd al-Khaliq within a healthy process of socialization, a process led by the "righteous believers" who acknowledge the right of the human mind to exercise the freedom of thought and the integration of its precepts with religious beliefs. "We are not desperate," writes 'Abd al-Khaliq, "that a healthy socialization would be processed on the basis of religious values to make of the populace a group free of the vices of greed, selfishness, and intimidation. What else do we expect from a power structure that deprives its following of reason and thought, and only forces them to comply with that? It would retard both the followers and the homeland to a state of a real *jahiliya* [ignorance]" (Mahgoub, Afkar, 1967: 8).

Exploring the need for a workable methodology to implement his program, 'Abd al-Khaliq criticizes the contribution of the Egyptian Islamic thinker, Sayed Qutb. He begins with an expression of admiration for the intelligible writings of Qutb in Fi Zilal Al-Qur'an (In the Shadows of The Qur'an). But 'Abd al-Khaliq rebukes Ma'alim fi al-Tariq (Milestones on the Way), Qutb's other publication, since it revealed Qutb's suspicion of all cultures or customs of mankind, in addition to his condemnation of much of the Islamic practices and sources of knowledge for being a *jahiliya*. Qutb was a distinguished thinker of the Muslim Brotherhood in Egypt. Accused of conspiracy to assassinate Jamal 'Abd al-Nasser, Egypt's president in the 1960s, he was put to trial and extra-judicially executed.

"Look at these ideas of the writer: Everything in this world is an absurd *jahiliya*, even those so-called Islamic bibliographies. He might have meant the books of jurisprudence and *Hadith* [sayings and deeds of the Prophet] that we call Islamic references. Is this really what Qutb wanted to say?" (Ibid.15).

'Abd al-Khaliq believes that the Prophet and his Wise Caliphs are examples that should be followed by all Muslims. The Prophet carried out the Mission he had been entrusted with by informing people about it. The Prophet struggled at the same time to guide them to adopt Islamic practice and faith. The Prophet had greatly influenced his followers with his magnificent personality. He was not only a Messenger, as some dishonestly claim.

"In truth," affirms 'Abd al-Khaliq, "the human self needs much treatment and impression upon it [to be persuaded with a new idea]. The process of faith is often rampant with doubt. But those who saw the Prophet with the miracles conducted by him and revelation conveyed to him were by far much more faithful and upholding to their belief in the Messenger [than any other succeeding Muslims]" (Ibid. 14).

Finally, the issue of rethinking religion for 'Abd al-Khaliq meant that Muslims should be aware of the progressive implications of Islam and, eventually, rely on that spiritual foundation for changing society, in principle, in the interest of the vast majority of the Sudanese have-nots and the productive forces. As a modern thinker, he draws heavily upon modern sciences, especially the social sciences and political economy, to change all aspects of the social and political life. In so doing, 'Abd al-Khaliq is not restrained from choosing what he thinks fit from all schools and trends of thought, especially the socialist thought that he develops into a profound social theory to achieve a program of political action.

The concepts of "reality," "progression," "jurisprudence," "revivalism," and the other relevant meanings attached to the crisis of thought in Sudan, as a Muslim-dominated society, have been used in a context of a political theory by 'Abd al-Khaliq Mahgoub, rather than an obscure version of religious revivalism. The emphasis on socio-economic and political development, however, does not blur the specific allocation of ethical, social and spiritual roles for religion in society. In that case, 'Abd al-Khaliq insists that society will be fully emancipated from backwardness and exploitation, as well as any manipulation of religion for "material advantages."

Obviously, Mahgoub was not a religious revivalist but a political theorist and activist. Turabi has been particularly concerned for Islamic jurisprudence affairs and challenges than 'Abd al-Khaliq was, regardless of the inadequacies of the Turabi thought.

The clarity of thought of 'Abd al-Khaliq Mahgoub seems to emanate from his political and ideological leadership, the idiosyncrasy of his party, the spheres of ideology it has largely disseminated in the Sudan. Hassan al-Turabi, on the other side, manages to assume leadership of the Sudanese Muslim Brotherhood, his politico-religious groups. But the survival and growth of his scheme has never been advanced through jurist lines, despite his law background.

Instead, the Turabi thesis, as previously discussed, suffers a serious lack of definitions, clarity of concepts, and coherency. Ironically, he fails as a jurist in utilizing these idiomatic tools that are typical jurist functions. This failure might partially explain Turabi's active involvement in the coup of June 30th, 1989, to exercise de facto, in the words of 'Ali 'Abd-Allah 'Abbas, President of the University of Khartoum's Professors Union, the conquering of Sudanese state and society" via an authoritarian model of a religious state.

To further the contrast between Sudanese thinkers on Islam and society in the Sudan, Sadiq al-Mahdi and Mahmoud Mohamed Taha are important thinkers who have devoted substantial portions of their thought and intellectual works to religious revivalism.

It may be true that Sadiq al-Mahdi, as a Sudanese Islamic thinker, made a practical contribution in his works to elaborate on the possibility of applying the broad theoretical assumptions of the Turabi model. Sadiq's intention seems to hinge on the establishment of "a new amalgamated science," as advocated by the High Institute for Islamic Thought in Washington, D.C., and to undertake a modern and scientific rehabilitation for the Muslim world today. Added to these aspects of his work are the ideas suggested by Sadiq al-Mahdi, the statesman and politico-religious leader, which reflect some of his own personal characteristics.

In his book <u>Al-'Uqobat al-Shar'iya wa Mawqi'a min al-Nizam al-Ijtimai al-Islami</u> (Shari'a Punishments and their Position in the Islamic Social System), Sadiq al-Mahdi presents some of his major ideas. He writes explicitly that, "The most enlightened picture of Islamic thought is the earliest one, the oldest stage of Islamic thought that was most lively and offering, a stage at which Muslims exemplified a society of mercy, justice, and forgiveness. Islamic thought was most persuasive to the whole universe in terms of reform, success, freedom, vividness, and creativity"('al-Mahdi, '<u>Uqobat</u>, Undated: 123).

This is a viewpoint that is completely contrary to the Turabi assessment of the earliest era of Islam, which was restrictive to the pioneer Muslims by limitations of jurist rules. Sadiq's evaluation is quite consonant with a number of Islamic revivalists, for example Ibn Taymiyah and Imam al-Mahdi, his own great grandfather, both of whom developed a revivalist thought based upon that of the earliest Muslims.

On the need for a "revision of the classical jurisprudence," Sadiq phrases "the Islamic vigilance," since the early 1980's to serve as an emblem for his religious scheme (*see* <u>Al-Sahwa al-Islamiya wa Mustaqbal al-Da'wa</u> (Islamic Vigilance and the Future of Islamic Call), issued by the Ansar Students' Movement, 1981). The Islamic Vigilance emblem may be related to the Islamic Revolution of the Iranian people that overthrew the rule of the Shah dictatorship and foreign domination over the country. The revolution was successfully planned and enforced by the people of Iran in the wake of their Muslim society to improve the economic, social, and political development of the country without foreign dependency or social injustices.

Sadiq al-Mahdi rejects the extremism of right-wing groups and the secularism of left-wing parties. He is equally resentful of "the rashness of persons who are enthusiastic [about Islamic revivalism] without planning, or the opportunists who have no real faith in their attempt to apply Islam [in society and the state]. Even if intentions are determined in good faith, contemporary Islamic application is challenged with problems that cannot be simply resolved by wishful thinking or enthusiasm. To straighten out Islamic applications, the problem of the [existing] rules of jurisprudence must be readily resolved" (Ibid. 24).

How does Sadiq evaluate these rules? He is satisfied with the fact that, "The references consulted by all those who desire to apply Shari'a are books of the *Madzahib* [schools of jurisprudence]. We have seen the *Mujtahideen* [scholars professing new rules of jurisprudence] inferring new rules with a thought addressed to the environments, social conditions, and customs of their own countries. Although the rules have been established according to texts and sources of the Shari'a, they were expressive of a reality that has greatly changed over time. Therefore, it is not right to establish a contemporary Islamic application with these rules" (Ibid. 124).

The conclusion reached by Sadiq was earlier shown in the criticisms of Turabi. The difference between the two writers is that Turabi only promises to create "a new amalgamated science" as an alternative to the "nullified" version of Islamic jurisprudence (which is not specified in his writings). Turabi anticipates such contribution only "if granted a wider opportunity to deal with the jurisprudence of religious sources and their systems, by using more accurate methodology and deeper analysis" (al-Turabi, Tagdid, 1980: 46).

Sadiq, for his part, is determined "to transfer the area of general research to a field of specific know-how of Islamic application" (al-Mahdi, 'Uqobat, Undated: 22). This is done by a series of discussions in some of his works on the needs, themes, and limits of a new *Ijtihad* to form a modern version of Islamic jurisprudence.

Al-Mahdi begins with a polite appreciation of the efforts of the ancestors, the older generations: "The consensus of the public Muslims in the issues [of jurisprudence] was a head of time as [that jurisprudence] had been the most just in the circumstances. But after 12 centuries passed away, a revision is necessarily manifesting itself [for that jurisprudence]" (Ibid. 124).

Sadiq then discusses the need to repeal seven rules of concern to the non-Muslims since they "degrade their status below that of the Muslims. This motivates the non-Muslim minorities in Islamic countries to reject the application of Islamic Shari'a" (Ibid. 125). He mentions that the remaining issues are pertinent to the imposition of *hudud* (punishment prescribed by Allah) on specific violations (for example wine drinking); women's rights; slavery; exercising authority of the state; transgression; apostasy; and the implementation of rules on citizens of the other states.

Based on intensive citations of authentic jurisprudence, al-Mahdi highlights a fundamental fact of Islamic thought, namely that a diversity of opinions has always existed among the *'ulama* and jurists.

A learned and enlightening dispute has consistently underlined that diversity because the scholars and jurists were originating their viewpoints in the fundamental origins and branches of religion, rather than any personal feelings.

Sadiq al-Mahdi explains that, "Apostasy is a crime punishable by a *hadd*. There is a disagreement [amongst jurists], however, about the rules of repenting apostasy such as the days required [to discharge an accusation]. Apostasy [Sadiq believes] should be punished as *ta'zir* [discretionary punishment, not a *hadd*]. The argument of the Imam Ibn al-Qayim to punish an apostate is the strongest because it reconciles between the [prescribed] punishment and the [Islamic] principle of 'no compulsion in religion.'"

"The argument of the bulk of jurists [that an apostate be killed if repentance is not pronounced within a few days] breaches the [Qur'anic] principle of 'no compulsion in religion.' This proceeding is not suitable for the forgiveness [and the mode of tolerance] of our times. It contradicts the interests of Islam nowadays since those who adopt Islam voluntarily all over the world are increasing [in population] in greater numbers than those who defect from Islam. The People of the Book [members of the other monotheist religions, i.e., Christianity and Judaism] expect an equal treatment on our part" (Ibid. 133-134).

Sadiq defends the potentialities of Islamic Shari'a to function creatively, in accordance with Islamic heritage. He claims that modern forms of behavior comply in spirit and texts with a wide range of [Shari'a] societal activities. His persuasion is to refute the rules of classical jurisprudence with respect to many topics and does not rest on a rejection of their "limitation" [as Turabi alleges]. Rather, Sadiq maintains that the conditions of the age are not suitable for these rules, hence Islamic rules might be reestablished should the need arise for that.

This logic brings him closer to the other Islamic liberals, like the Imam Mohamed 'Abdu.

Earlier, 'Abdu upheld the opinion that, "Islamic religion would not possibly be a social and spiritual force unless it is discussed and learnt in a liberal way." The Islamic thought, in 'Abdu's view, had taken a wrong path when it alienated itself from the public life before its downfall under influence of the Greek philosophy (Ahmed, Usul, 1960: 43). In contrast, "the epoch of the Prophet and his disciples" was the most flourishing time of Islamic thought (al-Mahdi, 'Uqobat, Ibid.).

Let us take another example to illustrate the liberal tendency of Sadiq al-Mahdi concerning the issue of succession in the Caliphate or the *Imamiya* (leadership over the believers). He alludes to the Shiite doctrine which ascertains the role of the grand jurist, one who inherits knowledge beyond the *Ijma'* (consensus) and *Qiyas* (juridical analogy) as popular tools of Islamic Authority.

The Caliphate in the Sunni doctrine hinges on a selection process controlled by a group of responsible leaders who are entrusted with the powers of legitimacy and prohibition. The responsible leaders are entitled to elect a Caliph because they constitute a group preeminent in piety, knowledge, and wisdom. Having briefly analyzed the experiences of the two doctrines in Islamic history, Sadiq concludes in this critique:

"The nonexistence of an infallible Imam or grand jurists, as is anticipated by the Shiite, renders the role expectation of the Imam in the revival of the Muslim *Umma* [nation] an impossibility" (Ibid. 161-171). The Sunni doctrine on leadership of the responsible leaders "continued to be redundant as the authority of the Sunni Islamic countries was forcibly encroached by a system of inherited political power."

In the final analysis, contends al-Mahdi, "We ought to overlook both the Sunni Caliphate and the Shi'ite Imamiya since the *Ijma'* of the majority jurists of these two groups was not practically useful in its historic times. It is unsuitable for our recent conditions, beforehand" (Ibid.).

The gist of Sadiq's argument is expressive of his actual Islamic thought: Due to the failures of the most influential doctrines of classical jurisprudence to achieve the Caliphate model of rule for Muslim societies, he rules out all forms of jurist elitist systems. Henceforth, al-Mahdi draws a lesson upon the experiences of Sudan: "Our homeland has been recently persecuted by authoritarian regimes sometimes in the name of nationalism, and at times in the name of freedom, stability, development, and socialism. After a third of a century, they left our countries in a state so largely divided, dependent, deprived of freedoms, subverted and impoverished – so remote from social justice" (Ibid. 171). This conclusion seems to be an implication of his liberal Islamic orientation.

A further note of Sadiq's concern for workable programs, more urgently than his philosophical concerns is his strong assertion: "Freedom and popular participation are prerequisites for governance. Even if they are not made available, dictatorial rulers must not be allowed to manipulate a despotic rule under any pretext. Shaikh Mohamed Abu Zahra should be praised for saying that, 'it is better for groups to commit mistakes while freely expressing their opinion than to be coerced to follow depression and a loss of will which are much more harmful to the process of nation building' (Ibid.).

Sadiq emphasizes this affirmative commitment to Islamic principle of *Shura* [consultation] and the condition of achieving it with justice and equality, the fulfillment of promises, respect of personal liberties, and the freedoms of opinion and political activity. With that, he is convinced that the full enjoyment of these rights would only be insured through the accomplishment of "human experience and reason," as values of Islamic antecedence. These are foremost premises for any Islamic model of rule. Hence, "No matter how many multiple forms of governance might exist [in the Muslim world], they ought to be committed to these principles since Islam does not ordain any single form of government" (Ibid.).

Guided by this liberalism in his political thought, Sadiq makes the attempt of designating a system of rule to be founded on a "modern Islamic base" by incorporating the "spirit of the age" to avoid any conflict or confrontation with religion. In his attempt to emphasize the compatibility of Islamic principles of Shura with modern political pluralism, Sadiq al-Mahdi affirms, "That a sacred war of Jihad spread Islam, or that Islam was expanded by the sword, is a lie. *Jihad* is not only a matter of fighting in war. It is a concept denoting all efforts made by all possible means for the sake of Allah. It is a steadfast stand against evil in all its forms, [a complete struggle] against wrongdoing as long as life continues to exist, forever. That is the reason why the Prophet enforced *Jihad* as a lifestyle up to the time of the other world" (Ibid. 84).

The criteria of integrating Islamic principles into international relations are another area of interest for Sadiq al-Mahdi. "Man is dignified by his very human nature. Justice is a permanent commandment. Honoring a promise is an obligation. Cooperation with people who do not belong to our folk is a must, unless they are unjust. And the freedom of religious beliefs [is another righteous criteria]," etc. (Ibid.).

These principles represent a broad Islamic umbrella under which provisions of international and regional laws could easily coincide, for example the Universal Declaration of Human Rights, the International Covenant on Civil and Political Rights, and the International Covenant on Economic, Social and Cultural Rights. They are stipulated "in recognition of the inherent dignity and of the equal and inalienable rights of all members of the human family, the foundation of freedom, justice, and peace in the world" (Preamble, International Covenant on Economic, Social and Cultural Rights, 1966).

The Preamble of the Universal Declaration of Human Rights (1948) reads that a world "in which human beings shall enjoy freedom of speech and belief and freedom from fear and want has been proclaimed as the highest aspiration of the common people." Sadiq al-Mahdi infers that, as a matter of fact, "the international politics dictated by the early Islamic jurists must be abandoned. It has to be looked at as theories of rules applied in the course of history as a phase of the development of Islamic jurisprudence."

"[These old rules] should be transcended at the present time by a new set of rules heavily drawn upon the texts and objectives of Shari'a, i.e., a new *Ijtihad*. Secondly, all charters and systems of the present international order must be reviewed, according to the principles [earlier explained]. We will support the rules [of the international order] compatible with these principles but those incompatible with them will be rejected. Thirdly, we have to submit to the principles in question such that any obligations or charters incompatible with them will have no bearing on us" (Ibid. 187).

Subsequent to this adaptation of international norms in close adherence to Islamic principles, Sadiq criticizes the ongoing international order, the United Nations and its organizations, the dominating position and actions of super powers over smaller countries, etc. He asserts that, "The international order is certainly a discordant system, if fairly evaluated." Nonetheless, Sadiq concedes that there are a few positive aspects of that order, despite its shortcomings.

"The specialized agencies of the United Nations in agricultural services, culture, and health are the best activities of the UN and they are the most favorable ones. But the agencies responsible for developmental and financial affairs, such as the World Bank and the International Monetary Fund, are totally biased toward the capitalist order because they are submissive to the will of rich countries."

He calls further upon the international community [in the early 1980s] "to undertake measures of protection versus the dangerous countries that threaten the word peace by their racism and repression, for example Israel in Asia and South Africa in Africa" (Ibid. 188-189).

Apparently, Sadiq is realistic in his statements. He agrees that the global civilization of our time with all its Western capitalist or (the defunct) communist systems "is an important civilization which plays a role in determining the fate of the world. It has not even resolved the crisis of its own civilization that enjoys a high level of freedoms, productivity, and facilities of life. But it is not a freedom of high ideals or altruism. It is a high productivity system but it does not allow any just distribution of wealth" (Ibid. 191-192).

"[Equally,] the Communist Bloc has an important civilization which plays a role in determining the fate of the world. The Communist Bloc managed to settle

68

many problems that had been caused by the East Civilization, and to correct its wrongs. The East, nonetheless, paid dearly for that settlement: Freedom as a price for social planning. It abandoned the spiritual meanings of life to advance materialistic gains. It did not know that a loss of freedom and spiritual values psychologically kills man just as a loss of food biologically diseases mankind" (Ibid. 191-192).

The 3rd World poor countries "are theoretically promised prosperity by the international order of the day; that, in fact, did not help the 3rd World to revive its origins. Nor did it help them to develop themselves with [the prevailing] modernity." In the light of this perception, the Islamic world is seen as an alternative civilization "if it realizes the power of Islam" (Ibid.). His central point is: How would the Islamic alternative be installed in place of both Western capitalist and the Eastern communist worlds? The solution put forward by Sadiq al-Mahdi is that, "a viable model has to be born out of an Islamic social order to reconcile Shari'a fixations with an advanced jurisprudence" (Ibid. 193). The ensuing economic and social systems, as well as a system of international relations, would thenceforth acquire both Islamic and contemporaneous elements.

Sadiq does not elucidate the features of his model in detail to convince the reader with them for he seems personally contented with the Islamic model as a possible alternative to the existing world system. In a broad theoretical approach, nonetheless, he criticizes the shortcomings of the model through a rigorous examination of old jurists' documentary material in comparison with systems of the modern political life. In contrast to Turabi and Taha, al-Mahdi does not claim any exclusive competence or that of a special party to perform the difficult tasks of creating an applicable Islamic order for our societies today.

He avoids Turabi's invitation to initiate a purely "new amalgamated science" because it disregards the conceivable possibility of integrating an Islamic model for the establishment of a new social order with the existing sciences and world experiences.

In general, it appears that Sadiq al-Mahdi's and Hassan al-Turabi's shared ideas might have molded them into a joint venture. Still, significant differences could be recognized between the methodologies the two thinkers suggest for the implementation of their projected models.

For one, Sadiq sharpens the idea of manifesting Islam as an alternative civilization in terms of a comprehensive social order: "Any speech about an Islamic insurrection empty of this orientation would only be a fallacy that only arouses dust without throwing any light on the subject matter" (Ibid.).

Subsequently, he asserts that "modern" conditions must be available to apply the Islamic social order, namely that "an Islamic insurrection must proceed with a strong faith in the Islamic model. This, in turn, should motivate a large wave of popular enthusiasm and assured popular response" (Ibid.193).

This very condition shows one of the deep discrepancies between Sadiq al-Mahdi and Hassan al-Turabi as Islamic thinkers. There is not a single mention in Turabi's work of the "freedom, popular participation, and assured popular response" needed "for the establishment of a modern Islamic state." Sadiq, on the other side, clearly maintains that Sudanese Muslim masses must not be isolated from modalities of the time so that the Islamic religion wouldn't suffer an increasing isolation from modern societies.

Sadiq appeals to all secularists to consider the suitability of Islam an alternative civilization and international social order through dialogue. Emphasizing, "the wide horizons of Islam and its broad teachings," he strongly believes that, "The establishment of an Islamic order is not parallel to the Inquisition Courts which put thought on trial and violated privacy. Islam is a strong guarantor of the freedom of religious belief and privacy because it does not allow any restrictions on them."

Islam values to a great extent "the right of religious minorities in Muslim countries to be well-informed about Islamic guarantees of human rights, Islamic provisions for their civil rights and religious freedoms, and the introduction of Islamic order in the society in agreement with them" (Ibid.).

This conceptualization does not overlap with that of 'Abd al-Khaliq Mahgoub and the other thinkers who anticipate a primary role for religion in the social life and conceive of the process of nation building according to the right of citizenship. A citizen who subscribes, or not, to a certain religion is worthy of all rights and is equally obligated to perform all duties of citizenship by law. The ideas of al-Mahdi despite his liberal views do not exactly fit in these concepts.

Can the ties created by citizenship achieve the objectives pursued in the present political and social life more than religion can possibly do? Would it be possible for a Muslim citizen today to interpret the meaning of the Qur'anic verse, "There is no compulsion in religion," without a correct assessment of the "material and moral progression" that allows a wide range of economic, political and social activities in society on its own right?

It certainly is clear that a careful investigation of these questions is critically needed beyond al-Mahdi's sketch of the Islamic principles for establishment of an Islamic state and a new international order.

Another paradoxical situation emerging from the emphasis on "freedom and popular participation" as prerequisites for installation of the Islamic state is that all trends of thought and ideologies must be allowed to exercise the right to define political identity of the nation and to guide its direction. This liberal attitude is a function of political competition rather than the call for an Islamic state.

Sadiq al-Mahdi, moreover, has not specified the limits to preserve an Islamic identity of the state. Thus, when it becomes expedient to spell out a workable program to ensure the right of minorities, for example, he upholds the same rules of jurisprudence without any attempt to 'adapt" them to the needs of minorities. This situation renders the problem unresolved in practical terms.

Hassan al-Turabi writes, "It is our good fortune in the Sudan that we lie in a country weak in inherited Islamic history and culture. This might appear, firsthand, as s a disaster. Nevertheless, it could be an advantage in some respect since there would be no vigorous resistance to stop advancement of a renewed Islam" (al-Turabi, Tagdid, 1980: 44).

This presumptuous judgment is vehemently rejected in the light of documented history of Islam in the Sudan through the writings of many historians, archaeologists, and the other researchers on the deep embodiment of Islamic religion in the worshipping, social, and cultural aspects of Sudanese society. A study written by Professor Own al-Sharif Qasim, Professor Osman Sid Ahmed with Ahmed Mohamed 'Ali Hakim and 'Ali al-Khatim *on* Al-Islam fi al-Sudan:

Dirasa fi Takween al-Shakhsiya al-Sudaniya (1984) (Islam in the Sudan: A Study on the Formation of Sudanese personality) illustrates the facts in question.

The study documents the fact that, "Islam came in the Sudan since the early days of its Mission … What we know about the spread of Islam in the Sudan is that it penetrated society without any official or missionary work. It was spontaneously spread among individuals and groups. We have much evidence about the presence of Muslims in the Sudanese hemisphere, amongst Christian Nubians or animist Beja … This Sudanese contribution to the Islamic movement was not marginal."

The study further asserted that, "We believe that it transcended a mechanical conversion to Islam through a sophisticated rational participation in the Islamic movement of thought and culture. Some Nubian personalities took part in the ongoing conflict that had been protracted in all spheres of thought, jurisprudence, grammar, and the Sufi activity. Many Islamic personalities including Zal-Noon al-Misri, the famous jurist Ibn Habib, and Lady Safiya the Sufi were actively involved in the movement."

The study illuminates a number of historical events on the permeation of Islam into Sudanese, as well as other neighboring societies. "The port of Izab, a center of Islamic thought and culture, became one of the world entrances for African pilgrimage. Hadith jurists, thinkers, and leaders of Sufi groups frequently visited Izab after the shut down of ports of the Fertile Crescent and Egypt by the Crusaders. It is worth mentioning that Muslim Nubian soldiers had regularly attended the mosques of Cairo. The mosques were overcrowded with Muslims at the time Salah al-Deen [Saladin the Ayoubite] was ruling" (Qasim et al., al-Islam fi al-Sudan, 1984: 56).

In a subsequent historical period, al-Haj Hamad Mohamed Khair tackled the origination of Islam in the early times of Nubian and Eastern Sudan. He investigated and evaluated the book Ibn Salim al-Aswani had earlier written in the mid 10th century AD. Khair demonstrated the intimate military and economic interaction that had cemented the close relations between the Islamic authorities of Egypt and the Sudanese parties of Nubia and the Beja. The ensuing common interests of these entities led to a stability and dispersion of Islam all over the lands of Sudan at that time.

In the introduction of the Aswani book, we came across Daif-Allah's stories about the Sudanese Muslim society during the centuries succeeding the rise of Islamic kingdoms in Sudan, chief of which is the "Black Sultanate of Al-Funj, the 'Abdallab dynasty (or Shaikhship) at Qarray, etc. These famous Sudanese medieval kingdoms testify to the strong, rather than "weak", existence of Islam in Sudanese history.

In conclusion, the Sudanese society is not simply lacking in "the inherited Islamic history and culture: as Turabi imagines it might have been so. The consensus of scholars and researchers is that Sudan is a society "deeply rooted in Islamic origins," and that Sudanese Sufi sects have acquired a massive popularity among the populace, regardless of the disputes frequently aroused on the extent of their jurisprudence knowledge.

The spread of Islam in Sudanese society, the relative tolerance amongst different Muslims and Sufi traditions, and the co-existence of Muslims and non-Muslims in peacefulness since the Sudanese Nubian kingdoms constitute intrinsic characteristics of the Sudanese personality. It is a personality strongly inclined to the full enjoyment of freedoms and popular participation in public affairs. This might be correlated in some way with the pastoral or semi-agricultural environment of the country. It is unbecoming and incorrect, however, in the light of the firm socio-political and religious background of the country to think of Sudan as a nation devoid of "inherited Islamic history and culture."

Sociologically speaking, a viable societal construct, such as a new science or order, cannot be established in a tabula rasa. The consent of people, their mood and full participation are necessary conditions for any installation meant to influence their social life. In these circumstances, a "renewed" religion can be based only on a people's inherited domains.

By now, a few features of the attempts made to revive religion in the Sudan, the convergence or divergence encountered in them, visions on society and its needs, and realities of the Sudanese society, in general, have been briefly discussed and assessed. The writer concludes that the only way to deal with Sudanese society in all parts of the country is to respect its values and internal composition in the first place, to think of its diversity with continuous appreciation and understanding.

Hassan al-Turabi, 'Abd al-Khaliq Mahgoub, and Sadiq al-Mahdi have been rethinking religion as a factual matter, an instrument of social change for the good life, each on its own right. The contrast is quite obvious between Turabi and al-Mahdi, on the one hand, and 'Abd al-Khaliq on the other.

At this point, it is suitable to highlight major ideas of the Islamic philosopher Mahmoud Mohamed Taha who has concentrated his thought, similar to Turabi and Sadiq, on the classical Islamic jurisprudence and the problem of adapting its rules to our present times.

A DIALECTICAL EXERCISE OF IJTIHAD

Mahmoud Mohamed Taha explores the possibilities of making an Islamic social order based on the fundamentals of Islam as a safeguard against deviations of the modern life and its worldliness. In what follows, we will elaborate on some of the most important ideas of Taha.

The Sufi religious thought as well as theories of empirical experimentalism influenced Mahmoud as is earlier mentioned. He diligently practiced politics in the opposition of the Rufa'a people in 1946 against a law issued by the British colonial authorities to prohibit female circumcision. Accusing the British of interference in their private life, the Rufa'a opposition was meant to rally people against the colonial administration to protect their cultural rights from foreign intrusion.[1]

Mahmoud benefited from his studies of engineering, an ancient science based on empirical research, at the Gordon Memorial College (thereafter the University of Khartoum). A unique blend of engineering studies and Sufi practices inevitably broadened Mahmoud's thought and deepened his world outlook. Mahmoud, however, was not clearly guided by a positivist doctrine that might have enabled him to contemplate pragmatically the problems of the Sudanese society. To explore this assumption, as well as the intellectual sources of Mahmoud's ideas, we will begin a discourse of the context of his agreement, or disagreement, with

---

[1] Mohamed Mahmoud believes that, "The "Rufa'a episode" effectively dealt the circumcision law a deathblow rendering it to all intents and purposes a dead letter... But in winning this battle in the name of the "honor" of Sudanese women, Taha had inadvertently contributed to the single greatest damage to the welfare of Sudanese women" (New Political Science: 23, Number 1, 2001, p. 72). Many Republican Brothers, however, believe that the "Rufa'a episode" was a serious challenge to the colonial conspiracy to prolong foreign rule in Sudan by imposing laws antagonizing Sudanese customs as "uncivilized" practices. See Yasir al-Sharif and Omer al-Garray replies to Mohamed Mahmoud's critique in the Sudanese Lists in the International Internet, for example sudannile.com and the Sudanese@list.msu.edu

the Western perspectives of social evolution, especially the Marxian doctrine for a representative of western thought.

Taking advantage of his broad intellectuality and his life of contemplation, Mahmoud studied Marxism in scholastic terms. This methodology allowed him to understand the positive as well as negative aspects of Marxist thought in a liberal way. With that, Mahmoud stands on an equal footing with Sadiq al-Mahdi and 'Abd al-Khaliq Mahgoub whose academic studies furnished them with an opportunity to evaluate Marxism in intellectual terms.

Sadiq, for instance, admits that the communists "achieved a success in the development of Central Asia" (al-Mahdi, 'Uqobat, Undated: 1992). He rejects, however, the surrendering of freedom and abandoning of the spiritual meanings of life as a price for social planning.

For his part, 'Abd al-Khaliq Mahgoub moves from a scholarly reading of Marxist thought to a serious analysis of Sudanese societal relations using a Marxist concept of class structure, production relations, social forces and their position in political authority and economic interests, etc. Mahgoub subsequently adopts a full consideration of Marxism as a "guide for social life that can be obtained to deal with the prevailing conditions of the Sudan." He holds that Marxist thought is adaptable and is capable of incorporating the diversified cultural and class differentials of the Sudanese society into an integrated whole.

At the opposite end of Sudanese thinkers, Turabi rejects Marxism as a secular atheism." So what would Taha see in Marxism? Writing in Al-Marxiyah fi al-Mizan (Marxism in a Balance), Taha thinks that, "Evolution, i.e., the fact that existence evolves in a continuous movement since it never rests, does not exit outside the facts of religion. Islam, indeed, is a total sum of all forms of activity in existence. Our Lord says in the Qur'an about Islam, 'What other than the religion of Allah do they claim?' So, Marx, and whatever is being brought by Marx, is contained in the general Islam" (Taha, al-Mizan, 1973: 6).

This viewpoint is based on Mahmoud's strong faith that Islam is a cosmological domain so absolute that it exempts no human thought, irrespective of its degree of faith, from falling within its existential web. One implication underlying this belief is that Taha appears as a philosopher who never defines Islam as exclusive rules of the Shari'a jurisprudence. Rather, Taha believes that Islam encourages full exercise of the freedom of thought. Despite the difference in context and scope between his definition and the meaning earlier suggested by Sadiq al-Mahdi (that "Islamic Shari'a is much larger than the jurisprudence developed within its milieu" (al-Mahdi, 'Uqobat, Undated: 135)), an encyclopedic vision of both thinkers on the cosmic mission of Islam is hardly negated.

Turabi agrees with this world outlook by saying that, knowledge is made submissive to "the worshipping of Allah" (al-Turabi, Tagdid, 1980: 8). All thinkers believe that Almighty God is All Knowing about His creatures, that Islam is the complete religion, and that there is nothing that can be occurring outside the knowledge of Allah.

The connotations related to Islam by Mahmoud Mohamed Taha are not only expressive of the general faith of Muslims that Islam is the complete religion revealed by God. What he additionally believes is that Islam is a special linkage of God with his creatures, their thought and action such that whatever they do is never outside His knowledge.

Mahmoud's study of Marxism consists of positive as well as negative evaluations of the Marxian doctrine. The positive evaluation includes an appraisal of the thorough research undertaken by Marx about the economic phenomenon. According to Mahmoud, "Marx made of socialism an issue that yields to supply, planning, and implementation. Colonialism is the evil of capitalism. History will continue to accommodate that fact. The economic order is governed, even created, by class struggles. History is a record of this Marxist display. The right to governance, according to Marx, lies in the hands of the exploitative class to exploit with it the exploited classes" (Taha, al-Mizan, 1973: 18).

Taha reiterates the age-old philosophical dispute: "Did Karl Marx believe that the mind is a superceding or an antecedent of matter? Yes! Is it his opinion that thought is nothing but a reflection of the movement of matter in the hemisphere upon the human mind? Yes!" And yet, for Mahmoud, "Marx was wrong in ignoring that there is a mind that has always existed before matter" (Ibid. 27-28).

Taha admits that there is a life-conflict of material interests among social forces, which signifies the fundamental role played by economics in the movement of history. He, nonetheless, is not fully persuaded by that Marxist discovery. Instead, he explores a religious reference which preceded the Marxian discovery, as it reads in the Qur'an, "Conflict is directed by the wisdom of Allah [but processed] via a law of chaos: 'If We desire to destroy a village, We will order its extravagant ones to act wrongfully at it; then the Word will be forced upon it, and We will destroy it completely.' The wisdom underlying this "eternal" conflict is what Allah says, 'And did not God check one set of people by means of another, the earth would indeed be full of mischief' [II: 251]".

Mahmoud mentions that he does not mean with the "law of chaos" that predatory power of the strong ones occurs over the weak aside from material goals or away from the will of God. But he concedes, "The struggle for living had been induced by a willingness to support the unjustly treated, or the weak, and to defend their rights. This good human impetus was not entirely absent from the theater … Human considerations have been articulated from time to time in an increasing manner by means of a special Islam that figures out from within the general Islamic religion" (Taha, Tatweer, 1971: 24-27).

Mahout Mohamed Tara draws heavily on positivist sciences in his theorization of Islamic evolutionism. For instance, he has repeatedly used some of the Western theories of evolution and concepts of progress. The following passage demonstrates the impact of Western thought on Mahout's ideas of worshipping God. "In the way to Mi'raj [the path of the prophet Muhammad to Allah in Heavens], light things emerge from heavy things. On the way back to earth, i.e., the Tana-zul, heavy things come out of light things. According to this rule of consecution, the Ingeel [Bible, New Testament] emerged from the Torah [the Old Testament] as the Umma [Nation] of Muslims will emerge from the nation of believers. The Ahmediya [Ahmedism] Message will come out of the Muhammadiya Message [that of Muhammad] as the Brothers will come out of the Companions. All creatures will continue to walk in the path, close to God" (Taha, Tariq Muhammad, Undated: 5).

In the picture just postulated in the preceding passage appears some influence of Muslim Sufis and philosophies (see for example, al-Maqrisi, 1996: 162-190). At the same time, we feel the influence of Hegelian thought which, in what has been known as the "Hegelian dialectics," poses idealism as a mode of thought developed over time in complementary stages. The Hegelian thought had been lately adopted by Karl Marx who converted some of its basic ideas into a doctrine of material evolutionism, class struggles, state relations, production relations, etc.

A mixture of these ideas, in addition to some Sufi configurations concerning "light and heavy [metaphysical beings]" is equally seen in the citation. This is one of the difficult applications of Mahmoud's republican thought. Here, he conceives the possibility of a "new" *Ahmedist* Message [of Islam] emerging from the [ongoing] Muhammadan Message [of Islam], the one believed by Muslims to be the only Message of Muhammad, the Seal of God's prophets and messages to mankind.

In the course of his critique of Marx, Mahmoud beholds that the implication of taking "matter" as presupposing the mind in existence is that, "matter" is more honored than the "human mind" is inasmuch as "matter" is seen as "the most dignified being" in existence. As a result of this favoritism, the individuals of a society [i.e., owners of the human mind] will be grossly reduced in status as opposed to society (Ibid.).

Because of Mahmoud's concern with human dignity, he concludes in a strong assumption that freedom is a precondition for the development of society. He criticizes the socialist attempts so far made to achieve communism (the final resolution of class struggles). In his words, "The individual became a unit of production without any supervision or motivations to entice him to work. Motivations were transformed into a material incentive to almost another form of capitalism" (Taha, al-Deen was al-Tanmiya, 1974: 46).

Despite all these objections to Marxism, socialism, and communism, Taha upholds socialism as a justifiable way to promote social development. He theorizes that, "There are those who negate socialism in the name of religion by claiming that socialism is heretical. Also, they may reject any thinking of social development. It must be clarified, however, that there is no social development possible without socialism" (Ibid.).

Mahmoud maintains that individualism is highly valued in both Islamic and socialist orientations. Individualism unravels the contradiction encountered between science and religion. Based on this presumption, Mahmoud is opposed to the idea of 'Abd al-Khaliq Mahgoub on the communist party as a vanguard organization of intellectuals, as well as the working and productive forces. Eventually, he stands in a direct contrast with Mahgoub: "Socialism cannot be accomplished unless Marxism is defeated," predicts Mahmoud (Ibid. 32).

With this commitment to individual freedom, Taha deals a strong blow to one of the major premises of Marxian thought. He raises a sharp controversy on the right of individuals to think and act freely against collective behaviorism and the need of society for a vanguard organization as adopted by communists. In so doing, Taha nullifies the broad agreement earlier contained in Al-Marxiya fi al-Mizan between Marxism as a secular thought and the theoretical formulation based on his own religious teachings.

Excluding the possibility of performing political activities independently from Islam, he places Marxism in a lower position to religion and attacks it openly. He has, nonetheless, noticed the positive aspects of Marxism in experiences vindicated by the peoples and societies, for example, the [former] Soviet Union, China, and the other socialist countries. Still, his criticism of Marxism is firmly grounded.

Utilizing classical Islamic jurisprudence, Taha makes an attempt to find answers for the problems facing Muslim societies within modern cultures and sciences – a situation equally handled by Hassan al-Turabi and Sadiq al-Mahdi.

With a knowledgeable liberal mentality, Taha contributes to solving the dilemma of modernity in traditional societies. He mobilizes a wide range of scientific disciplines and objective sources of human knowledge to augment his spiritual constructs. Because of his rational thinking, Taha incorporates his theoretical formulation into a religious doctrine that is somewhat peculiar in both context and form. Consequently, traditional Muslims met his thought with adamant opposition. But he continued to pursue his thought with a consistent commitment until his death for the crime of apostasy under the gallows of Nimeiri.

In this book, some of Mahmoud's ideas have already been discussed, for example, the *Ahmedist* Message of Islam. This is an idea raised within his opinions about evolution and religious revivalism, the compatibility of contemporary life with Islam, and the use of *Ijtihad* to establish a workable scientific method of religious adaptability in the present era. These are complex problems to which Taha addressed himself to the last day of his life.

We have to remind ourselves at this point that Hassan al-Turabi cautions against any restrictions imposed on the freedom of *Ijtihad*. Turabi affirms that, "Jurisprudence must be free. There must be a public authority, however, to look after, organize, and implement that jurisprudence to guide society and to control its movement. It should be appreciated that such a project may lead to a great danger, for if the freedom of *Ijtihad* is completely allowable, the well-controlled fundamentals of interpretation would be at risk of a loose flexibility of jurisprudence. Such flexibility [will lead to a conflict between] the techniques of *al-Masalih* [comparing interests], and *al-Istishab* [rules extracted by association] which makes it possible to have a great difference amongst schools of jurisprudence" (al-Turabi, <u>Tagdid</u>, 1980: 36-37).

Turabi subsequently advises that, "The role of the public authority of society is to approve of reasonable opinions by enforcing them as a law, that alone is obligatory over any other suggested interpretations" (Ibid.). Turabi announces in another place that, "Whatever official qualifications may be, the Muslim public is the judge, the authority entrusted with the distinction of the most knowledgeable and the most righteous [opinion]. There is no church in Islam or any other official authority to monopolize the *fatwa* [scholarly opinion], or to act as a decisive authority [upon society]" (Ibid. 32-33).

Furthermore, Turabi believes in the right of individuals to participate in public affairs. "Each individual [in the *Umma* of Islam that which never agrees on mischief, the nation that is a successor and owner of authority upon itself] is entitled to participate in the process of developing a public opinion with his own knowledge. He has to acquire for himself a personal share of knowledge to enable him to distinguish whatever is exhibited for sale in the market of that knowledge" (Ibid.).

What is understandable about Turabi's speculation is that freedom of thought is a necessity of *Ijtihad* as an Islamic practice. Notwithstanding, he has serious reservations about the "danger" anticipated from freedom. Moreover, he confers upon the authority of society the task of selecting "the reasonable opinion." But he does not specify that authority in jurisprudence terms, accurately.

Additionally, Turabi envisages the possibility of practicing authority by the "Muslim public" of "a nation that does not commit mischief." What actually are the characteristics of that nation? Does it exist in our world today? And if it does not exist, how would it be established "as a successor and owner of authority"? These questions amidst others that have to be answered in detail are not adequately addressed in his work.

The individual in Turabi's announcements has a great status as is equally lamented by both Taha and al-Mahdi. 'Abd al-Khaliq Mahgoub lends a profound thought to the significance of the human mind remarking that, "By the power of thought, mankind has been searching for its own existence to discover the mysteries of nature, thus ascending with that thinking in both perception and faith. Had the human mind gone astray from this activity, man could have been sunk into a life of backwardness in submission to nature, with no power to explore its mysteries, a captive of witchcraft and rituals" (Mahgoub, Afkar, 1967: 24).

Despite their ideological disagreements and political hostilities, the Sudanese thinkers agree, in general, on the significant status and role of individuals with reference to the Qur'anic verse: "And behold! Ye come to Us bare and alone as We created you for the first time" (Al-An'am: 94). In truth, Taha concentrates on the individual Muslim more than the other thinkers did.

Sadiq al-Mahdi and Turabi refer to the individual as an active member of Muslim society. They cherish the power of Muslim society in exercising decision making on Muslim groups and institutions. Sadiq usually mentions the Muslim society is "a united entity" in a broad sense, while Turabi calls for "the masters of prohibition and admission" - a distinguished group within Muslim society, as well as institutes of Islamic research - to recognize contributions of the Muslim individuals to their adaptations.

Emphasizing the will and interests of organized groups over individualism, 'Abd al-Khaliq encourages organizations of the party, those of the other parties, and the social forces to form a "National Democratic Front" independently from any religious commitment by any individual. He urges all forces of society to rally around a general political vision guided by programs of the National Democratic Front.

Judged by his analytical works, Taha concentrates on the individual Muslim rather than the other thinkers did. Contrary to what Mahgoub emphasizes, individualism is the spinal cord of the philosophy of Taha and his scheme for religious revivalism. He talks about "the need of individuals to enjoy absolute individual freedoms and the need of society to ensure social justice for all its members. Individuality is an end in itself, and social groups comprise the largest means of preserving its tenets" (Taha, al-Mizan, 1973:26). Interestingly, Taha appears in his early writings to be a "realistic" author who is gravely concerned for the direct material needs of society. It appears that he might have moved gradually from realism to a romantic glorification of individualism. This impression is well exemplified in his early correspondence with Sudanese educators.

In a letter dated December 24th, 1958, addressed to Osman Mahgoub, Dean of the Bakht al-Rida Institute, regarding the Abu 'Akar Committee on Educational Curricula, one feels an air of realism in Mahmoud's suggestions to the Committee. "The educational curriculum must aim to educate a student how to learn on his own, how to adapt to the environment, and how to reconcile individual freedom with collective freedoms to behave spontaneously in the best manner with his society" (Taha, Rasayil, 1973: 10-23).

Attention is also drawn in that letter to Taha's sociological awareness of the reciprocal relations between man and the social order. "Before living in a society, man was an individual animal. The conditions of life forced him to invent a social order for the group by foregoing a considerable portion of his individual freedom for freedoms of the group. Certainly, there had never been a specific person existing in a specific time who might have been invented by his group's order. This in fact is a common heritage. Individual freedom is the origin of mankind. Collective freedoms do not survive by restricting the individual freedom. They are actually a means of ensuring it since there is no contradiction spotted between them" (Ibid. 11-12).

In 1974, Mahmoud writes that, "Individuals existed before societies. The individual invented society." Mahmoud's interest is largely centered on struggles of the individual to survive. This is reflected in his critique of a number of upheavals, chief of which is the Russian socialist experience and the gradual collapse of the Soviet Union (Taha, al-Deen wa al-Tanmiya, 1974:46).

Mahmoud's book Al-Deen wa al-Tanmiya al-Ijtima'iya (Religion and Social Development, 1974) elaborates on many comprehendible ideas of the needs of Muslims in contemporary societies to emancipate their minds from traditional interpretations of Shari'a law, i.e., the classical jurisprudence. This leads us to the unique approach of Taha to the substantive themes of religious revivalism that have been thoughtfully explored by him using a complicated set of creative concepts and meanings. Taha's approach distinguishes him as an Islamic philosopher from the other Sudanese thinkers who, in general, either employ simple conceptualizations or adopt programs of action based on a direct political strife rather than rigorous theological thinking.

The concern of Mahmoud Mohamed Taha for religion is ingrained in his continuous emphasis on freedom of thought, the most vital condition for the establishment and maintenance of a healthy society for the individual Muslims. Referring to the Qur'an, he explains that "Our Lord says, 'We have revealed unto you the recitation,' i.e., the whole Qur'an, 'to explain to the people what has been revealed unto you,' i.e., the Shari'a, 'so that they may reflect on it.' This [sacred order that God created for man] is the cause of all causes, for man cannot sublime to the higher degree of dignity without thought. Religion came to scrutinize thought, that it may not deviate from righteousness" (Ibid. 50).

In a historiography of the social evolution of slavery, feudalism, capitalism, and classes, Taha ascertains that, "Society is the greatest invention made by man. The mind emerged from within the struggles of man in the environment" (Ibid. 36-37). But the philosopher does not correlate all these incidents and historical events with any particular activity, a specific political organization, or a certain class structure. He affirms that, "Science is the infrastructure while religion represents a supra-structure. Between the two structures there is an entire unity because both of them make [the grand science]" (Ibid. 8).

The methodology adopted by Mahmoud is enclosed in these descriptions: "Scientific investigation into the nature of things does not stand solely on the methods advocated by empirical science. Rather, it conjoins materialism and metaphysics. It is a science of knowing Allah, a science founded on every letter and word of the Qur'anic verse "Soon will We show them Our Signs in the (furthest) Regions (of the earth) and in their own souls" (Ibid.).

The need of this epoch for this grand science [i.e., the science of knowing Allah] is clearly included in Taha's definition of mankind. "We are the mankind of the 20th century, the mankind promised to spread about justice all over earth as it has been pervaded with injustice" (Taha, Ta'alamou, 1972: 96).

This auspicious claim of mankind's redemption echoes the persistent belief of Muslims in a redeemer to purify society from injustices. The redeemer, however, for Mahmoud is not simply an individual person. He is much greater than that. Redemption implies the meaningful exercise of the freedom of thought and the full enjoyment of scientific progression by the individual members of the human race. Again, Mahmoud's liberalism enables him to compose theoretical approaches from a large pool of Islamic jurisprudence, Western thought, and Sudanese Sufi traditions.

Mahmoud takes advantage of the Marxian theory by assuming that society is divided into infra-and-supra-structures. These structures may be consciously linked via political organization to transform a society for the interest of forces desirable of that transformation. Earlier, Karl Marx asserted that class struggles and production relations had always been developed and gravitated towards social change due to the contradictions occurring between social forces. This is a Western configuration that is deeply rooted in the Hegelian thought of Germany and the French classical socialism.

Mahmoud, furthermore, undertakes major changes in the Marxist theoretical model as he "compromises" some of the Marxian concepts with his own parallel terms. For example, he replaces "production relations" in the infrastructure of society with the notion of "a materialist empirical science." The "praxis", as a practical connection between the two structures of the Marxian model, is replaced by Mahmoud's Sufi perception that teaches that, "Materialism and metaphysics are a science of knowing Allah." Earlier, Mahmoud speaks decisively about "the creation of existence, conscientiousness and non-conscientiousness, by God" (Taha, al-Mizan, 1973: 6). He has certainly used the theory; but he is not a Marxist thinker.

The reader may note that Mahmoud has been more actively engaged in contemplative thinking to promote the Republican Brotherhood movement than any political concern for Sudanese State of Affairs. Indeed, he has consistently focused his thought on the idiosyncrasies of the individual Muslim, the significance of individuality, and the role individuals play in a society's religion, social change, and modernity.

In contrast with the other Sudanese thinkers, whose ideas handled the issues of governance and public affairs, Mahmoud's thought is not easily translated in political terms although he has undoubtedly practiced politics in the course of his public life. But he appears to be a philosopher rather than a political activist. Some of his political contentions include this social equity project: " For a society to be an integral system, it has to be based on three equal premises. Economic equality is a socialist function that develops into communism whereby the bounties of life would be a common good for all people. Political equality comes about as a parliamentary democracy transforming itself into a direct democracy with a prevalence of social equality such that marriage would be possible among men and women in all levels of society. Added to these three levels, the tolerance of public opinion must be enhanced so that it will not be impatient with the liberality of free thought" (Taha, al-Mizan, 1973: 26).

OLD MISSIONS, NEW APPROACHES

Taha's versions of socialism and communism have been briefly explained in the preceding discourse of his ideas. His definition of parliamentary democracy is quite different from that of 'Abd al-Khaliq Mahgoub, although in theory it is much more congruent with Sadiq al-Mahdi's views.

'Abd al-Khaliq blames bitterly "the parliamentary system of rule practiced in context of the social and class situation of our country. [The parliamentary system] became an impediment of economic and social development. To say that there is a possibility of being a stable parliamentary regime in this fashion means nothing but the in-continuity of an authority of classes and social strata that is ardently opposed to the task of completing the national democratic renaissance [of the Sudan]. Not only that, it equally implies that the authority is stable and that the struggles necessitated by the conditions of this country and its historical needs must be abated" (SCP, al-Marxiya, Undated: 152-153).

Mahgoub affirms that, "The problem of our country is exacerbated by a rule of reaction that is based on the use of violence under a cover of a formal parliamentary system. Equally, the forces of reaction and the executive apparatus of the State use violence directly, especially the senior bureaucrats of the Armed Forces. [The alternative] is an advancement of our country towards a political, economic, and social life that would move the homeland into modernity of the 20th century. The only path possible for such an advancement is to be paved by victory of the National Democratic Revolution" (Ibid.).

Sadiq al-Mahdi says, "For an Islamic system of succession to arise on the basis of popular representation, the political movement of society must liberalize society of all coercive regimes, and to render the political will of society determined via free and fair election of people. The ensuing parliamentary order shall oversee and decide by majority votes the system of rule desirable for a majority of people by their majority representatives" (al-Mahdi, 'Uqobat, Undated: 196).

Hassan al-Turabi has already spoken about, "the authority of society", "the power of society", and "the masters of prohibition and admission" without any adequate explanation of the whereabouts. By the same token, there is not a clear definition available to elucidate Taha's conception of "a parliamentary democracy" in light of the "Second Message of Islam," the foremost socio-religious mission of Taha's group, the Republican Brotherhood.

We have previously mentioned a special project of Turabi. The "new amalgamated science," which is entrusted with the pioneering role of resurrecting an Islamic movement capable of leading the Nation of Islam in thought and in practice. We have also reiterated al-Mahdi's agreement with Turabi in that particular sense. Mahmoud calls for the rise of Islam through the implementation of a contemporary viable science and a competent authority. However, Mahmoud's concepts and spiritual constructs are strikingly different from those of Sadiq and Turabi.

Taha (al-Deen wa al-Tanmiya, 1974:16) believes that, "A meeting with Allah can not be held by crossing over distances, but by science. Ours is an age of science, even though it is not perfectly truthful since it assumes that only materialist empirical science is scientific. We are the ones who called for the establishment of a new science, namely 'the New Islamic Call.' People must accept this call because if they refuse to do so voluntarily, they will do it compulsorily ... It is a fact that, 'who would not walk in the path of Allah by good acts will be ordained to Him by the chains of ordeal.' This new call rests on a scientific level of Islam, not its level of belief, for this is the rule of time.

Taha elaborates his new call in this critique of the First Message of Islam: "It must be clear for us when we talk about religion and social development that religion in the level of belief, i.e., the First Message, inhibits social development. This is because it is not a matter of faith … In this level, religion does not treat women equally with men; hence, the religion's system of rule negates both democracy and socialism. It is only based on guardianship and a modified version of capitalism, … the *zakat* as quantified alms giving. The hopes of mankind in this age is unquestionably bound to Islam, but only on the scientific level (not on the level of belief) … the level of 'the second Message of Islam' for which we have been calling since a long time" (Ibid.).

In pursuit of the contributions of Mahmoud Mohamed Taha to religious revivalism, we are now approaching the Second Message of Islam, the most sensitive core of his thought and the most criticized. We will make an attempt to grasp that Message. We will begin with his revivalism of the existing "lag of intellectuality" between the rules and applications of classical jurisprudence (i.e., the Shari'a of the First Message of Islam) and the modern contemporary life of Muslim societies. This is a very problematical dispute that has persistently invited the philosophy of other thinkers on Islamic affairs.

Spending long years in contemplation of a broad scientific approach to amalgamate the rules of Shari'a with the empirical innovations of the age, Taha believed in the relevance of Sufi to the rational thinking that emphasizes individualism rather than political maneuvering or insurrection. With this unique approach, Taha, a philosopher, educator, and religious thinker has strongly influenced his disciples.

The Republican Brothers issued many *fatawi* (opinions) on Islamic institutions and activities; for example, they attack the Shari'a Courts as "courts of reactionary judges" who are only dedicated to humiliate women through the application of outlawed rules of private law, etc. These *fatawi*, however, are not the major concerns of Taha.

Taha's main agenda centers on a life-mission to carve out an Islamic science that finally resolve all problems of Muslim societies. Because of the complexity and diversity of his sources, Taha's writings and sophisticated arguments are sometimes confusing. The subsequent discussion examines briefly a few aspects of his complex thought.

Like the other Islamic thinkers, Turabi and al-Mahdi, Taha envisages the need of the age for Islam, the complete religion – a religion for the future that is ahead of time. Muslims should therefore work very hard to capture "the most advanced meanings of religion," those originally inherent in it, to strengthen their debilitated systems.

The means of achieving this redeeming mission of Islam, claims Taha, begins with a progressive understanding of "the Second Message of Islam." As an "advanced version of Islam," the Second Message requires scientific knowledge, awareness, and continuous liberalization of worshipping practices and workaday transactions from dogmatism or obsessive conservatism.

Let us compare, here, Taha's ambitious scheme (which subjects the *'Ibadat* [worshipping practices] and *Mu'amalat* [worldly transactions] to a religious revision) with the ideas of the other Sudanese thinkers that only involve the Shari'a transactions of classical jurisprudence.

Turabi, for example, avoids in his scheme a revival of Islamic jurisprudence or intrusion in the sacred practices of Muslim deity. His opinion is that, "The highest degree of religiosity is that attainable by worshipping Allah. It is an objective that binds all Shari'a rules. If we examine that meaning carefully, we will decide that the core objective of Shari'a includes all activities, except for those the Shari'a rules out as non-achieving practices" (al-Turabi, Tagdid, 1980:12). In the final analysis, the Shari'a determined the religious control of society.

Turabi does not specify what he technically means by "Shari'a" although he has strongly criticized rules of the "old" jurisprudence. Despite these criticisms, the inherited jurisprudence continues to rule the daily life of a billion Muslims all over the world whose majority is dissatisfied with the failure of modern alternatives to the inherited Shari'a.

Sadiq al-Mahdi believes in the constant validity of Shari'a transactions. He speaks admiringly of the early Muslims. He depicts the *Imams* (leaders) of the *Madzahib* (schools of jurisprudence) as "pious and enlightened men who studied the fundamentals of Islamic texts with an insightful rationality. They recognized the significance of thinking and the fields of intellectual interest, incorporated the beneficial traditions of the other cultures of their times [into Islamic jurisprudence], appreciated the needs of their societies, used cleverly efficient means of judgment, and inferred accurately just and good rules."

For al-Mahdi, "[The early jurists] pleased the Lord, served the Nation [of Islam], and left behind them a rich knowledge of jurisprudence. It is a real honor to understand and follow up their ideas to be able to overcome the challenges facing us in our present times to infer just and useful rules from the Islamic Shari'a. This is not meant to abide by their *fatawi* [scholastic decisions] blindly since such biases will make of a beneficial rule at a certain time a prejudicial one at another time. The best we can say about them is what Mohamed Ahmed ibn 'Abd-Allah, the Grand Mahdi, said. 'God bless them for what they accomplished and conveyed [to Muslims]. They are men; so we are. We have to make the effort as they did'" (al-Mahdi, 'Uqobat, Undated: 121).

Having shown his strong commitment to the traditional Shari'a, Sadiq suggests a special procedure to deal with the *Ibadat* [worship] as a universal concern for all Muslims. The procedure realizes the need "to amalgamate the Islamic schools of jurisprudence on the basis of the Qur'an and Sunna, in origin. The new synthesis of jurisprudence should allow a fair chance to mold the existing differences in interpretation and inference. All Muslims are entitled to participate in the process of organizing the united form of worshipping and religious ritual" (Ibid: 186).

Sadiq is further concerned with Shari'a transactions and socio-legal arrangements, and the advantages provided by a newly phrased Shari'a to satisfy the needs of modern life in politics, economics, and social organization. Both Sadiq and Turabi are quite close to each other in the fundamentals of their thought, despite the discrepancies evident in a few cases.

'Abd al-Khaliq does not intervene in *'Ibadat* for he takes them as a matter of faith. He does not analyze Shari'a transactions with a view of changing them as Sadiq, Turabi, and Mahmoud tried to do. Instead, he is interested in the role religion plays in the service of "basic needs of the public," according to his political program.

Mahmoud Mohamed Taha wishes to revise *'Ibadat* and transactions to establish a new conceptual scheme. Namely, the idea that worshipping God constitutes a special relation between a Muslim and the Creator, the highest ecumenical sentiment for an ordinary Muslim, the major duty, the hope of a Muslim in Mahmoud's thought to please the Lord if faith is fully maintained. Worshipping occupies in Mahmoud's thought the supreme practice of all religious activities: "To know how to behave with people, there must be worshipping" (Taha, al-Thawra al-Thaqafiya, 1972: 40).

Assuring his will to abide by the Prophet Muhammad, the Example," Taha claims that he has been inspired by the Prophet: "Knowing the reality of Muhammad, in itself, is a prayer upon the Prophet that is deemed much greater than the ordinary prayers Muslims say upon him. What actually prevents a possible blend of the two types of prayer, the one based on knowledge and the other literal saying of prayers? Wouldn't that blend be more complete and fulfilling "than the ordinary prayers"?

Mahmoud announces at this point that, "For me, the answer is left to the knowledgeable individual and his own vision because it is a matter related to his individualistic method [of worship]. This is a new Mission, starting from where the First Mission ended with sanctity and literal prayers upon the Prophet, moving with open eyes along the path of the real knowledge of Muhammad where sacredness and worshipping is complete" (Taha, Rasayil, 1973: 34-35).

Thus far, the reader is certainly aware that this philosopher calls upon believers to pray in a sincere way to make of their literal prayers a meaningful activity. A question is that if Mahmoud's prayers differ from Muslim ordinary prayers, what characteristics do his prayers have, once exercised by individuals "knowledgeable of the reality of Muhammad and his closeness to Allah?"

Because the prayers he is calling for are meant to be meaningful and contemplative, Mahmoud elaborates on the religious origin of these prayers. "The *M'iraj* Prayer [i.e., the Shari'a ordinary prayers to worship Allah and pray upon the Prophet] is a means to attend the *Silah* Prayer [i.e., the prayer suggested by Mahmoud for the knowledgeable believer, presumably a Republican Brother]."

Taha explains that, "We have two types of prayers. The first type is a major prayer that the Archangel Gabriel was not present when it had been imposed on the Prophet at the time his contact with the Lord was no more inter-mediated by Gabriel. The other prayer is a minor one that was revealed by the Archangel to the Prophet with a certain method and designated times. The Lord ordered the Prophet to ascend with the *Mi'iraj* Prayer. We [the common Muslims] were entitled to pray our *Mi'raj* Prayer everyday to ascend through it to our *Silah* Prayer. We pray the *Mi'raj* Prayer the way the Prophet had been praying. But the Prophet is original, while we are imitating him" (Taha, Ta'alamou, 1972: 92-93).

Taha taught the Republican Brothers how to pray properly the *M'iraj* Prayer to reach out to the *Silah* Prayer. In addition, he calls upon leaders of all contemporary religious sects to act as "guides of their followers to adopt the example of the Prophet in worshipping practices" (Taha, Tariq Muhammad, Undated: 28). It is timely for Muslims "to dignify themselves, respect their minds, and be liberated from the servitude of sectarianism and the incomplete ways of life by returning to Muhammad, prayers be upon him" (Ibid.).

Taha points out his own classification of the Shari'a, apart from the Sunna. In the First Message of Islam the Prophet transformed an illiterate nation into a nation of believers who essentially became the Companions (i.e., disciples of the Prophet). The Muhammadan Shari'a "was addressed to people, according to the level of their perception and needs. Their needs were simple. Therefore, a descending occurred from the level of the verses on fundamentals of the Qur'an to the verses only consonant with that [simplicity in perception and needs]. These verses thus abrogated the [higher] legislation available in the verses of fundamentals" (Taha, Tariq Muhammad, Undated: 16).

Mahmoud assumes that the Message of the Prophet Muhammad is in fact consisting of two messages. "The First Message is *Muhammadist*, the Second Message is *Ahmedist*. You may refer to them as the First Message, i.e., the Shari'a that Muhammad detailed to the Nation [of Islam], and the Second Message that was also summed up by the Prophet but he has not elaborated on it, except for the meaningfulness underlying his performance in life" (Ibid. 15).

What is the difference between *Muhammadism* and *Ahmedism*? Mahmoud elaborates on this division by saying that, "*Muhammadism* is a version [of Islam] that emerged from *Ahmedism* [the other version of Islam]. It is a bifurcation necessitated by the rule of time and formed into a certain level by the needs of the Nation of Islam in the 7th century and its capacity. There is a difference between these two versions of Islam. That indicates the continuous distance between Sunna and the Shari'a. We have repeatedly informed that the Prophet did not belong to the society of the 7th century. He came from the future; from the 20th century ... the nation of believers responded to him ... Muhammad will come [again] with an *Ahmedist* prophecy and an *Ahmedist* Message. He will call upon the nation of believers and the other nations to follow Islam" (Ibid. 15).

Subsequent to this classification of the Nation of Islam into knowledgeable believers, nation of believers, *Muhammadist, Ahmedist*, and other entities, Taha calls upon mankind. "Simulate the example of the Prophet whose self has been endowed with an intrinsic purity, and to imitate that example so perfectly that every man and every woman attain the unity, personal integrity, and liberality of personality" (Ibid. 18).

To contrast all these ideas with the other Sudanese thinkers, a brief summary may be presented on these few points. First, Taha envisages a "Muhammadan Shari'a" as "being addressed to people according to their perception and needs." This assumption appears to be very close to a statement by Turabi on the rules of classical jurisprudence. Turabi's labels them "[as rules] established on a narrow base of knowing the nature of things, the facts of the universe, and the laws of societal living for Muslims at a time of establishing and developing the Islamic jurisprudence" (al-Turabi, Tagdid, 1980: 8).

Second, Taha's conceptualization is different from the ideas of Sadiq al-Mahdi and 'Abd al-Khaliq Mahgoub, as earlier analyzed, concerning the issue of religious integrity at the time of the Companions in the life of the Prophet. 'Abd al-Khaliq says, "Those who have witnessed the Prophet with many miracles made by him and revelations revealed to him were strong believers who continued to be greatly committed after the death of the Prophet" (Mahgoub, Afkar, 1967: 14). Sadiq al-Mahdi considers the epoch of early Muslims "a postulation of the most brilliant Islamic society ... a stage of the most vibrant Islamic thought" (al-Mahdi, 'Uqobat, Undated: 123).

Third, Mahmoud Mohamed Taha urges Muslims to "liberate themselves from the servitude of sectarianism." With this view, he stands equally with 'Abd al-Khaliq Mahgoub and Hassan al-Turabi.

Fourth, Mahmoud has uniquely conceptualized Islam into a First Message and a Second Message. In addition, he has perceptibly categorized Muslims into "believers" and "Muslims" by claiming that, "Muslims are much closer to Allah than believers are; their prayers are more complete than believers; their prayers on the Prophet are more integral and fulfilling than prayers of the believers are. A Muslim whose truthfulness is fully realized will have his Shari'a path emerging; thus, he would be possessive of an individual Shari'a by praying to Allah and upon the Prophet, without restrictions of the believers' prayer. Once his truthfulness is fully realized, his individual Shari'a [path] would figure out, God wishes, as an outcome of his imitation of the Prophet. There is no Muslim who has not passed through the stage of believers. The Muslim nation began with the stage of the nation of believers" (Taha, Tariq Muhammad, Undated: 20-21).

Taha reminds the reader that his book, Tariq Muhammad (The Path of Muhammad), "has been written without reference to the literal prayers [traditionally said] upon the Prophet." The whole book, asserts Taha, "is made of prayers upon the Prophet at a level higher than that of the ordinary prayers" (Ibid.).

For this writer, it is extremely difficult for the ordinary Muslim to accept Taha's perception of "a practice not bound to the method of prayers adopted by the believers." An ordinary Muslim normally takes the prayers he or she performs as an imitation of the Prophet. In their daily traditional form, these prayers, for which there is no alternative, are the backbone of religion – the legitimate prayers for which a Muslim would be accounting in the Hereafter.

It is true that Mahmoud Mohamed Taha refers to the Holy Qur'an in his arguments. He draws the attention of readers to the "Islam of Abraham" to indicate the ancient existence of Islam, an "evolutionary religion" consisting of different kinds of faith: "We will understand the Qur'an perfectly well if we make a distinction between the stage of believers and that of Muslims" (Ibid. 20).

In Taha's speech on the Prophet, he ascertains that, "Being a prophet is an honorable status to which the Prophet prepared himself with the favor of God bestowed on him, besides the long experience of seclusion which provided him with an awakening sense and a clarity of thought" (Ibid. 12). Here is an indication of the role the Prophet played as a human being, who had been exercising a life of seclusion and deep thinking, in addition to the great merits that enabled him to carry out the glorious Message of God.

In truth, Mahmoud challenges the idea by some "ordinary Muslims" who question the personal merits of the Prophet that enabled him to convey the Message of Islam in the best manner possible. He affirms that, "it is a serious lack of knowledge to think, as some people do, that the Prophet was only told to report [to mankind] what he had known from his Lord" (Ibid. 11). 'Abd al-Khaliq Mahgoub equally censured this same criticism. But Mahmoud was more deeply involved in the Message of Muhammad than 'Abd al-Khaliq was.

A question arises:

The Prophet had been endowed with great merits and miracles, for example the great miracle of the *al-Isra* and *al-Mi'raj* (the trip to Heavens and the meeting with the Lord, respectively) that took him far beyond the Archangel Gabriel to meet directly with the Lord. Wouldn't these events mean that the Prophet had been uniquely selected and entrusted with the Message of Islam?

Wouldn't these attainable miracles ordain all Muslims to imitate his deeds and follow his words inasmuch as they can? What are Muslims required to do other than what the Companions, the well-guided disciples of the Prophet, did? Shouldn't all Muslims alike submit to the Qur'anic verse: "Glory to (God) who did take His Servant [Prophet Muhammad] for a journey by night from the Sacred Mosque to the Farthest East, whose precincts We did bless - in order that We might show him some of Our Signs" (Sura al-Isra: 1). Isn't it clear that the Qur'an glorified the Prophet without reference to any other individual or a special group of Muslims?

The Prophet himself ordered Muslims in an authenticated *Hadith* (sayings) "to adhere to his *Sunna* and that of the well-guided Companions" (al-Nawawi, Riyadh al-Saliheen, Undated: 51). The *Hadith* on the Companions is highly regarded by Muslims because it recognizes deeds and sayings of the Companions a significant aspect of revering the Prophet. It is quite logical to expect a greater warning, on the light of this *Hadith*, against innovating Muslim worshipping practices. The learned Imam al-Haziz Imad al-Deen ibn Kathir (d. 774H) ascertained the Hadith of *al-Isra* (the Prophet's trip to Heavens) as confirmed by the well-guided Companions (al-Saboni, Mukhtasar ibn Kathir, 1979:364).

It is inconceivable for the common Muslims to believe that a Muslim could ever ascend in a lifetime to Heavens through an "individual *Mi'raj*" to meet with God.

Only the Prophet Muhammad, Muslims believe, has been made an Imam of all prophets and messengers of God in the trip to Heavens. The prayers of *al-Mi'raj* and *al-Silah* have all been combined, one and the same prayer, for all Muslims for "prayer forbids mischief and misdemeanor," in the words of the Holy Qur'an. Prayers empower Muslims with an overflow of psychological restfulness and spiritual sincerity if initiated by the right form of Islamic ablution and then practiced with humility and concentration of the mind and the soul before the Lord.

True, Mahmoud Mohamed Taha emphasizes the need to follow the example of the Prophet who is the complete man, "the one with the great morality," as bestowed on him by God. But the idea of Taha to extract from Sunna prayers an ambiguous version exercised by "the knowledgeable individual according to his own vision" is an unauthorized superimposition of a prophetic privilege, a special miracle, upon the common Muslims. Moreover, many believers might be knowledgeable of jurisprudence and theology. But they do not aspire to acquire a special knowledge with the Lord, like Prophet Muhammad had. Muslims contemplate on these Sufi matters, "in fear and hope" that they might please the Lord and His Messenger.

The Muslim's hope to follow the path of Muhammad is much less than the imagination of Taha to approach the Lord Himself. Only Prophet Muhammad had been exceptionally privileged with that approach in a way that only the Lord knows how and where it took place beyond the highest limits of Archangel Gabriel. Because of all these reasons, Taha's predisposition in this particular subject is a great spiritual illusion. It might be imaginable in the form of a grand abstraction based on the *Mi'raj* prayer of the common Muslim. Taha theorizes an architectural construct in which the ascendancy of the Prophet to Heavens through a *Mi'raj* prayer (possibly attainable by the 'knowledgeable Muslim individual' in the 20th century) represents a spiritual supra-structure.

Apart from these theological aspects of his thought, it is the opinion of this writer that Taha surprisingly shares with the Islamic conservative thinker Sayed Qutb some of his condemnations of the contemporary civilization of mankind, the one relevant to the sciences and life styles of the 20th century. Mahmoud contends that, "Nowadays, in the 2nd half of the 20th century, mankind lives in a Second *Jahiliya* [ignorance], at a level much higher than ignorance of the seventh century" (Taha, Tariq Muhammad, Undated: 16).

In the early 1960s, Sayed Qutb sorts out in his book Ma'alim fi al-Tariq (Milestones on the Way) the *Jahiliya* of the 20th century and condemns its contradictions with classical Shari'a Law. But the adaptations of each thinker (i.e., Taha and Qutb) of a way to salvage mankind, in general, and Muslims, in particular, from *Jahiliya* are quite different.

One difference at hand is that Mahmoud confines the task of salvaging humanity "with God's will, from the darkness of the Second *Jahiliya* into the light of Islam" (Ibid: 27) to *Ahmedism*. This is the Second Message of Islam, exactly as *Muhammadism*, the First Message of Islam, formerly saved humanity from the darkness of the First *Jahiliya*.

Sadiq al-Mahdi, Hassan al-Turabi, and 'Abd al-Khaliq Mahgoub (who partially criticized the capitalist mode of the century) do not approve of this condemnation of the century at large. On the contrary, 'Abd al-Khaliq, for one, attacks Sayed Qutb vigorously on his assessment of the century (see Mahgoub, Afkar, 1967). These Sudanese thinkers, including Mahmoud Mohamed Taha to some extent, admire the remarkable achievements of the century's "rational sciences," "materialist evolution," "progression," etc. They insist on calling upon society to take advantage of the fruition of science and technology, although they disagree with each other about many ideological concerns regarding modernity of the age.

Taha has earlier emphasized the significance of modern sciences in the promotion of Muslim societies: "We have to be perfectionists, scientifically planning to implement and to evaluate all fields of modern sciences, economics, technology, and the other areas [of knowledge]. We have to acquire the know-how of experimental science, increase our qualifications in scientific abilities, as well as thinking. We have to move ahead of the modern inventions and the philosophy underlying them to explore horizons of the unknown. In other words, we have to utilize all that which is produced by experimental science to make of this world the best means to reach out to the other world" (Taha, al-Deen wa al-Tanmiya, 1974: 16-17).

A clear contradiction is that this magnificent civilization, which Mahmoud further views as a suitable ground for the *Ahmedist* Message, the Second Message of Islam, is looked upon by the same thinker as a Second *Jahiliya* - a clear contradiction. What portion of this civilization, with its beloved modern sciences, is a Second *Jahiliya*? Is it true that "material evolution" is a *Jahiliya*?

The conclusions of Taha throughout his writings are not harmoniously interrelated with his comprehensive theoretical approach. The critique of this writer of the Turabi scheme of modernizing classical jurisprudence by means of a "new amalgamated science" holds true in the case of Mahmoud. Both of them advocate a number of presumptions to project the rise of a "new" Islamic entity. But they do not present the details required to delineate the prerequisites, relations, and interrelations of the "new" Islamic society or nation of Islam with respect to the existing global doctrines and world powers.

It is now appropriate to sum-up the outcome of this analysis on trends of thought and the innovating ideas of religious revivalism. It is clear that, as a consequence of their individuality, the thinkers are neither fully in agreement nor disagreement on the topics in question.

It might be argued, furthermore, that had these different schools of thought enjoyed freedom of expression on a permanent basis, they might have come in agreement with each other to the extent needed to prepare their adherence to co-exist with tolerance and peace in the same society. This assumption indicates the same archaic code of ethics that had earlier prevailed in Sudanese medieval systems, as explained in the introduction of this book. The validity of this fact recalls the rich background of the social and psychological development of the thinkers.

Being citizens of Sudan, they have been continuously attached to the familial settings, Sufi practices, and the other activities of Sudanese society. Politics provided a bridge that connected them with one another since all of them assumed political leadership over parties or popular organizations. All of them contributed to the major events of the 1960s - the 1964's October Revolution, which overthrew a military dictatorship via civilian struggles that shocked the Sudan, and has since affected the world's outlook about popular uprisings versus tyrannous regimes.

Some of the thinkers were involved in political negotiations during and after the April Popular Uprising 1985. By then, unfortunately, 'Abd al-Khaliq Mahgoub and Mahmoud Mohamed Taha were extra-judicially killed by the Authority to silence their active opposition against the May dictatorial regime.

All of these thinkers passed through arbitrary detention, prisoners of conscience. In July 1971, most gravely, Nimeiri approved the extra-judicial killing of 'Abd al-Khaliq Mahgoub. The same president supervised the arbitrary arrest of al-Mahdi several times from 1969 throughout 1985. Following many arbitrary arrests in the mid 1970's, Hassan al-Turabi became a presidential assistant for foreign affairs before the eruption of the April Popular Uprising in 1985. In January 1985, Ja'far Nimeiri, president of the May regime, approved a death sentence passed on Mahmoud Mohamed Taha by a court of Turabi's supporters.

Again, a few days before the Popular Uprising of April 1985 that overthrew his government, Nimeiri arrested Turabi, deposed him from his position as presidential assistant for foreign affairs, and announced his intention to put him to a harsh trial. From behind the prison bars, Turabi and Sadiq witnessed the 1985's Popular Uprising in which Sadiq al-Mahdi had played a distinctive role in overthrowing the government that incarcerated them.

Ideological struggles, by their very nature, are more tolerable than political conflicts are. On recognizing this fact, both leaders and members of political parties or ideological groups should observe human rights and civil freedoms, especially the right to free expression and assembly, to promote the social life for the whole community, Muslim or non-Muslim.

This is a civil compromise that can never be attainable by fear. It is a voluntary agreement that springs from the right to exercise thought and private preferences freely. It must be strengthened by the strongest guarantees possible, including the free exchange, competition, fertilization, and incorporation of thought.

The actual worth of these agreements will evidently materialize if all parties resolve in a permanent commitment to preserve civil rights by democratic rule so that Sudanese thinkers will not be killed or imprisoned for an expression of thought. This national commitment must be equally adopted and further inculcated in the minds and souls of the new generations. Although other problems will continue to exist in society at large, the diversity of Sudanese cultures and schools of thought can only be maintained by that commitment, the best guarantor to protect thought from cheapness, frustration, or abhorrent animosity.

To provide another example of the impact of freedom of thought on Sudanese national issues, the following section focuses closely on the constitutional debate of the mid 1960's which involved additional aspects of the diversity of thought among Sudanese thinkers and political groups.

THE CONSTITUTIONAL DEBATE

Up to this point, we have analyzed contrasting views of the Sudanese thinkers in the issue of religious revivalism. In the meantime, political struggles have actively ushered economic disputes into the national arena. This culminated in the emergence of a major crisis whereas the country continued to oscillate, without a stable economic growth, between capitalist and non-capitalist development administration.

The ensuing conflict was sharpened by the competing ideologies although instances of congruity occurred along the debates over religious revivalism. This need to rally political support from Muslim masses in the northern parts of Sudan motivated thinkers to manipulate religious revivalism in their efforts to influence the constitutional dispute on the national identity of the homeland. The dispute also included the distribution of wealth, systems of administration, the right of political organizations to assemble, and so forth.

Sadiq al-Mahdi is one of the leaders who call for the establishment of an Islamic constitution to rule Sudan with a modern parliamentary system of rule. Fairly administered national elections, thinks Sadiq, will bring about "a parliamentary order to oversee and decide upon by majority vote the system of rule desirable for people by their majority representatives. The Islamic Movement will be engaged in this election under the banner of Islamic Revivalism with the required mandate."

Sadig believes that, "As soon as the Movement is mandated, it will submit to the parliament a draft constitution on governance of the country. The constitution will stipulate a clear commitment to the principles nominated by us political obligations of Islam (*shura, adl, mussawa, and horriya*) [i.e., consultation, justice, equality, and freedom, respectively]. The constitution will provide for the principle of adopting the Qur'an and the *Sunna* as sources of legislation" (al-Mahdi, 'Uqobat, Undated: 196-197).

On approval of the Islamic Constitution by election, the Islamic Movement, in Sadiq's Islamic scheme, would achieve Islamization of the political system. A "modern Islamic constituency" would apply the political principles of Islam and the rules of Shari'a. In addition, Islamization of the legislative authority (the judiciary and the legislative) would ensure guarantees of the fundamental freedoms and the organization of constitutional security apparatuses.

Accompanying his call for Islamization of the economic system "according to rules of Islamic Shari'a," he recognizes that, "the Islamic economy is theoretically and practically an infant" (Ibid. 197).

In a covert reference to "Islamic banks," Sadiq criticizes "the banks that work through a system of profiteering, partnership, and competition, instead of using interest value of the non-Islamic banks. These banks have not resolved the problem of ensuring a just distribution for the revenues wielded from investment. The revenues reaped by these banks are even higher than interest value. The problem of the hidden usury generated by inflation and the disruption of currency exchanges is also unresolved [by these banks]" (Ibid. 198).

Evaluating the experiences Sudan passed through in the exercise of constitutional drafts, Sadiq reiterates the perplexity of "adopting Islamic rules under the contemporary [non-Islamic] systems of rule." He admits that, if the old ages' rights of non-Muslims are not fully recognized in the "modern" Islamic State, the situation will result in a nation-wide sedition.

"The jurists of Islamic jurisprudence have allowed the abrogation of a religious text if its provisions lead to sedition. The best alternative of such a text must be implemented in its place. This is well illustrated with what we did in 1967 in the draft of Permanent Constitution since we had not included any principle that might discriminate against citizens on the basis of religion. We subjected the provision on that issue to a apolitical decision by the majority" (al-Mahdi, al-Islam wa Janoob al-Sudan, 1985: 17).

Sadiq al-Mahdi recognizes the suspicions of non-Muslims in the deliberations of the Permanent Constitution. He criticizes the political regime ruling the country between 1983 and 1989, which claimed to be "an Islamic rule." "It had been unfair to Muslims even before it began to Islamize the other citizens. The first citizens imprisoned for opposition of the regime were the Muslims who uncovered the falsifications of the regime. But the non-Muslim feelings of injustice were greater than Muslims because they had been religiously persecuted" (Ibid. 15).

Sadiq then mentions the rights of non-Muslims in the "modern system of Islam" he is calling for. These rights embrace "the political, economic, and social rights of a citizen so that he will not be a citizen of a lower grade. [They also embrace] the equality [of citizens], share the responsibility of financial burdens, and [observe the principle of] non-discrimination in religious beliefs. Equally important, they [prohibit] the rules that impose on non-Muslims an Islamic obligation by coercion, [and sort out] Islamic rules in criminal and civil law to which non-Muslims are not a party."

In addition to these clarifications of the rights of non-Muslims in a "modern Islamic polity," Sadiq contends that, "the contemporary international law is a constituent of peace and international cooperation, while the rules of Shari'a are addressed to a continuous state of war" (Ibid.116).

The solutions of these questions in the opinion of non-Muslims, theorizes al-Mahdi, follow this logical argument: "We, the non-Muslims, have no reason to support policies of a State of War. We do not want our State to be involved in a permanent state of war. We do not raise a banner of *Jihad* [holy war]. It is a right that Sudanese non-Muslims be opposed to any Islamic orientation that ignores these fears or questions and to fight, if necessary, against such an orientation by force" (Ibid.).

The strong commitment of Sadiq al-Mahdi to an Islamic constitution draws heavily on his attempts to find an optimum blend of both contemporaneous thought and classical sources of religion. He is a thinker who has no special impetus to keep up with the heritage when he emphasizes the need to adopt newness. A critical question, however, is: How could al-Mahdi persuade non-Muslims to trust his claims about the competency of Islamic justice and the relevancy of Shari'a rule to contemporary life?

Sadiq declares that, "Shari'a is not a penal institution. Nor does it involve people in it [by force]" (Ibid: 10). Accounting for features of the "new Islamic State," he mentions that, "The Shari'a sources [as constitutional sources of the State] are more conscientious to ethics, social life and humanity, and are more flexible than positivist sources are. The preservation of Islamic Shari'a [being the fundamental source of legislation] does not rule out the constitutionality of customs. Nor does it exclude the other humanitarian sources that do not contradict a fundamental source of Islam."

Sadiq then makes the point that "Rather, the full adoption of Shari'a makes it necessary to incorporate the other sources of the law into state legislation. The reason is that the sources of Shari'a are broad and just. The Imam ibn al-Qayim depicted Shari'a in these words: Shari'a is all justice, all mercy, and all wisdom. Any decision that goes astray from justice to injustice, departs from mercy, turns a good cause to corruption, or converts wisdom into recklessness has nothing to do with Shari'a" (Ibid. 21-22).

The preceding citations contain some of the most important views and beliefs of Sadiq al-Mahdi on "Islamic Constitution and State." Indicated in these statements is the fact that the Islamic Constitution and State would have to be installed in the

Sudanese society today without any need to change its social structure. Sadiq anticipates the establishment of an Islamic State by persuading the people of Sudan to adopt his Shari'a Program (the Program of Islamic Vigilance) optionally by using national elections.

What does Turabi and his supporters say?

Turabi rejects "the largest portion of the structure of our modern political societies and their governmental systems [because they are] a product of Western colonialism, or an implementation of dominant patterns of the Western civilization. The greatest blame of this reproduction is placed on the prevalent non-religious traditions of Western rule" (al-Turabi, al-Islam wa Nizam al-Hukm, 1984: 6). He announces, "Today, the failure of liberal parliamentarian party systems, the single party rule, military rule, and socialist systems is evident by trial and practice" (Ibid. 7).

At this point, there appears a major difference between Sadiq al-Mahdi and Hassan al-Turabi. Sadiq holds that political liberalism is a popular path of the modern life to install an Islamic state "by freedom and popular participation." Hassan al-Turabi considers political liberalism and its parties an ordained failure. Turabi continues with that stance in mind to document and evaluate instances of the Islamic Movement's struggles to establish an Islamic constitution and state in the Sudan.

"When the Sudan started to consider the formation of a Permanent Constitution in the late 1950's, some Muslim youth, accompanied by religious personalities, established a front calling for an Islamic Constitution. That youth was committed to an Islamic Movement previously spread to combat the post World War communism. Communism was further pushed by elements socialized by the movement of Egyptian Jewish communists and British patrons in the Sudan. The call for an Islamic Constitution was somewhat strange in the post-independence nationalist climate. It motivated, however, a wide response on the part of people, thus embarrassing negligent party leaderships on the issue of religion since they had been leading religious groups and they always seized power by virtue of that religious leadership. Upholding their liberal political beliefs, the politicians succeeded in avoiding an open confrontation with the Islamic [Movement for] Constitution," asserts Turabi (Ibid. 10).

Turabi peculiarly tackles the availability of "freedom and popular participation" which is a necessary precondition for Sadiq al-Mahdi to establish an Islamic constitution and state. Unlike al-Mahdi, Turabi looks at the possibility of building up an Islamic state through "a front [formed] by some Muslim youth accompanied by religious personalities. This political trend was called the Front for the Islamic Charter" (Ibid. 10-11). With this elitist approach, Turabi, nevertheless, relegates the other leaderships of Islamic orders and their mass following to a degrading position.

Even more, Turabi insists that during the deliberations conducted on the Islamic Constitution at the political forums, including the Constituent Assembly (1965-1969), the debate on the Islamic content of the Constitution versus a secular state led the "traditional parties to surrender to the doctrine of Islamic constitutionality. [This shift of opinion came about] either by persuasion or through the pressure exerted upon these traditional parties to appreciate their own popularity" (Ibid.).

Secondly, Turabi asserts that, "The [constitutional] dispute touched upon the situation of non-Muslims within an Islamic constitutional framework. The

Christians of the South were intended for that dispute, and yet the continuous dialogue ended up with an initial agreement whereby the Southerner parliamentarians gave their consent to the Constitution, in principle, in condition that their religious, cultural, and political freedoms be fully guaranteed. They considered, in particular, the fact that the draft of the Constitution suggested an autonomous rule to preserve for them the type of governance they have long yearned for. The third point with reference to the Constitution was to provide for the nature of an Islamic state with respect to the direction of State, the meaning of its supremacy, and the principles guiding state policies. The final issue was to decide upon the rule of Shari'a over statutory law. This had been resolved in a proposal to set-up a transitional rule in the country even before supremacy of the Shari'a over statutory law was decided upon" (Ibid.).

It is striking to note in the foregoing citation "the initial agreement" mentioned between Muslims and Christians during deliberations of the Islamic Constitution at parliament after the October Revolution of 1964. Equally important is the statement stressed by Turabi on the "reconciliatory formulations of the draft constitution, including Islamic terminology and religious meanings, in addition to phrases and slogans of the prevalent tradition of liberal culture" (Ibid.).

For Hassan al-Turabi, this latter heritage is only a masquerade that does not have any bearing on Islam: It is nothing but a pretense of Islam. The reader might have sensed that Turabi, starting with the dispute on the Islamic constitution at the Constituent Assembly, imputes an impression that his group had been the sole political and ideological leader of the Islamic constitution. He tries, furthermore, to consolidate a special patronage over the idea of an Islamic constitution by claiming that the ensuing results of the political situation had been originally a function of his own group.

The propagandized patronage Turabi claims over Islamic activities in the Sudanese public life is remarkably different from the liberal orientations of Sadiq al-Mahdi. Apparently, this is a situation so conflicting that it does not help to reconcile the intellectual contradictions between these two thinkers. Another evidence of this deplorable situation is made available by the writings of 'Abd al-Khaliq Mahgoub and Mahmoud Mohamed Taha that will be shortly discussed.

Turabi informs us about the steps taken by the political regime of 1983-1985, which promulgated Shari'a formal system of rule for the whole country since September 1983, and had earlier engineered a presidential election in 1977 towards that goal. "The elections of 1977," views Turabi, "advocated a program consisting of a completely religious plan to achieve Islamic rule. Guided by State endeavors to originate national problems and their solutions in Islam, the Islamic Movement was enormously strengthened among intellectuals and the people [at large]. The Islamic inclinations of [state leadership] were integrated with the popular movement to enlarge Islamic applications."

"The third term of office came to the President of the Republic in 1983 who promised to implement a full application of Islamic Shari'a in the public life of the Sudan. The President fulfilled his promise after the elections. But the implementation of Islamic rules in the judicial and administrative levels faced political and other practical difficulties. External media campaigns were strongly launched and opposition forces moved to obstruct the Islamic Scheme inside the Sudan. It was expedient to implement the third stage by enforcing a state of emergency that was not meant to control a security crisis of the ruling regime, as some might have thought. The state of emergency was actually enforced by a regular mobilization to allow the Islamic legislation to influence the public opinion and the criminal justice system. The forth stage was directed towards Islamization of the Permanent Constitution" (Ibid. 13-15).

Turabi sums up the proceedings undertaken to stabilize the Islamic State of 1983-1985 in constitutional terms in the following statement: "Perhaps the first project in that concern was to re-establish leadership of the State on the basis of *al-Bay'a* [Islamic oath of allegiance]. This was superseded by a project of amending the Constitution to complete the Islamic installation so that the main document [of the State] would go hand in hand with the spirit of laws and policies."

To conclude, Turabi ascertains that, "The Islamic transformation of the Sudan was not born of a contradiction between ruled peoples and the ruling leadership. The transformation was not an outcome of a revolutionary coup de'etat. It was created in a mood of integration combining all political forces of the country, government and people - a gradual and delicate transformation" (Ibid.).

Hassan al-Turabi has generously given a great appreciation to the "virtues" of "integrating political forces of the country, government and people," with the political regime of 1983-85. He expands his evaluation of that regime to depict Islamization of the State "a gradual and delicate transformation." He also considers the state of emergency through which the Islamic Shari'a rules were promulgated and forcibly applied in Sudan, "a regular mobilization of Islamic legislation to influence the public opinion."

Four years before in 1984, the date in which Turabi wrote his evaluation of the 1983's "Islamic State," Turabi had been holding this opinion. "If we will not bring up Muslims in the era of Islamic Call and Movement through the respect of free *Ijtihad* and broad-minded disputes, prior to any rule of Shari'a on the basis of consultation and consensus, obligation and compliance, we will face a great sedition. That will lead us to chaos or rigidity when the [Islamic] state is established. This is due to the fact that public tranquility must be founded on the will of the individual" (al-Turabi, Tagdid, 1980: 45).

It is indeed difficult to reconcile the two quotations.

The Sudanese Islamic Movement has issued the assessment of al-Mahdi and his supporters of the "transformation of Sudan" into an "Islamic State" in the years 1983-85 in June 1984. Sadiq also elaborated on these issues in subsequent works. The Movement states that, "The [1984's] Constitution of the Sudan, the Charter for National Action, and the Socialist Union are the basic institutions and documents of the ruling Sudanese regime. It is clear that they have a negligible relation with Islam. Therefore, the Sudanese people have been astonished at the regime's promulgation of adopting an Islamic orientation [for the State]. They did not believe the regime." The Movement makes the point that, "The practices of the regime indicate that, in the first place, most of the regime's political leaders are reputed for non-Islamic political and ideological tendencies, plus their non-Islamic social behavior" (al-Mahdi, al-Nizam al-Sudani, 1984: 17).

How did the Movement evaluate the state of emergency? Was it "a regular mobilization of Islamic legislature to influence the public opinion," as Turabi maintains? The Sudanese Islamic Movement announced that the state of emergency inflicted on the country from 1983 throughout 1985 aimed "to repress the escalated strikes that have been well-planned and firmly implemented." The emergency came "to smooth out the contradictions of the Constitution and the new [Islamic] laws, and to consolidate allegiances of the regime's [diminishing] loyalists" (Ibid. 23).

The Islamic Call and Movement observes that the 1983 regime also abused the state of emergency "to absorb repercussions of the deteriorating situation in the South where the regime has been massively defeated to the extent that large developmental schemes ceased to function [in the South]. It was meant to impose exceptional summary trials via emergency tribunals to terrorize the citizens. Finally, it was imposed to expand police action by delegating police jurisdiction to the Armed Forces with wide powers of inspection, arrest, and penalties to subdue citizens. [In conclusion], the regime covered up proceedings of the emergency law with an application of Shari'a Law. The regime used a reformative dress against the administrative, financial, and immoral corruption that has been ravaging the country for 15 years (the regime's reign of governance) without any checking or measures of accountability"(Ibid. 23-24).

The critique by the Sudanese Islamic Movement repeats the same adaptations of Sadiq al-Mahdi to "return to the Holy Qur'an and the Sunna, the enlightenment of the *Madzahib* [schools of jurisprudence] and the *Ijtihad* [scholastic decisions]. Added to these sources, an incorporation of useful sections of the secular laws is required to establish a new *Ijtihad* capable of inferring modern Islamic rules." Sadiq concludes in that, "The Sudanese Scheme [1983-85] has not committed itself to any of the well-reputed *Madzhab* or *Madzahib*. It has not issued a new up-dated Islamic "formation". It enacted rules and laws of which some originated in the Shari'a's jurisprudence but some originated in a secular source. These two approaches have been confused, admixed, hence violating justice both Islamically and secularly" (Ibid. 29-30).

The Sudanese Islamic Movement ends its critique of the "Islamic transformation of the State" with this reprimand: "The Sudan today is suffering from a wrecked economy, a people living in injustice, a civil war, and a ruling regime held responsible for the destruction afflicted on the country and its people. The regime lifted up a slogan of Islam to protect its own existence having had all of the other slogans irrevocably nullified" (Ibid. 51).

What were the ideas of the Islamic philosopher Mahmoud Mohamed Taha on the Constitutional debate?

Although we will not retract to political stances to analyze the ideas of Taha on the Islamic Constitution and the experiences of the political regime in 1983-85 to promulgate and implement Shari'a, we will first analyze his major opinions in constitutionality compared to other thinkers.

A thoughtful thinker, who prohibits for good any use of force to change society - an ethics to which he has been strongly committed against the Marxist thought - Taha abhors the acts of violence as a means of religious revivalism. His own stand is to assure the rise and growth of Islam on the basis of individual voluntarism and peaceful argumentation.

Taha attacks vehemently the forces and groups that reversibly understand, in his assessment, the noble message of Islam in the past, present, and future times. "Violence is forbidden in Islam; but the Shari'a of Islam is not the whole Islam. Shari'a is an approach to Islam. The original [Qur'anic] source of Islam dictates: "Call for the path of thy Lord with wisdom and good preaching, and discuss with them in the best manner." When the real legislature of Islam comes about in its most flourishing time, it will not rest on anything other than a rejection of violence" (Taha, Rasayil, 1973: 33).

Blaming the groups that strive for an Islamic Call without perceiving the ethos of Islam, in essence, Taha criticizes, "Those who speak about 'Islamic Call and the sword": misunderstand the ethos of Islam and the rule of the time, simultaneously. They would do good to themselves, as well as Islam, if they abandon this inhibiting call" (Taha, al-Thawra al-Thaqafiya, 1972: 26).

He attacks, on the other side, the religious and political forces that reject the Islamic Call: "There is no constitution for this country other than an Islamic Constitution. Yet, we have to be clear. The Islamic Constitution the existing propagandists (i.e., the Front of Islamic Charter, sectarianism, Ansar al-Sunna, and Shari'a jurists) are calling for is not an Islamic one. It is ignorance hiding behind the sacredness of Islam. They pursue an Islamic Constitution in the Islamic Shari'a; but the constitution is interwoven in the Qur'an (the actual Islamic Constitution) not in the Islamic Shari'a, which has nothing to give in political affairs but guardianship. The Shari'a does not have any [place for] socialism in wealth. Women have no equality with men in Shari'a."

Finally, Taha holds that, "The fundamental rights, which are the spirit of constitution, are based on these three domains: democracy, socialism, and the equality between men and women. The Qur'an embodied the constitution. And the Qur'an needs a new interpretation to give rise to the origins abrogated in the past by its branches" (Ibid. 28).

Mahmoud presents an alternative conception for the Islamic Constitution, which has been so vigorously disrupted by intellectual and/or political groups. This writer, however, believes that Mahmoud only presents a philosophical perspective that eloquently analyzes the serious contradictions involved in the constitutional debate. He does not offer, in fact, any program of action that political competitors usually do. Instead, Taha sketches broadly a "Second Message of Islam," which is so complicated that an additional effort is unusually required to grasp the practical implications of its theoretical abstraction.

It is irreversible, however, that Mahmoud Taha shares with the other thinkers a concern for the general challenges of the Sudanese society. Mahmoud Taha asserts, for example, that social development hinges upon "the geographical, political, and national unity of the Sudan. The first step is to bring the remote areas of the country into a close connection with each other, using a modern technology of communications and transportation." For him, this national unity is so critical that it deserves a special handling.

"Political unity," thinks Mahmoud, "takes place in a number of levels that must start with peaceful co-existence among all ethnic sections of the population, including their different and hostile tribes. A stoppage of the armed conflict between North and South is the best start to make. National unity means that the multitude of tribal groups, nationalities and ethnic groups of the Sudan be molded in a melting pot to make of themselves a united population with a common destiny, similar characteristics, and a shared perception."

"National unity requires [the collaboration of] all scientific, cultural, and intellectual efforts. It does not become true, as a rule, unless all activities are sufficiently utilized. We maintain in principle that the Cultural Revolution and the Intellectual Revolution will not arise until all activities are energetically pursued. In our point of view, the Cultural Revolution and the Intellectual Revolution will not materialize until they are firmly founded on a religious revivalism" (Taha, al-Deen wa al-Tanmiya, 1974: 20-22).

This important citation figures out an educational strategy for an idealist group that believes in religious revivalism as a life outlook much more than political and social struggles. The solutions sought for the bitter realities of Sudanese diversity and civil striving, nonetheless, require detailed policies and practices within a well-defined plan of action. Mahmoud Mohamed Taha has not offered such details but rather confines his intellectuality to the Second Message of Islam, the focal point of his philosophy. We will examine in the subsequent section specific characteristics of the Second Message of Islam that helps to delineate Taha's concern for Islamic revivalism and constitutionality.

Primarily, Mahmoud manipulates a few construes of thought as ideal models to explain his new message of Islam. This methodology is quite comparable in some aspects to the ideas of the German thinker Hegel as already discussed. For example, Mahmoud employs a notion of the "Ideal Thought" that presupposes and encompasses the cosmos of all existing things for eternity. Although the foundations of this thought are quite different in the light of Mahmoud's Islamic orientation, Mahmoud seems to be influenced by the logical structures of the Hegelian thinking. Moreover, each thinker believes that his own thought is an apex of human thought.

Ironically, Mahmoud criticizes Marx in this particular point: "In all aspects of his scientific socialism, he was blinded by the fact that socialism could only be a stage not a final destination. Marx erred in assuming permanency of his thought and taking that assumption as a base for the future of evolution [of the human race]" (Taha, al-Mizan, Undated: 21).

What does Mahmoud hold, in turn?

Apparently, he has viewed his "mission" "a last solution" to the problems of mankind in the 20th century, exactly as Karl Marx has earlier seen in his intellectual work a legitimate seal of political thought and social evolution in the 19th century.

Mahmoud begins with a broad framework to explore the path to Allah. He starts with a complex conception of renewing religious thought through a refutation of the general precepts of the public in the present day Muslim societies. "A new thought and a new science" should be processed to lead Muslims to "a new horizon." He draws heavily upon a new realm of ideas to prepare the ground for the Second Message of Islam.

"The rule of time stipulated that *Muhammadism* had to depart from *Ahmedism* a great deal to be able to guide people, according to the level of their rationality, applying rules addressed to their simple needs. That departure occurred by a shift from the verses of origins in the Qur'an to the verses of branches of the Qur'an. The latter became the rule of the time, abrogating in legislative terms the verses of origins" (Taha, Tariq Muhammad, Undated: 70).

This ideal construct is further elucidated in this statement: "It is better to decide firmly that there are two forms of Shari'a, the classical Shari'a which is the Shari'a of the First Message of Islam [*Muhammadism*] and the new Shari'a, that of the Second Message of Islam [*Ahmedism*]. The difference between them is a matter of degree. The Shari'a of the First Message is a base that of the Second Message is a step forward towards the top of a pyramid whose basis in a Shari'a and its top is morality. This pyramid picture generates a clear impression that the Shari'a of the First Message is not locked up; it is opened onto the Shari'a of the Second Message."

"There is also an inter-relationship between [the two forms of Shari'a] that renders some postulates of the First Message's Shari'a valid alongside the Second Message. This includes, for example, the Shari'a of '*Ibadat* [worshipping], *hudud* [God's penalties], and retribution. The continuity of these valid aspects of the First Shari'a is explained in our book Al-Risala al-Thaniya min al-Islam [The Second Message of Islam]. The remaining transactions' Shari'a in political, monetary, and social affairs has inundated much of its functions to the extent of exhaustion. Its development thus became a necessity" (Taha, Tatweer, 1971: 71).

Mahmoud wrote this elucidation in 1971, maybe earlier. In another place, he confirms his contentment with the same ideas by asserting, "I am, naturally, a preacher seeking a revision of religion via a new perception" (Taha, al-Deen wa al-Tanmiya, 1974: 54). He mentions further that, "The Shari'a of '*Ibadat* [worshipping] is valid, as practiced in the First Shari'a, and is equally valid in the Second Shari'a," the one innovated by his thought.

Previously noted, Taha has earlier divided Muslim prayers into the usual forms of *Mi'raj* prayers (the ordinary practice of Muslims) and the *Silah* prayer, a new prayer to be practiced, according to Mahmoud, by "the knowledgeable Muslim via his own vision." These ideas continue to be an object of criticisms by a vast majority of Muslims, in general and Sudanese Muslims, in particular.

Mahmoud stretches out his concepts of the Second Message of Islam to establish a most efficient remedy for the current deformities of religious rules by incorporating the traditions of the age and their inventions. Related to this, women's rights constitute fundamental constitutional rights in Taha's outline. "The level of Shari'a of the branches [represented by the Meddinese verses of the

Holy Qur'an] is that of the First Message of Islam, the message for which we have confined our lives in dedication" (Taha, Tatweer, 1971: 68).

The origins refer to the Meccan verses of the Qur'an, as he sees them. He gives an example of marriage contracts: "These are defined and applied as 'contracts for a deliberate possession of pleasure', according to Shari'a of the Branches - definition of the *fiqh* that falls short of [our] definition of the Shari'a. The shortcoming of *fiqh* is quite known compared to the tenderness of Shari'a" (Ibid.).

Up to this point, we can compare Mahmoud's opinion on and critique of marriage contracts to the views of Sadiq al-Mahdi and Hassan al-Turabi since they have all drawn attention to the need to develop *fiqh* for the purposes of modernity. However, Mahmoud adds: "When this Shari'a is appropriately placed in congruence with the rule of time, it certainly is the most authentic, the best in wisdom, justice, and tolerance. It liberated women, at that time, a great liberalization - a wise and daring leap at the same time. There are no shortcomings involved in Shari'a unless it is moved away from its time reference to accommodate the concerns of contemporary women, to organize their [struggle for] rights, and to solve their present-day problems. Even though the ensuing shortcomings should not be attributed to the Shari'a."

"It would be a shortcoming of the minds to transmit Shari'a from its [appropriate] environment to another one, that is not located for it, in the pretext that the Islamic Shari'a is fit for every place and every time. We have talked about this ignorance in many parts of our books. All verses stipulating guardianship over women are abrogated, starting from this day, by the [Qura'nic] verse, 'And women shall have rights similar to the rights against them, according to what is equitable; but men have a degree of advantage over them' [II: 228]. All verses of guardianship upon men, and upon women, are abrogated from this day by the verses "Remind, you are only a reminder. You are not mastering them'" (Ibid. 69-70).

The same views are said about capitalist economy: "All verses on capitalism in the Qur'an are abrogated by the verse: 'They ask you about what to spend. Say: forgiveness.' Forgiveness has a top and a bottom. Its top will be reserved for the area of morality. What concerns us here is its base because it is the lowest degree of socialism, i.e., the prevention of ownership of the means of production by a single person, or by a few individuals. With that, the path would be opened to develop a legislation on which the Second Message of Islam relies" (Ibid.).

Mahmoud Mohamed Taha manipulates several intellectual constructs to explain a complex perspective a dualism derived from the fundamentals of religion in an unprecedented manner. He is a creator of a new "Islamic" thought. The extent to which jurists accepted this thought is not difficult to predict. The classical jurists, in general, rebuffed his ideas and have thence resisted them. The public, at large, expressed much wonder about his thought and has continued to question him about it. Among other layers of the Muslim population many scholars thoughtfully discussed his doctrine in academia, at the halls of philosophical studies and research.

Indeed, it would be difficult to do away with the ideas of Taha concerning the need to pursue religious revivalism peacefully, regardless of the rejection of his Second Message of Islam by the majority of Muslims.

Mahmoud greatly suffered for the sake of his thought. Finally, he challenged the authority of Nimeiri's "Islamic" state, which had been strongly supported by

Hassan al-Turabi and his Muslim Brotherhood, by a strong rebuke of the May regime's Shari'a application to make war in the South and to terrorize the opposition. Accompanied with a strong call upon the regime to check its policies wisely, Taha issued *fatawi* (scholastic decisions) disdaining the religious transformation of the regime. His political enemies connived with the Authority to deal with their long-lived hostility. In January 1985, led by Ja'far Nimeiri, the Authority executed Mahmoud Mohamed Taha extra-judicially.

What remains now is a discussion on 'Abd al-Khaliq's views on Islamic constitutionality. Besides his thought to solve problems of the Sudanese society, which constitution does he adopt?

'Abd al-Khaliq perceives Islam in congruence with his political commitment, "a religion that allows Muslims to think about politics and economics. Islam allows them, furthermore, to contemplate freely so that [a person] can touch upon an ideal form of the good life. Islam does not permit distinctions between people if they hurt humanity. God said, 'And made upon you into nations and tribes, that ye may know each other (not that ye may despise each other). Verily the most honored of you in the sight of God is (he who is) the most righteous of you.' Colonialism is the thoughtful and practical side of the Crusade, and religion is the unconditionally motivating force to support what the Church was calling upon" (Mahgoub, Afkar, 1967: 11).

'Abd al-Khaliq differentiates between Islam, a religion transcending the abilities of mankind by knowledge, and the other religions. Islam encourages *Ijtihad* (independent thought or interpretation) in politics and economy to establish "the good life". He criticizes the use of religion by the Crusade to support the politico-religious institution of the Church, which is an experience Islam never encouraged.

'Abd al-Khaliq believes in the role to be played by reason and scientific knowledge. As he puts it, "The path of knowledge identified by Muslims is a firm perception, that is expressive of reality, according to evidence" (Ibid.) Highly appreciative of these elements of "rational cognition," 'Abd al-Khaliq conceptualizes Sudanese society as a class-society whose major problem centers on "the capitalist path of development with its negative impact on the advancement of the country. That path may increase development growth rate under certain conditions. But it soon declines the living standards of people as a consequence of the low level of local capital. It is a path leading to the entrenchment of neo-colonialism. It has exhausted out the prerogative of the homeland by moving it increasingly to dependency and a loss of national independence" (SCP, al-Marxiya, Undated: 97).

"Still, backwardness continues unabated and its social and production relations incarcerate the vast majority of our people in anachronous epochs that have no opening for enlightenment or social progression. It is indeed true that national resurrection for the peoples who have recently obtained national independence is impossible in the present world the way it had occurred in Europe in the 18th and 19th centuries through a capitalist path of development. This path is blocked in historical terms" (Ibid.).

Within the capitalist path of development, there are social forces that are bound to take advantage of that path politically and economically in the auspices of neo-colonialism, heir of the benefits and conspiracies of the decayed colonialism since the momentum of national independence. "For the Sudanese Revolution to successfully accomplish the tasks that antagonize colonialism it should have to struggle firmly against the backwardness of social and production relations" (Ibid. 69).

'Abd al-Khaliq does not rule out the interests of social forces in political economy or the impact of bureaucratic apparatuses of the State on society. His evaluation of Sudanese politics and social change is primarily undertaken regarding the position of social forces in relations of production. For whose interest are the processes of production and their final outcome utilized? Upon what do the ensuing social injustices impinge? In what direction are the social energies of society directed and engineered? Whether the system of rule is military or civilian, how is Sudanese labor force used and abused?

'Abd al-Khaliq's insights into these socio-economic and political issues draw heavily upon his study of the Marxian theory. Mahgoub and his party members made a great effort to make of this western theory an indigenous part of the Sudanese political thought by injecting into it local dimensions of the Sudanese struggles, past and present. With that, he projects a horizon of a continuous popular struggle for the future of the country, "the march of the Sudanese Revolution" in his own words. Hence, a question arises: What role does Islam play in this adaptation?

In the mind of 'Abd al-Khaliq Mahgoub, the linkage of Islam with the "Sudanese Revolution" does not cancel out disparities of class affiliations or positions of social forces in production relations. And yet, Islam can be a binding drive of all forces of the political arena for the worship of God, if they so believe. This collective faith, nonetheless, does not necessarily discriminate between Muslims or non-Muslims. Nor does it eliminate the persistent differences between these groups with respect to the accumulation, utilization, and distribution of wealth.

These differences are not determined by faith although they might be molded to a certain degree by justice and righteousness. A greater degree of the good life, however, would only be reached in 'Abd al-Khaliq's view when individuals and groups abandon class exploitation for the service of "the basic interests of the Masses." This alone could maximize a spiritual and material reconciliation in society.

With these political assertions, 'Abd al-Khaliq Mahgoub approaches the cause of ensuring democratic rights through the state administration of a socialist economy and the observance of the right to religious beliefs. The Constitution should tackle these vital issues to define clear provisions for the establishment of a democratic state, the freedoms of people and their civil associations, etc. The Constitution must adopt a progressive orientation in all legal and social stipulations, including a consistent commitment throughout its provisions to international norms.

Why is it that 'Abd al-Khaliq does not advocate an Islamic Constitution although it has generated much support for many political and/or intellectual individuals and groups after the October Revolution in the mid-60's?

Mahgoub and his group are certain that, "The enemies of the Democratic Revolution, i.e., the colonialists and all classes and local elements collaborating with them, are working to deepen and to enlarge the collapse of the Arabs [resulting from the 1967 war with Israel]. This attitude has been determined by the forces of reaction to reinforce the colonial power by setting up a reactionary regime [in Sudan] to destroy all the strongholds of the [democratic] revolution of our country ... to eradicate the Revolution for good. Relying on the Constituent Assembly and the Council of Ministers, the forces of the right wing marched on, using a variety of techniques to isolate the revolutionary forces from centers of the popular struggle, under the banner of religion. They theorize the political striving of the country in terms of a conflict between forces of Islam and the forces of agonist" (Ibid. 138).

The real conflict, for 'Abd al-Khaliq, is not a conflict of religion. He reaffirms that "A violent conflict between the democratic movement of the country and the anti-revolutionary forces clustered around the democratic rights. Having gripped the positions of Authority, these forces started in a desperate attempt to crush all strongholds of the Revolution. In so doing, they have been using different forms of violence and resorting to the legislature to deprive the masses from the right to association and expression. They tried their hardest to control the popular democratic organizations, splitting them, and appointing right-wing leaderships to supervise over them in the hope that they might constitute a social base among the revolutionary masses to weaken their will and to blind their vision" (Ibid.).

This conflict will not grow quiet in his opinion. Many factors came into play "after the October Revolution [the popular uprising of 1964] and the emergence of a popular attitude towards social change. Regardless of the forms of violence that persecuted the revolutionary movement, the preeminence of the causes of democratic revolution and the historical need to resolve them, in addition to the disastrous failures of the traditional path of economic development in the political and social life, [developed]. The reactionary forces would have to find an outlet other than violence and persecution alone to delay the advent of the Revolution or to abort it. The social forces calling for a capitalist path of production and relying on its motives and bases in our country are the forces working for a right wing reformation, the same forces that push hard for a capitalist revolution" (Ibid.139-140).

The forces of the Democratic Revolution in the thought of 'Abd al-Khaliq Mahgoub would continue to be permanently ready "to lay out in a multi-faceted thrust different forms of democratic development in the areas of economic, social, and political insurrection. The masses of the modern sector are the forces that directly influence popular activities. They comprise that bulk of the population, which is most receptive to the ideas of social change. It is impossible for a political regime to live in stability if the modern forces are seriously opposed to it or if these forces view the regime or a section of the regime a speaker antagonizing their wishes" (Ibid. 141)

'Abd al-Khaliq further asserted that, "Inasmuch as the struggle of the revolutionary masses led by the communist party is rallying against violence and persecution to gain democratic freedoms, the struggle of these masses and the purity of their corps would be maintained. This maintenance is possible in spite of the negative propaganda of the right wing reformists by the spread of reform and public support. The path and the techniques necessary to deter the counter-revolution would be prepared, and our country will enter a new phase in the stage of the National Democratic Revolution" (Ibid.).

From the early 1950's up to the late 1960's, the ideas of 'Abd al-Khaliq Mahgoub and his party comprised a new political scheme in formulation and terminology, involving concepts that do not focus on Islam as a major concern in governance and public affairs. It is a political scheme addressing itself to the economic, social and political state of the Sudanese society from a positivist point of view: What characterizes the state in question? What needs does it require in economic, social and political terms? How would a social change be enforced and for whose sake?

The nature of this political innovation is not embodied with faith and spiritual commitments, although these religious obligations and their impact on individuals and groups are not denied at all. But religion is not the political top agenda for 'Abd al-Khaliq and his supporters in the sense that the priorities of their political program are strictly reserved for a renewal of the social life. The accomplishment of this program hinges upon a salvage of society from economic servitude, backward technology, exploitation of the labor force, cultural stagnation, etc. In challenging the Authority, this political program is collectively organized to permeate society by a day-to-day participation of the masses.

The ideas of Mahgoub manifest the will of his party to fight a political and intellectual battle to foil the attempts of religious thinkers and groups to change the Sudanese society and state into some religious entity. 'Abd al-Khaliq, however, has not ignored the religion of Islam in that battle even though he continues to emphasize the class dynamics of the conflict apart from religion. Equally important, he restricts the role played by religion (being a unified system of spiritual beliefs) to the strengthening of morality and ethics in the social life. Towards this end, he stresses the impact of Islam, in particular, and the other monotheist religions, in general, on Sudanese society.

In theorizing his political scheme for the social change of Sudanese society, 'Abd al-Khaliq hopes that a settlement of the political crisis of the country would discern itself in a fair competition between the social forces, that maintained vested interests in production and development administration. In this aspect of his scheme, he comes in conjuncture with Taha and al-Mahdi that also think that civil liberties are a precondition for intellectual and political competition.

This is a partial consensus, however, that does not indicate any political overlapping between their schools of thought or political programs. It is a consensus which carries with it a possibility of avoiding violence, coercion, and persecution - the very atrocious policies and actions that only take place in the political arena when, by the abuse of Authority, absurdity overrules the honor of wisdom, and ignorance masters over rationality and conscientious awareness.

Nothing in the ideas of the Sudanese writers, Hassan al-Turabi, Mahmoud Mohamed Taha, Sadiq al-Mahdi, and 'Abd al-Khaliq Mahgoub has advocated force, as far as their personal under-writings are concerned. The political schemes of these thinkers, however, have not coexisted in peace. The dispute escalated with an increasing involvement of the Sudanese Armed Forces since the late 1950's, throughout the 1980's, to the present time. The analysis of these crucial developments of the use of force in Sudanese society and state lies beyond the scope of this book.

THE MOVEMENT OF INTELLECTUAL WOMEN

An interesting question pertains to the ideas of the thinkers on women's rights. To answer this question, the subsequent section focuses closely on important aspects of the critical cause of women's advancement.

Hassan al-Turabi tackles the promotion of women's movement in one of his books, as does al-Mahdi. Mahmoud Mohamed Taha dedicates a part of his works to women's rights. Mahgoub's views on women's progression have been indirectly voiced through the writings of Fatima Ahmed Ibrahim, a prominent leader of the Sudanese women's democratic movement, who has been influenced by the guiding principles of the school of modern socialist thought.

Fatima Ibrahim believes that there is a need to emancipate Sudanese women from the forces precluding their development, which are caused by ignorance and remoteness from entry into the labor market. Pressures of the household and its familial obligations also affect them with all their backwardness and tiredness. The Sudanese women have also been incarcerated in a captivity of old customs and traditions, lethargy, superstition, and sectarianism" (Ibrahim, Hasadona, undated: 761).

The context of the predicament is not alien to "the stage of complementing our economic independence or the task of directing it towards a path of socialist growth to accomplish the National Democratic Revolution. This installation of a democratic society will essentially drive the country along the enlightening path of socialism to a complete emancipation of the Sudanese women," asserts Fatima (Ibid.).

Fatima Ahmed Ibrahim struggled soon after the eruption of the October Revolution in 1964 to consolidate the democratic movement of the women's urbanite organization, the Sudanese Women's Union (SWU). The SWU aspired to become "a massive popular activity, empowering women of the country for a greater participation in the challenges of the National Democratic Revolution" (Ibid. 77).

Since the early 1950's, Fatima has been repeatedly elected to lead the Union. To highlight female struggles and intellectual disputes on women's rights and social change issues, a brief comparison is made on the ideas of the other Sudanese thinkers, concerning these rights.

Sadiq al-Mahdi employs a broad perspective of liberal thought to handle the problems of religious revivalism with new formulations of Islamic jurisprudence from within the classical heritage, carefully avoiding any split or fraud. Sadiq's style is penetrated in the following text with respect to women's rights: "When the teachings of Islam were revealed, they resembled a revolution that assured the humanity of women their rights. The secularist revolution of Europe enhanced the rights of women hence ushering them into a new epoch of rights. Today, the doubt casting upon Islam is that the rights of a woman in Islam are much less than her rights in contemporary society. It is therefore expedient for the Islamic Call to show that the rights of a woman, as a human being and a Muslim, are equal to those of a man" (al-Mahdi, al-Sahwa al-Islamiya, 1981: 20).

But, for Sadiq, "there is a functional distinction [between males and females] ... for a man there is a 'headship over the family" ... for a woman there is a 'specialty in motherhood and child guardianship' ... in such a way that these functions would be performed in affection, mercifulness, and cooperation. That a woman is entitled to only one half of what a man inherits is adjusted to the mandate of males to spend [on the family], and since females experience the weaknesses of pregnancy, child bearing, and child feeding which hinder their energies" (Ibid.).

Sadiq mentions some rights guaranteed for woman in the Islamic Shari'a: "For the women, there is a social security made of her share in inheritance, her dowry, and any other income that she might gain from work. That a woman is entrusted with only one half of a testimony in financial matters is due to her lacking in experience. If that lacking is alleviated, the reason for the half testimony rule will be removed. This is said in reference to the [saying of] the Imam Ahmed [that] ... 'One woman's testimony is accepted if the testimony is valid.'"

"Even the traditional Islamic thought admitted the political rights of women. Ibn Hazm is one of those jurists who conceded the women's holding of the public office, except for the Grand Imam's [leadership office], which is the only exception. Ibn Rushd conveyed in his book fi Bidayat al-Mujtahid that al-Tabarri said, 'A woman is allowed to be an absolute ruler in every respect, except for the aspects specified, in consensus, for the Grand *Imamiya* [leadership]'" (Ibid.).

Finally, Sadiq argues that, "The Islamic Call explains the basis of equity between males and females, the functional distinction [by sex], and all of the legislation needed in light of the new conditions [of the social life]. This is to be done so that a woman who is conscientious, outgoing, and ambitious would not be forced to find her position outside Islam ... if not in the camp of its enemies" (Ibid.).

Through his persistent study of the rules and *fatawi* of the master jurists of Islamic *Madzahib*, al-Mahdi presents his own resolutions: "There are premises for equity between males and females and legislation must respond to the new conditions of life." Still, many explanations are required for his statements: What are the detailed provisions of the legislation Sadiq emphasizes in the context of life in Sudan? What characteristics would the Grand *Imamiya* have that restrict a qualified woman from assuming its office? How would that inhibition be overcome if a feminist *Ijma'* [consensus] surpassed that of the male's population and scientific qualifications, according to the rule of the time and its ever-rising transformations?

These and other questions are challenging problems in the arenas of Sudanese political and intellectual life, even if many organizations and assemblages have already made the attempt to resolve them.

Another modern Islamic trend toward women, other than that of the Sudanese Islamic Movement, which supports al-Mahdi, is concerned with the women's rights that are guaranteed and practiced in Islamic terms with regard to the family, society, and the individuality of women. For example, there is the study of Zakiya Ahmed Satti presented at the 1st International Conference on the Application of Islamic Shari'a in The Sudan (1984).

Zakiya mentions in a paper on al-Usra fi al-Islam (The Family in Islam) the Qur'anic verses that have risen up the status of women over their subordination in pre-Islamic times. One of these verses is that 'I will not waste the work of anyone of you, male or female' [al-Imran: 195]. She refers to a _Hadith_ [speech] of the Prophet praising the good socialization of girls whose only reward is Paradise.

Zakiya ascertains the equal rights of women and men to attain an honorable life since Islam guarantees both of them full employment of rights and equitable obligations. "Islam prescribes marital relations and the rights related to them such as dowries, as well as the rights of childhood and motherhood. Islamic teachings have promoted the status of women," writes Zakiya (Satti, al-Usra, 1984: 6).

Practically, Zakiya's work provides for general indications of Islamic guidance. But she has not discussed in her brief study particularities of the problems in dispute. These embrace the right of women to work and to occupy positions in the judiciary, political leaderships, and the high echelons of state apparatuses including _al-Imama al-Kubra_ (the Grand Leadership of the Nation), the right of women to free movement and traveling without a close male relation for protection, etc.

Some Islamic modernists have considered the possibility of urging society to allow a greater exercise of women's rights than is actually realized in Muslim societies today. For example, they emphasize the right of women to wear female dress on the basis of cultural modesty rather than the veil, which is a rigid model of women's dress.

Of these modernists, 'Abd al-Halim Mohamed Ahmed Abu Shiqqa presented a paper on the issues of women's rights in Islam at the Fourth International Meeting of the International Institute for Islamic Thought, Washington, D.C., in the University of Khartoum (15-22 January 1987).

Abu Shiqqa holds that, "Another *Ijtihad* to classify verses of the Holy Qur'an and the *Sunna* would help to advance the kind of scholastic work required in [Islamic] jurisprudence. What is now critically demanded is the establishment of a new categorization of *Ijtihad* to serve the requisites of specialization, whether old (e.g., bibliography and history) or new ... and to serve the causes and contemporary issues... related to women)" (Abu Shiqqa, al-Maraa, 1987: 1).

Shiqqa mentions that he has earlier prepared an encyclopedia on women, a preliminary phase of a far-sighted project, "which consists of Qur'anic verses and citations from the two authenticated books of [the jurists] Bukhari and Muslim on the *Hadith*" (Ibid.).

Another example, explains Abu Shiqqa, is shown in connection with female dress and adornment. This includes, "a) the unveiling of the face was originally prevalent amongst pre-and-post Islamic societies. b) Necessarily, there was some adornment made in the face, hands, and clothes that believers had been accustomed to do. c) No single pattern of dressing was ever imposed on women; but modesty was a virtue highly respectable with due allowance to the diversity of women's dresses, in accordance with climatic and social conditions" (Ibid. 2).

Abu Shiqqa stresses that, "Both staying at home and the veil were a private attitude specifically for the wives of the Prophet. The wives of the Prophet's Companions did not follow suit; and they would not have been obliged to do so. The meeting of Muslim females with men was pervasive in all fields of the private and public lives, without any complexity or sensitivity. Nothing restricted the movement of women in society or their meeting with men, except for etiquette rules that aimed to maintain women's status rather than undermining it" (Ibid.).

"The fruition of these serious meetings bore a high degree of maturity. Women participated actively in charity campaigns as a part of their full participation with men in the public affairs of society. In the sphere of family relations, the right of a woman to select a spouse was assured, in addition to the right to be divorced if she disliked the husband. There was a clear division of responsibilities between spouses, and a prevailing state of equality in the rights of wives and husbands" (Ibid.).

Abu Shiqqa concludes that, "The role of women in the family is the primary task that, nonetheless, does not negate the other tasks of women in society. The development of social consciousness and the availability of close cooperation between spouses are two factors on call to help coordinate the major task of women [in the family] and the other tasks of women [in the public life] in the interest of society" (Ibid. 2-3).

Abu Shiqqa's views seem to be ambiguous when it comes to "close cooperation between spouses" in the context of "the major task" he allocates for the women "within the family." His notion of "social consciousness" is not well-defined, especially that the concept of "consciousness" means the rationality of (women's or men's) independence in opinion and actions from traditional forms of emotional commitments, or does it take another meaning? Furthermore, the limits of the "major tasks" of women in the family and the "other tasks in the interest of society" need to be clarified.

All in all, it appears that Abu Shiqqa shares with Sadiq al-Mahdi some of his views since they rely on the inherited jurisprudence to find legitimate connections of Islamic affairs with modernity. Moreover, as previously discussed about Sadiq's methodology and viewpoints, they endeavor to associate classical rules of religion with the concurrent novelty of their liberal interpretations.

In the area of women's professional activities, including social and political work, Abu Shiqqa emphasized the fact that women "participated in all spheres of the social life in accordance with the needs of the Muslim society at the Prophet's time. This participation embraced women's activities in the fields of knowledge and sciences [of the era] by attending forums of scientific knowledge and taking up responsibilities of education, acculturation, and literacy."

"Regarding politics, women took part in supporting with their faith a religion that had antagonized the values of society and its dominant groups. The Muslim women stood bravely against the persecution of Muslims by the ruling aristocracies. They migrated outside Arabia and experienced political exile. They maintained an active interest in politics, public awareness, political opposition, and the *Jihad* [wars] for the sake of Allah" (Ibid.).

Based on these facts, Abu Shiqqa lays his emphasis on the necessity of "removing the hull of having to conceal whatever is related to sex ... by returning to the Sunna of the Prophet and his Companions for a healthy sex education" (Ibid. 5). He does not feel any need to "renew religion" by departing from the origins. The shortcomings involved in the existing Muslim society are simply embodied in "the inability of minds" to grasp the origins of Islam. Abu Shiqqa, nonetheless, does not discuss in any elaborated fashion the conflicting views or interpretations of the schools of Islamic thought about women's rights. There is not yet a clear consensus among Muslim modernists on the necessity to grant women the full enjoyment of human rights, without any discrimination on the grounds of gender.

Many difficulties, in theory and practice, spring out of the fact that the women's movement in predominantly Muslim societies is comprised of both Muslim females and a considerable proportion of non-Muslim females, for instance the case of Sudan. Additionally, the movement must forge ahead amidst a plethora of social and cultural realities that do not overlap perfectly with the inherited Muslim jurisprudence.

In this conjunction, many Sudanese female intellectuals contributed with significant works to document their movement to advance women's rights in the country.

Haja Kashif Badri's book Al-Harakah al-Nisaiyah fi al-Sudan (The Feminist Movement in The Sudan) and Hasadona fi Ishreen 'Ama (Our Outcome in Twenty Years) by Fatima Ahmed Ibrahim document the participation of Sudanese women in public life. Many feminist organizations contributed to the formation of a progressive modernist movement by raising awareness among women of the country, independently from ruling political parties.

144

The Sudanese Women's Union (SWU), the largest voluntary activity in the women's contemporary movement, announced formally that, "It is not biased to any party. Its mission is to activate women to enjoy their political rights. Every member of the Union, in the rank-and-file or in the leadership, is granted a right to exercise free political activities with the parties to which she belongs or supports. The only condition is that the name of the Union, its branches, or assets, shall not be used for partisan propaganda" (Ibrahim, Hasadona, undated: 68).

The Women's Movement started with "a conglomeration of the wives of senior officials of the government [in the early 1940s], both Sudanese and non-Sudanese, who joined together in a women's club to entertain the membership as a major objective" (Badri, al-Haraka al-Nisaiya, undated: 103).

The idea of the club was practically developed "when Fatima Talib invited a number of educated females to her house in Omdurman to discuss the idea of setting up a women's organization. Those invited were namely Khalda Zahir (who was also calling for a similar organization), Zakiya Makki Osman Azraq, Aziza Makki Osman Azraq, Um Salama Saeed, Soad 'Ali Badr al-Deen, Amna 'Ali Badr al-Deen, Zeinab al-Fatih al-Badawi, Asia Abbas, Zarwa Sarkisyan, and Amna Hamza" (Ibid. 105).

As schoolgirls, "they decided to engage attention to the illiteracy of women, among other important social problems, through the league they subsequently formed for that purpose in June 1947 ... Khalda Zahir was elected chairperson with the other founding members, officers of the executive committee of the League" (Ibid. 105).

During the late 1940's throughout the 1950's, many female organizations were established, including a Union of English Speaking Women that came about a British reaction to the success of the League. Another association, "The Society for Promotion of Women, was inaugurated by the women of the Mahdi family, but this association did not survive for a long time" (Ibid.).

The Sudanese Women's Union was established and enhanced by prominent women activists of whom many had been founding members of the schoolgirls' League of the late 1940's. These include Dr. Khalda Zahir, Fatima Ahmed Ibrahim, Aziza Mekki Azraq, Soad al-Fatih, Thoriya Umbabi, Nafisa Ahmed al-Amin, Haja Kashif, Amaiym Adam, Batool Adhm, Mahasin Gailani, Um Salama Saeed, Fatima 'Abd al-Rahman, and Khadija Mustafa. Fatima Talib headed the first executive committee with Nafisa Ahmed al-Amin as secretary general in 1952. The names of these founding members of the Sudanese Women's Union have been collected from the two books of Kashif and Ibrahim earlier mentioned in this section.

The constitution of the Union adopted the objectives of "promoting the social, economic, and political standards of Sudanese women and raising their awareness on national issues and participation in philanthropist activities. These objectives have been directed to satisfy the needs of Sudanese women. They also constituted a major factor for the success of the Union and the positive impact of its activities within the Sudanese society" (Ibrahim, Hasadona, undated: 110-111).

The groups opposed to the Union were composed of *Imams* (leaders) of the mosques, "the Mahdi's family members and the Muslim Brotherhood led by Babiker Karar and Merghani al-Nasri. But this opposition soon withered away when the Union manifested itself in practical terms ... moving cautiously to stimulate social awareness with due respect to the prevailing customs and traditions. Some of the significant factors that enabled the Union to stabilize its activities in society embraced the labor organizations, students, farmers, writers, artists and many other sectors of the intellectuals. In addition to the Sudanese Press (led by Al-Saraha Journal which dedicated a special issue for the Union in its day of inauguration on September 1, 1952), they made it possible for the Union to maintain a prestigious status and role in the Sudanese community" (Ibid. 111-112).

Like the other non-governmental popular organizations, the Sudanese Women's Union has been severely persecuted by authoritarian governments of regimes, notably with confiscation of property and the freedom of expression, besides attempts of tutelage and subjection. In 1959, the Union was banned by Act disbanding all organizations and social associations. After the October Revolution 1964, Haja Kashif asserted that, "the Union was reinstated for political activism more than social work."

The Union continued to struggle for the cause of Sudanese women until many economic and political rights had been realized. In 1968, the Sudanese women were granted the right to equal pay for equal work with men. Political equity was established by recognition of the right of women to elections and competition in public office. Fatima Ahmed Ibrahim, the first woman to become a member of the legislature, was elected a member of the Constituent Assembly (the Sudanese Parliament) (Ibrahim, Hasadona, ibid.113-114).

The Union engaged in several external contacts with the outside world. "It strengthened relations with women's organizations in African, Asian, and European countries and became a member of many international groups. It was democratically handled to allow the renewal of leadership and adaptability of programs to social change. Within the first 7 years since its inauguration, the Union reached out widely to pursue its objectives: a popular educational institution that maintained solid traditions, rules, a world outlook, and principal stands" (Ibid. 113).

The Sudanese Women's Union overcame many problems through the political and social efforts the Union made to raise awareness of the masses about social change and women's concerns. But the Union never functioned in a complete consensus since many conflicts occurred among leaders and members of the Union in the course of time.

Fatima Ahmed Ibrahim points out a major dispute between her supporters and those with Haja Kashif "on implementation of the decision undertaken by the Union's Committee in its first session to create branches for the Union in every town. [We] argued for the expansion of services to the women in their households, instead of waiting for them at the Center" (Ibid. 46-47).

Fatima reports: "It was our viewpoint that a centralized organization would not help to expand the Union or to convert it into a popular organization. Centralization, moreover, will not open up training opportunities for leadership or grass roots activities. Led by Haja Kashif, the majority of the executive committee, however, was opposed to this opinion. Their view was that a decentralization of the Union's work would result in a multiplicity of leadership that, in turn, would weaken the influence of the executive committee. It would make it possible for enemies of the Union to undermine its well-being. The conflict was acutely personalized by the division of the Sudanese Communist Party (SCP) which was taking place at that particular time."

Fatima makes the point that the political preference of each group had earlier been determined (as the Fatima-group joined the CP while the Haja-group stayed with Awad 'Abd al-Raziq party after he had defected the CP). The dispute overshadowed the Union despite the objective discussions of the committee. "The strategy used by Haja Kashif's wing against us was to accuse our group of trying to convert the Union into a communist front. That strategy proved to be successful for Haja gained the support of most members of the committee" (Ibid.).

The first parliamentary elections held after these events were conducted on a national scale for the post October Revolution era. Fatima ranked the third in the list of Graduate Representatives at the Parliament of 1965.

It is interesting to note that the Sudanese women's struggles to promote the status and role of their counterparts have not been linked with a dialogue on the problem of modernizing the old Shari'a jurisprudence with a new Islamic approach. This writer feels that even the women who could have thought it that way might have been equally discouraged by the intransigence of *Imams* or some other religious personalities.

The efforts of women to harness their energies for the mainstream functions of the Union have been properly motivated and channeled by organizational activities, rather than religious inclinations. Enlightened with modern education, they have been actively absorbed in intellectual and/or political struggles to improve their status in Sudan's male-dominated society. The objectives of the women's movement have been clearly phrased as vital issues for their social well-being and lively aspirations rather than any religious revivalism.

One might assume that had Islamic thinkers who believed in the social and political equity for men and women supported the women's movement, the outcome of the movement might have been enormously different. It is, however, difficult to accept this assumption since most women have been exercising modern methods of thinking by adopting liberal democracy a political framework for participation in public affairs. Their movement eventually succeeded in the attainment of their goals regardless of religious commitments in the household or the private life.

Haja Kashif summarizes the situation in these concluding remarks, "The Union provided its members with democracy." This explains to a remarkable extent the successful movement of the Union. She mentions the close cooperation between SWU and the other Sudanese trades unions. "The invitation to review the organizational performance of the Union emanated from the other trades unions that recognized the significant role the Union played in the 1950's throughout the late 1960's" (Badri, al-Haraka al-Nissaiya, Undated: 97).

In her book, Fatima Ahmed Ibrahim confirms, "This period was one of the most prestigious periods of the women's Union. Many accomplishments were achieved, chief of which a major transformation occurred in the lives of women who [became aware] of their position in society and have already started to make of themselves an influential political force" (Ibrahim, Hasadona, Undated: 81). The achievements of the Women's Union included the election of a Sudanese woman a member of parliament, recognition of the women's right to public service pension, and a full paid 4-weeks maternity vacation before and after child delivery.

The women's movement had forcefully struggled for the realization of these rights for a very long time before they finally convinced a democratically elected government to adopt them formally. Instead of the democratic government, however, the May military coup implemented a "revolutionary" program leading to the enjoyment of women's rights in 1969. "The fact that the Union had developed itself into a massive movement by employing democratic programs impacted upon the Authority to recognize the women's rights, " says Fatima.

Ibrahim attributes this progress to the continuous struggle of Sudanese women for democracy, side-by-side with the other public organizations, the victories of women and the realization of their human rights. "We are convinced beyond any doubt that the women's attainment of their political rights would enable them to occupy an influential position in society that, in turn, would enable them to enforce their will [and the women's rights] in the long run. We have been a target of sarcasm and attacks by the Muslim Brotherhood and gangs of the Authority [during 1958-1964]. Zeinab al-Fatih, editor of Al-Thawra, a daily newspaper published by the ruling junta, launched a ponderous campaign against us" (Ibid. 60).

The author of this book collected the bibliographies from the sources authored by Kashif and Ibrahim. (See for example, Ibrahim, Hasadona, undated: 163-197)). The bibliographies of the leaders of the women's movement of Sudan demonstrate the existence of important relations between the women and the external organizations that have always supported them. The list of books further indicates the impact of modern politics upon their attitudes added to their superior characteristics as community leaders committed to the advancement of women's rights in the whole country.

Indeed, modern contacts and politics provided the women activists with the opportunity to struggle, without any conservative drawbacks, for the full participation of Sudanese women in the public life.

Khalda Zahir Sorour, the first Sudanese woman who entered the university and graduated together with Zarwa Sirkisyan as the first female physicians, had been politically organized since her early school days. She participated in the late 1940's and early 1950's in the newly established women's democratic movement, leading the famous demonstration of the Graduates' Club (1946) to protest the British-controlled Constituent Assembly - an act for which she was arrested by the colonial authorities.

A founding member of the women's movement, as well as a leader of many distinguished academic and scientific meetings on women's development, Zahir led the Sudanese Women's Union until the late 1950's. Also, she was a founding member of the Women of Sudan Popular Association, a member of the World Peace Conference throughout the difficult times of the Cold War, and a regular participant of many medical conferences. Dr. Zahir was a founder of the Associations' Front, a creation of the October Revolution in 1964 which played a prominent role in the overthrow of the 'Abboud's dictatorial regime (1958-1964).

Fatima Talib Ismail, the first female principal of a high secondary school, was also the first to call for the establishment of women's social organization. She participated in planning the education of the Yemen Peoples' Republic, created the first women's organization in Sudan (i.e., the League of the Educated Young Women), and contributed to the formation of the Women's Advancement Association at Omdurman in 1949 with the women of the Mahdi's family.

Fatima Ahmed Ibrahim, the first Sudanese woman elected to the Parliament, was one of the leaders of the first strike that schoolgirls organized in opposition to the British educational system in Sudan. She was one of the prominent activists in the women's movement and organizational activities, a founder of Sawt Al-Maraa Magazine [the Voice of the Woman] and its editor-in-chief. The magazine published strong criticisms denouncing the first military rule of Sudan (1958-1964) for which the authorities repeatedly disbanded it.

Fatima participated actively in the creation and success of the October Uprising [or Revolution]. She led many regional and international conferences, a member of the Associations' Front, and has served elected president of the Sudanese Women's Union since 1956 to the present time.

Soad al-Fatih al-Badawi, the first Sudanese woman appointed as dean of a university college, obtained an MA and Ph.D. in Arabic Arts from the University of Khartoum. She was a member of the first executive committee of the Sudanese Women's Union and the first to represent the Union outside Sudan in 1952. She participated in the establishment of the Sudanese Women's Popular Association during the military rule of 1958-1964. She was the initiator of the Women's Front in 1967, a founding member of the Associations' Front to protect the October Revolution, and Dean of the Girls' College at the Riyadh University in Saudi Arabia through a UNESCO grant in 1969 to advance women's education in the Kingdom.

The other pioneers retain bibliographies with distinguished intellectual and/or socio-political activities so much similar to, if not greater than those of the men. They have demonstrated publicly their opposition to policies and practices of the authority as far back as the colonial times. They have created with their male counterparts political parties, professional associations, educational institutions, etc.

The interaction, interdependence, and divisions practiced by the male thinkers and/or politicians of the Sudan have been equally encountered in the women's movement. The women met, disputed political issues, agreed and disagreed. Originated in a common cause of national activism, their movement concentrated on the advancement of women, the largest minority of the population. They have consistently raised the most demanding needs of education, employment, political participation, and involvement in international activities for the women than any issues of the religious revivalism in which their male counterparts have been so heavily engaged.

Was it true that the women's movement oriented itself in practical terms to solve the most urgent problems of women in contrast with the men who devoted their thought to design far-sighted strategies for a societal transformation of the Sudan? The author feels that the Sudanese women's movement has successfully empowered the urban women of Sudan, at least in the modern labor sector. The women lost no time in philosophical disputes, as the men did.

There are certainly growing concerns about the future prospects of the women's movement. If the same controversies on religious revivalism that have increasingly divided Sudanese thinkers and politicians among themselves, also prevail over the women's activities, the lack of Sudan in political stability and development administration will certainly continue for generations to come.

The success of women's struggles has been partially achieved as a result of their deep appreciation of the cultural diversity and social intricacies of the society more than any emulation of the male-dominated activities. True, the women's movement has not exerted a great effort to help Southern women, or the other women of rural Sudan, to promote their living standards, although the rural areas of the country have been largely deprived of adequate social, political, and economic attention.

The Sudanese rural women must be commended for their struggles in the war-affected zones, as well as the areas hit by famine and drought all over the country. The needs of rural women are critical and ever increasing, being a determining factor in the national development of the Sudanese people.

To conclude, the women's movement contributed to the innovative attempts by Sudanese thinkers and politicians to drive society into modernity and social progress. In so doing, the women have certainly transcended with their independent movement many ideas emphasized by the male thinkers on "the necessity for another Shari'a, "the need for a new science of Islamic jurisprudence, a philosophical approach for new relations," etc. The struggles have clearly reflected the knowledgeable practicality of the women's leadership and broad membership.

Finally, the women's movement has decisively illuminated, irrespective of the shortcomings entailed, the political competence of the Sudanese female. The women's movement documents the organizational ability and will power of Sudanese women to cope with both religious and modern values. The efficiency of women's activities to realize their social and political goals materialized in spite of a labyrinth obstructing their march, a skepticism frustrating their ambition and aspirations, and a plethora of conservative rules against their equity with men.

Based on this information, the development of Sudanese society seems to have been hinging on the need of men, rather than women, to promote their world outlook and theoretical formulations on women's status and role. Despite the fact that a few men have been encouraging women to struggle for their just cause, Sudanese men continue to act conservatively towards women. The men exercise the power of guardianship over public and familial affairs. The Sudanese women's democratic movement, nonetheless, enabled many families to reduce the monopoly of men over their lives by the encouragement of male participation instead of male-domination.

In many instances, the Sudanese male thinkers appear to enjoy consensus than disagreement in the disputes between them. Their political ideologies, however, tend to undermine that consensus. Conversely, the Sudanese women thinkers have been firmly united in their perspectives to promote women's rights. Supported by trades unions and progressive groups, the women's struggles have been largely strengthened by political activity.

The women's political ideologies have not strengthened their political integrity. Documented in this chapter, the activists' political and ideological conflicts were rarely resolved in positive results. Some abandoned the struggle for good, while many continue to fight for the cause. In conclusion, the Sudanese women's activism was tremendously influenced by intellectual rivalries and ideological diversities more than any religious revivalism might have possibly done.

SUDANESE THOUGHT: A CONSENSUAL DIFFERENTIAL

INEVITABILITY OF DEMOCRATIC LIBERALISM

The closing chapter of this work finds the writer caught between a reality so broken with bitterness and illusive pictures of ideal thinking.

In the case of Sudan, one questions the nature of Sudanese thought, whether it is consensual or uncompromising. If it is consensual, i.e., apt to contain conflicts and absorb disagreements, no matter how they may be, Sudanese thought will comprise an integrative propellant for the good life. It will eventually develop a respectable life for people based on human rights and the ability to utilize the energies and limited resources of the country effectively for the public use.

A foremost task is bestowed upon all Sudanese intellectuals to deepen the awareness of people about the ability of intellectuals to reconcile differences, to meet urgent needs to harness their thought for the perseverance and advancement of humanity, the ethos of that thought.

However, if the Sudanese thought is contentious and contradictory, it will create a serious catastrophe in a society characterized by poor levels of technology and an impoverished majority. It is almost impossible to steer Sudan to the shores of the 21st century - a century already bewildered with scientific novelty, space travel, and large discrepancies in social welfare programs and fluent economies - while still caught in a persistent deprivation of technology, liberalism, and professionalism.

Another dimension of this episode considers the Sudanese thought simultaneously consensual and contradictory. If that is really the case, it will be difficult to define features of the Sudanese thought clearly, let alone follow its intrinsic logic.

How do we find the essence of Sudanese thought, according to the ideas intensively analyzed in this work? How much agreement, or disagreement prevails among the thinkers? Is their thought an amalgam of conflicting extremes? How would that thought manage to mold the differences ensuing in the conflicting ideas?

Recalling the earlier chapter on the Sudanese diversity of culture and thought, it has been assumed that the Sudanese thinkers, Mahmohd Mohamed Taha, Sadiq al-Mahdi, 'Abd al-Khaliq Mahgoub, and Hassan al-Turabi are not devoid of commonality on the issues of social change. Despite the partisan loyalties of their supporters, which have been politically influenced by the thinkers, many compromising deals were readily acceptable in Sudanese political fashions. This occurred throughout the post-independence era, for example the Round Table Conference after the October Revolution 1964.

We will now make an attempt to delineate a few converging aspects that may be appraised amongst our thinkers.

All of the Sudanese thinkers called for freedom of thought and expression: Turabi called for "a new amalgamated science." Mahmoud emphasizes that, "a Second message based on thought, science, and a high level of spirituality." Sadiq adopts "an Islamic Vigilance ... an intellectual movement." And 'Abd al-Khaliq demands "new interpretations ... for a rational social change." In all these appeals, there is an undeniable agreement, a general consensus of thought; however it is an agreement swollen with differences of conceptualization, almost as much as the land and people of the Sudan are themselves diversified.

The thinkers regard the freedom of thought and expression indispensable to a healthy social life. Sadiq insists that, "the installation of an Islamic regime does not mean the imposition of Inquisition Courts or the launching of a campaign that violates personal taboos." Turabi says, "There is no church in Islam or a formal authority to monopolize the _fatwa_ ... To issue _fatawi_ or _Ijtihad_ in our contemporary conditions is a matter of brave opinions, a consistent perseverance versus the pressure of conservatives [to behave otherwise]."

Mahmoud calls upon Muslims "to review religion with a new understanding since religion is refined, exact, and righteous. ... Thought is a purpose of religion ... [and all individuals are capable of thinking]. There is no master of mankind but _Allah_." For 'Abd al-Khaliq, "Democratic freedoms are preconditions for any serious thought. ... Islam allows Muslims to think about politics and economics. Islam frees their ideas and perception and recognizes new interpretations [of the social life]."

Is it possible then that the agreement of these thinkers on the indispensability of thought and freedom of expression testifies with living evidence to the impact of intellectuality, as well as the high value their Sudanese society attributes to freedoms and human rights? The answer to such questions could be quite positive. However, the thinkers continue to disagree, in practical terms, on the impact of religious and cultural exigencies on the substantive issues of politics and public interests.

This, in reality, seems to be a code of political behavior that has no exception anywhere on earth. The human bondage of thought has to give way in many instances to the expediency of political interest. Liberties of thought are frequently subjected to the needs of action, and the influence of political agenda overshadows intellectual works.

We are not convinced that there is an end of thought beyond which new ideas never exist. Contrariwise, we are more convinced that thought is endless. This fact shines from within the controversy of thought this analysis shows about Sudanese writers. Apart from any biases, each one of the thinkers expresses individuality unique in its own right. Each one of them exhibits a trend of thought accumulated by the individual experiences they passed through.

It is the freedom of thought they have more or less acquired in the course of life that is responsible to a considerable degree for their intellectual activities. Hence, it is important to ensure the right to free expression to the whole populace, individuals or groups, to enjoy their own intellectuality.

Within the consensus observed between Sudanese thinkers and their freedom of thought a differential still lingers in their handling of material evolution, progression, modernity, and the other contemporary concerns for they all pointed out these themes with varying concepts and theoretical formulations.

Sadiq, Mahmoud, and Turabi discuss the problems of evolution and progress using concepts of modernity and revivalism in a broad "Islamic" perspective. This perspective has been caught in a labyrinth involving difficult choices between origins of religion and their branches on the one hand, and secular sciences and modes of the social life on the other.

'Abd al-Khaliq prefers to confront these problems with a "positivist" perspective, which considers religion a motivational "factor" of advancement "serviceable to the basic needs of the public and the national cause." He prefers to struggle for that cause "with all its conflicting realities" than to adopt religious revivalism as a goal-achievement in Sudanese society.

Another indication is that Sadiq and 'Abd al-Khaliq uphold a similar view on the prominent role the early righteous Muslim intellectuals played to accumulate and disseminate religious knowledge and to widen religious interpretation in accordance with "Sources of religious *Ijtihad*."

Here, Turabi and Mahmoud seem to be more agreed on the need to establish a religious *Ijtihad* emancipated from "traditional jurisprudence," although they are in greater disagreement on the degree required for that emancipation than other thinkers are. Turabi, for instance, asserts that the interpretations of classical jurists "available in our jurisprudence heritage are dormant theoretical assumptions that create an endless dispute." Mahmoud thinks that, "Religion in the level of the First Message hinders [the] social development [of our present time]."

In truth, Turabi does not claim another Message of Islam, as Mahmoud does. Nor does Turabi condone that sort of thinking, in essence. Nevertheless, this writer believes that the difference between the intellectual assumptions and expectations of both Mahmoud and Turabi falls, to some extent, in their own ideological commitments rather than their sense of the existing crisis and its resolution.

Turabi's claim that "the old jurisprudence is based on a limited knowledge of the nature of things, facts of the cosmos and rules of sociology," almost overlaps with

Mahmoud's evaluation that "Our reactionary Shari'a is only a stage that does not go rightly with our contemporary life."

For Turabi, the reason is that: "Science has been expanded to a great extent. But the science of scriptural texts had been limited at that [early] time by the difficulties entailed in the means of study, research, and publication. We have been impelled to rethink the *fiqh* of Islam with a new perspective which utilizes all knowledge of the worship of Allah, and to formulate a new structure amalgamating sciences of the human mind with those of the scripture," asserts Turabi.

Here, as well, Mahmoud's doctrine does not contrast with the Turabian scheme. In Al-Tanmiya al-Ijtima'iya, Mahmoud writes, "For the old Shari'a to be able to incorporate this [present] life and to direct its enormous activities, the Shari'a must open up, develop, and ascend high above branches of the Qur'an to reach its [original Qur'anic] fundamentals. If this claim of us fails to occur, religion would have been defeated because it would have helplessly failed to face out challenges of the time. This opinion can not be upheld by any person who knows about the realms of religion."

The revivalism Mahmoud hopes to establish for Islam is motivated by his contention that "Man was created on earth to live freely with no one mastering him until he submits in servitude to the Lord. Science is [destined] to serve man. To know Allah and to fulfill man's servitude to Him, man must experience worshipping." Mahmoud calls for a return to the fundamentals of religion. So does Turabi.

Regardless of this convergence, the planning proposed by the two thinkers to implement their schemes is quite divergent. As the political situation turned out in the most recent history of the country, Mahmoud continued to persuade people in a peaceful dialogue to follow his doctrine. But Turabi devoted his energies in pursuit of political power, which finally led him to usurp al-Mahdi's authority by the Islamic Front's coup de'etat in June 1989.

Mahmoud and 'Abd al-Khaliq approach democracy from a shared perspective. "Democracy is a precondition to socialism," states 'Abd al-Khaliq. "Economic development could only be accomplished through socialism," ascertains Mahmoud. "In our era, socialism is the decisive element of development," confirms 'Abd al-Khaliq. But Mahmoud Mohamed Taha moves along with socialism and democracy to prepare the ground for the Second Message of Islam, his ultimate goal-achievement.

'Abd al-Khaliq envisions that socialism is a concluding chapter of political struggle, a progressive completion of the movement of Sudanese Revolution. There is no other way for these countries to be developed other than the non-capitalist path of development. By nationalizing foreign capital, accumulating resources of national wealth in the hands of State, eradicating feudalism, and developing agriculture on the basis of cooperatives and large-scale production, etc., they will make for the industrial and agricultural revolution. This way socialism will remove the backwardness of pre-capitalist relations to regenerate life onto the reins of progress" (SCP, al-Marxiya).

The concepts used in the preceding statements indicate the difference between the thinkers in objectives and action plans. Note, for instance, the different uses of the concept of "progression." Turabi thinks that progression is a source of resistance.

He predicts, "We are prone to launch, while we embark on, a huge campaign of revivalism. Undoubtedly, a conservative reaction will be surrounding forces of revivalism when they proceed on." He draws an analogy between his scheme and the case of Ibn Taymiya [a well-celebrated Islamic jurist who endeavored to renew jurisprudence on the basis of fundamentalist thought and doctrines] whose movement "faced strong resistance when he rose to revive the matters of religion from dormancy."

Mahmoud calls upon religious conservatives to "do good to themselves and the missionary work they perform" by abandoning "their unfruitful methods." Sadiq al-Mahdi criticizes "all ill-practices made in the name of Islamic Vigilance. The strongest allies of secularist thought and action are founded on a misunderstanding of the Islamic Vigilance and a wrongful application of Islamic Shari'a." In this statement, al-Mahdi differentiates secularism from Islam in a way that posits secularism an antithesis of Islam.

We have read 'Abd al-Khaliq's version of secularism that concentrates on the notion of progression without having to deny religion or to antagonize it. Equally, we are aware that Mahmoud condemns the Marxist intellectual and practical trend "that uplifts group interests over the individual, and advocates violence to enable one class to subdue the other classes."

Also, Sadiq, 'Abd al-Khaliq, and Mahmoud agree that the political movement of society must "emancipate society from all forms of coercion in order to make of a society's political destiny a free choice for people to express their will power via fair elections. Such elections should lead to the establishment of a parliamentary institution to decide with majority vote the system of governance that is selected by the majority representatives" in the words of Sadiq al-Mahdi.

In spite of this partial consensus, conflict is neither hidden nor forbidden. 'Abd al-Khaliq rejects a democracy "that does not open up for progression. The problem, in essence, was not a conflict of distributing electoral constituencies or a matter of allocating some constituencies for workers, modern farmers, and the intellectuals. The context is a new democracy that paves the way for a National Democratic Authority. The context refers to the enjoyment of fundamental democratic rights [by the masses]. The context equally refers to the restoration of activities thus far controlled by the counter-revolutionary forces of the Democratic Revolution. It also requires the confiscation of activities of the classes that have been associated with colonialism without paying attention to our national resurrection."

Sadiq does not condone this obvious differentiation between strata and classes. The Sudanese Islamic Movement criticizes the political alliance of the communist party in 1969 with the ruling junta and its Nasserist elements. "This coalition did not stay for long because the communists considered these alliances with the "petty bourgeoisie" a short-term strategy. The conflict pulled together most of the coup officers, the Nasserists, and members of the major political parties which supported the coup on one side, and with them leaders of the communist party. On the other side, the party took a different stand. The conflict intensified, then violently quashed in July 1971 for the interest of the former [i.e., the Nasserist] group."

In its very nature, the conflict was deeply underlying an intellectual dispute, which had been coexisting before the Authority made it into a bloody confrontation. In the meantime, the masses never enjoyed the right to free expression and association, or any other fundamental right. This isolation of intellectuals from participation in national decision-making escalated the conflict until the advent of popular rising in 1985.

Previously mentioned, the failures of Authority to allow a peaceful dialogue with different schools of thought, led to the disastrous elimination of some thinkers, as well as arbitrary arrest and torture of the others. The May Authority assassinated Mahmoud Mohamed Taha with a mock trial. Turabi was detained before he finally collaborated with Authority and became a senior member of government. Sadiq was forced to live in exile, condemned to death in absentia, and imprisoned and tortured several times (until the date of writing this work). 'Abd al-Khaliq Mahgoub was imprisoned, repeatedly forced to live in exile, imprisoned, and finally executed by the Authority via a military mock trial.

The competition anticipated between schools of thought was only allowed to survive in peace for a very short period of time. Another Authority came about using ghost houses (clandestine centers of torture, fire squads, and the gallows to deal with intellectuals. God be with you, oh People of Sudan! It is only with parliamentary democracies that the people managed to resolve ideological and political conflicts. This surely is a well-documented experience throughout the popular uprisings of October 1964 and April 1985 that enabled the Sudanese to enjoy freedoms of thought and expression.

SUFI SECTS AND SUDANESE INTERACTIONISM

In the remaining pages of this chapter, two important tasks remain to be completed. The first task explores the laws or codes of behavior that regulate the social evolution of the Sudan. The second task evaluates the present and future modes of thought that influence individual and group behavior. A valuable contribution by Mohamed al-Mekki Ibrahim is immediately consulted on the evolution of Sudanese thought since the Turkish-Egyptian rule.

For many writers, the Sudanese nationalist personality embraces a complex admixture of knowledge and wisdom, as well as a personality deeply interacting with different cultures, religions, etc. Own al-Sharief Qasim, Osman Sid Ahmed, Ahmed Mohamed 'Ali Hakim, and 'Ali al-Khatim Ali (1984: 5-6) emphasize "the spontaneous spread of Islam" during the early times of Islamization of the Sudan. This spontaneity "was further developed into a rational and cultural participation" and an Islamic movement was intellectually enhanced which exerted a special impact on Sudanese nationalism."

A different reading of historic events reversibly sees this viewpoint. For example, a study on Medieval Eastern Sudan and the Arabs: a Study on the Evolution of Economic Relations. (This is a region that includes the Nuba and the Beja peoples). The study analyzes the interaction of civilizations with the Sudanese Muslims that became a strong stimulant for the adoption of Islam in the region.

Haj Hamad, writer of the study, says that, "The Arabs who entered the region nearly represented all major branches of the *Adnans* of North Arabia, who had earlier settled in Egypt since Muslim conquest, as well as *Qahtans* of the South. A developing division of labor and the Arabs economic interests rendered blood ties and socio-tribal systems incompatible with the ongoing transformation. In other words, the realities of production relations expanded the economic interests far beyond the bondage of blood relations" (Mohamed Khair, Medieval Eastern Sudan, 1982: 332-333).

"If the terms Arabs and Beja were accurately used to depict the autonomous units that showed up in historical times, new forms of production were lately endorsed by the social groups of the Eastern desert. These forms made of ethnic differentiation a meaningless domain" (Ibid.). The economic utility, which spread over and exchanged all around the mines among the Beja and the Arabs trading with them, "led the Beja to ignore their own tribal affiliations. The Beja submitted to the [new] leadership of their alliance with Rabi'a [an Arab tribe] that was generally known in the aftermath as the Hadariba. Rabi'a itself was engaged in a sharp conflict among its own factions, the Beni Yunis and the Beni Hanifa, on control of the Izab port. Al-'Umri of Beni Makhzoum, a branch of Mudar, was granted asylum first of all with the Hadariba. But when he became a source of disruption to the production of gold, his own tribe [the Beni Makhzoum] assassinated him. The Arab migrants from Yemen and Mudar became followers of the leaders of Rabi'a and the Beja [i.e., the Hadariba]. This is a unique event in the history of Arab tribalism" (Ibid.).

The cultural interaction between the Sudanese Arab-Beja groups in Eastern Sudan was not an outcome of "a spontaneous spread": "The rational cultural participation" was not more effective than "production relations and the economic exchange" were. Compared to the former, the impact of the latter was clearly reflected in a tremendous transformation of the population structure, as well as the tribal affiliations that resembled a specific culture and a base of expanding Islam in the region. The study undertaken by Haj Hamad Mohamed Khair makes it possible to infer these interesting facts on the interaction of civilizations and cultures in Sudanese society at these ancient times.

"Neither the Arabs nor the Beja were discrete identities in isolation of historical development. The best that can be thought about them is that they had transformed themselves into transitional structures involving a central chiefdom and different groups of followers. In this context, one can understand how the alliance of sections of the Beja and Rabi'a developed into the one main group of the Hadariba. This new group recruited a following interested in the natural resources of their territory, i.e., gold, trade relations, and community life to increase production. In turn, these new interrelationships strengthened a cultural radiation that helped to develop a cultural identity for all these groups in its own right" (Ibid. 323-334).

Khair ends with a finding that the depiction of the Hadarba as "urbanites" by the Mamlukes (of Egypt) should not blur the occurrence of economic and cultural interaction between the rural and urban groups of Eastern Sudan. "These groups controlled the mines, the roads to the mines, and the ports of Izab and Suakin. New centers were also created, old [tribal] centers were renewed through the input of feudal estates, coalitions, or by invasion, and, above all, many changeable varieties of economic activity that subsequently surfaced [in the social life]" (Ibid. 334-335).

Haj Hamad Mohamed Khair concludes that, "The mines played an important role in the late stages of cultural interaction. The Arabs were not to stay on ethnic or cultural grounds as McMichael's classifications of the tribes suggest. Mixed with the local inhabitants, who were a majority population, they almost assimilated them" (Ibid.).

How did Islam, an ideology of the Arabs, spread about within these transformations? Haj asserts that "Islam was described by Ibn Hugal as being influential on the Beja in the period taking place since the Arab infiltration of the Eastern desert until the death of Khalifa [Caliph] al-Mutawakil. Ibn Salim reported the lamenting of Beja clergy that the will of God meant that they submit to their own leader, Kanon, and to the Rabi'a [the Arab tribe]. Islam was not a dominating ideology over the ruling strata. Throughout this period, nonetheless, it appears that - as a lifestyle - Islam was gradually penetrating society to prepare the ground for the rise of the political entities of its advocacy" (Ibid. 341-342).

The influence of the economic factor and the relations it bore came to an end "When the mines deteriorated, and trade moved southwards, new forms of living started to regress into the former patterns. This direction, however, does not imply that the process of cultural interaction was totally exhausted. The process continued to have an impact on the Bashariyeen and Beni Salim until the present days" (Ibid. 349).

Finally, Khair observes a pattern emerging from these processes in the Arab-Nubian relations, especially after the *Baqt* Agreement (625 A.D), and a drive of the resident population and the Arab migrant corporate groups to pursue their interests. Signed by the Egyptian Arab Emir and the Sudanese Nubian king, the *Baqt* brought about peace in the region, ascertained freedom of religious beliefs, and increased trade between the two neighboring states. The prevalent peace and stability helped to bring about flourishing Sudanese cultures and arts. New kingdoms figured out with an Islamic lifestyle and faith, and the depths of the country were eventually opened to scholars, jurists and Sufi leaders (see the opening discussion in introduction of this book).

A significant lesson can be heavily drawn from the unique amalgam of Sudanese cultures and Islam in connection with the new production relations. "The Arab migrants from Yemen and Mudar became followers to the leadership of Rabi'a and the Beja." This process is suggestive of a sophisticated rule, or rather a social code, that elucidates the important role that domestic factors played in shaping our societal relations of a multiethnic society. The study undertaken by Haj Hamad demonstrates the validity of this particular aspect of Sudanese society.

Another important work attempting to theorize the evolution of Sudanese thought, in close relation with socio-economic and political development, is a book written by Mohamed al-Mekki Ibrahim on <u>Al-Fikr al-Sudani, Usulu, wa Tataworu</u> (Sudanese Thought: Origins and Development), including critical remarks on the recent development of thought.

Bearing in mind the condition of medieval Sudan that was earlier described by Daif-Allah, Ibrahim writes, "The trend of the juridical culture in the Sudan was so weak that it could not survive in the face of Sufi sects and their mysticism. The Sufi tradition was stretched out without resistance. Five centuries of Sufi traditions stamped the Sudanese thought with a mystical color that is a reason for the negligence of scientific thought as well as the shortcoming of Sudanese generations in writing skills and oracle. It is also responsible for a prevailing state of emotional simplicity, weakening of logical and rational thinking, the tendency to use self-assertions instead of persuasion, and exhilaration of the [Sufi] moral life as content, austerity, and leaving out the pleasures of life. The Sufi impact has created in the Sudanese thought an irrevocable romantic and emotional aptitude of which only a few thinkers disengaged themselves, particularly those educated in Western institutions" (Ibrahim, <u>al-Fikr al-Sudani</u>, 1976: 9).

How can we develop this critical opinion in the light of what Daif-Allah earlier mentioned about the long list of Shaikhs, learned jurists and saints, starting with the great *Manjuluk*, al-Shaikh 'Ageeb, and the learned jurist Idris wad al-Arbab, accompanied with the other jurists?

Mohamed al-Mekki underestimates the contributions of these Muslim intellectuals as occurred over the long centuries through medieval ages to the present time in his assessment of the heritage of northern medieval Sudan. "The principles of Sufi traditions Sudan had received were not more than a trivial layer. Not a single Sufi was known [in intellectual terms] throughout the Funj time to have understood the genuine spirit of Sufi life, to have studied the basic books, or to have displayed a Sufi philosophy" (Ibid. 10). However, the writer of the Tabaqat, the only authenticated book on that period, did not say that.

Mohamed al-Mekki admires the Al-Funj dynasty's era of originality and creativity. He condemns the Turkish rule of the Sudan for its traditionalism and superficiality. "The Turkish Empire continued to rule Sudan for sixty years and never convinced the people that they had been defeated, or that some master dominated their own destiny. The people have always been infuriated, intact, and high above the atrocious rulers. The masses continued to pursue their inherited cultural activities without being seriously affected by the Turkish invasion. Popular poetry maintained an original Sudanese heritage. Folklore was kept free from impact of the invasion, and the followers practiced Sufi tradition exactly as it had been observed in the old days. Despite the failure of the Turkish culture to precipitate in the daily life of the masses, it laid its anchorage in the intellectual section of the populace" (Ibid.).

Ibrahim emphasizes that, "It was necessary for the *Mahdiya* to uproot the Turkish roots from the soil of Sudanese culture, and to eradicate undesirable habits, lethargy, and superstition. This was not an easy job because the Turkish [elitist] culture had been ruling the Sudan for sixty years. The [Mahdist] revolutionaries were confronting this sacrificial civilization with a weak cultural tool, an incomplete tool. The intellectuals were taking a shameful stand about the Revolution, and some of them were collaborating with the Turkish authorities" (Ibid. 18).

Ibrahim thinks highly of the *Mahdiya*, a Sudanese revolutionary movement that asserted Sudanese culture versus the foreign culture of the Ottoman-Egyptian rulers. "The *Mahdiya* generated ingenuity of the people" in innovation and creativity. He numerates many forms of the [social, economic, and political] revivalism initiated by the Grand Imam al-Mahdi and his efforts "to write the four Islamic *Madzahib* in one school of jurisprudence by selecting the best [views] from each *Madzhab* into his new doctrine."

Ibrahim believes further that "The Sufi tradition came to a stop [during the *Mahdiya*]. Its influence shrank because it was enclosed in a few secretive and small pockets. Jurisprudence was being liberated from the [old] spirit of argumentation and bickering. The poetry and prose began to emancipate from the impact of Turkish ornamentals" (Ibid. 20).

This author does not see that Sufi tradition "ceased from growth." The Grand Imam al-Mahdi himself was a student of the Sufi tradition. He had grown up among the Sufi groups, and he had selected from Sufi ranks *Emirs* [governors] and leaders of the Mahdist armies. An innovative trend that had been culturally intertwined in some cases with lethargy and superstition, the Sufi movement did not spread about in society due to the persecution policies and practices of the Mahdist Authority against Sufi rivalries.

Mohamed al-Mekki recalls that the Sudanese modern parties, particularly those established by Sufi families, "did not have a specific class affiliation or social context in the beginning. One class would be fighting among itself not in the interest of its factions, but in the name of sectarian allegiance and spiritual following. The existing aspects of the class formation of parties is actually attributed to recent changes in political status, that have not been originally part of their nature" (Ibid. 76).

Ibrahim's evaluation of the Sudanese politics indicates that the national causes that normally engage different social disputes resolve in practical and intellectual agreements of disputes. But class conflicts are prone to consolidate intellectual disputes into categorized political entanglements. This conclusion reminds us of the class affiliations of Sudanese thinkers of whom the works of Sadiq al-Mahdi, 'Abd al-Khaliq Mahgoub, Hassan al-Turabi, and Mahmoud Mohamed Taha included different views about Sudanese social classes.

Ibrahim's remarks suggest further that, other than the prominent role Sudanese cultures and domestic life played since the old times to help advance the interaction of Arabs, Islam, and ancient Sudanese peoples with each other, another significant domain was related to the enhancement of intellectual and political activities. This domain functions through the advancement of class awareness in Sudanese society.

As it appears, Sudanese thinkers use the notion of social classes, society, and social change to generate different meanings and implications. Mahmoud Mohamed Taha, for example, believes that, "the four principles of Marx are 1) the movement of history is determined by economic forces; 2) history is nothing but a record of class conflict; 3) a government is an instrument of a class to subdue another class; and 4) violence and power are the only means to incur a major change in society. Dreadful as they are, [these principles] have much truth in them. But, fortunately, they are temporary facts contrary to what Marx believed them to be a permanent reality of mankind and society" (Taha, Tatweer, 1971: 26-27).

'Abd al-Khaliq Mahgoub adopts many Marxist principles, except for the use of violence, to impose social change. 'Abd al-Khaliq emphasizes that democratic competition among political parties is a viable way to change power relations. He has many reservations, however, on the compliance of reactionary groups with political liberalism, in the first place.

There is no support for Marxist thought in the ideas of Sadiq al-Mahdi and Hassan al-Turabi. Notwithstanding, these two Islamist thinkers stress in their writings the significance of economic factors in societal affairs. Turabi, for example, speaks to the International Conference of Islamic Call at Khartoum (1981) as follows: "The common factor in the cultures of mankind is the initiation of religiosity that springs from the human nature. This is a state clarified by experiences of mankind and validated by civilization. One aspect in mind is the oneness of God and the meaningfulness attributed to it for the liberalization of mankind, emphasizing the unity and dignity of man, and the equity of all people without racism of discrimination" (al-Turabi, Khitab, 1981: 12-113).

"Other aspects include a reluctance from pagan lethargy and a commitment to freedoms of man within the economic and political relations that are based on equality, freedom, justice, and solidarity. This illuminates the ethos of religion that facilitates the accomplishment of economic interests, as a top concern for the believers. This is a special area of interest in which awareness has been greatly centered on economic needs, competing standards, and plans for the growth of wealth. Most likely, economy may thus have been the [most influential domain] to preserve religion in contemporary times" (Ibid.).

The aforesaid text calls openly for the use of economy "to preserve religion." It is a clear-cut acceptance of the power of the economic factor and its influential effect on this era. The class context of this direction, which Turabi never mentions, suggests the possibilities of strengthening certain strata of the population while weakening the others, unless this particular result is nationally rectified by political agreement.

Turabi's concern for the economic factor aims to maximize economic utility to keep pace with contemporary life and its prerogatives. This concern appears to be a rational orientation to ascertain worldly affairs more than a means to solidify religious behavior. Because Islam strongly calls for the veneration of modesty and simplicity of life, a question still lingers. How would the "just Islamic principles" be implemented in the era with all its overwhelming material and economic concerns? How could we avoid class division and class conflict if the economy is used to divide societies into rich minorities and an impoverished majority? If class stratification is an indispensable result of economic development, what are the proceedings needed to guide economic growth within "the required ethnic and religious hegemony" that Turabi perceives to enhance "equality, freedom, justice, and solidarity"?

Sadiq al-Mahdi does not write about class struggles. He has no tendency to use the concept in his analytical works. And yet, he discusses the Marxist theory that is essentially founded on economic and political class models. Sadiq originates the Marxist thought in the "European environment that equally produced capitalism and its antithesis." He sorts out the functional roles of social classes in both capitalism and socialism (al-Mahdi, al-Manzour, undated: 20-29) with respect to "the modern thought of development." For al-Mahdi, "the teachings of Islam allow the incorporation of the beneficial and the righteous [aspects of life] according to certain jurisprudence techniques. These teachings include standards and principles to correct any deviance from the right path of Islam, thus they provide solutions to correct the miserable conditions of the Third World" (Ibid. 55).

Sadiq's statement seems to be reconciliatory for it accepts, in essence, the coexistence of capitalism and communism models of modern paradigms that involve "huge economic and military power." Islam, for al-Mahdi, does not negate the "beneficial and righteous" elements engendered by these paradigms. He is particularly interested in the middle class since it is "historically entrusted with the task of capitalist development."

Pointing at the strong impact of the capitalist market in the present time, Sadiq criticizes "its negative effect on the attitude of the middle classes of the 3rd World since it has converted them to mere agencies or fronts in the service of international companies. The policies imposed by systems of rule over middle classes exert a strong impact negatively upon them. They are unstable systems because they exchange political allegiance for privileges and loans to their favorites. They deprive the qualified [persons or groups] by that bias while parasitic elements excessively abuse financial resources" (Ibid. 33-35).

With this middle-class critique that reminds us with 'Abd al-Khaliq Mahgoub's working class criticisms of capitalism, Sadiq states, "The rich classes in the Islamic world are frightened of the hazard that nationalization present to their ownership. Also, they smuggled the largest portion of their money abroad. These classes will not be able to invest in the 3rd World or in the Islamic World compared to economic development of the European and American middle classes [in the preceding times]" (Ibid.).

"The leftist systems of 3rd World Countries raised a slogan of relying upon the working class, which constitutes a small proportion of the undeveloped countries. Therefore, the left-wing governments resorted to the establishment of a coalition of many classes. They organized political parties to lead that coalition. The alliance was superimposed from the top and, in its name, totalitarian regimes ruled these societies while still promising in the name of "progressive" alliances the achievement of a speedy and just socialist development" (Ibid.).

"But all these systems and claims did not bear any fruit," claims al-Mahdi. "Instead, they were abused by elite regimes so isolated from the people. They persecuted people in the name of socialism, and wasted the national wealth. In addition to political spending to buy off supporters and to enable the favorites to live a soft life, for which they never made the least effort, [these elite groups] ruined the national wealth with spending on security apparatuses and false propaganda" (Ibid.).

Sadiq's analysis of the ongoing conditions of the Islamic, as well as the non-Islamic, 3rd World Countries touches upon social classes and their roles in development administration. It is an analysis parallel to similar adaptations by both leftist and capitalist economists. Above all, Sadiq elaborates on liberalism and his firm belief in "freedom and popular participation by fair elections, "according to his version of Sudanese political evolution.

On the other side, 'Abd al-Khaliq Mahgoub adhered consistently to the Marxian class-dialectical model of human behavior to understand problems of the politico-economic and social development of the Sudan, which was clearly exposed in al-Marxiya.

Mahgoub affirms the commitment of the Marxist doctrine by saying that, "After the transformations taking place after the July 1961's presidential decrees in Egypt and the strong strokes they dealt to the bourgeois capitalist ownership, a class direction started to manifest itself in the arena. President Nasser expressed this reality in the Charter for National Action. The Charter emphasized that class-conflict is determined and has to be taken in consideration. There is no healthy resolution possible for this conflict unless the economic and political tools [of power] are withdrawn from the hands of reaction" (SCP, al-Marxiya, undated: 50).

After these declarations, it can be resolved that the contemplation of Sudanese thinkers on the existing class-oriented models of social change testifies to the possibility of some potential agreement concerning aspects of the social and political life of society. Still, there are many disagreements about the dynamics of that life, namely the underpinnings of economic structures and the distribution of political power among forces of production.

Turabi admits that economy is vital to "the need for and the growth of wealth." Obviously, he has reserved a lion's share for the Muslim Brotherhood to transform Muslim societies both politically and economically. But he does not elaborate on the issue beyond assertion. Nor does he use analytical methods in his work. Marxist thinking is "secular and atheist." Hence, he believes it has no direct bearing on his thought. The other writers mentioned in this juncture, such as Mohamed al-Mekki, believe that class formation and stratification is one characteristic of evolution of which Sudanese society is no exception.

This conclusion ends up the first task sought in this chapter. The second task summarizes some dispositions on the present and future conditions of Sudanese thought.

CONCLUDING REMARKS:
INTELLECTUALITY AND CULTURAL DIVERSITY

There are many questions raised about the main constituents of Sudanese society: Is cultural diversity a significant feature of society? What role does diversity play to ensure tolerance in the social life and to smooth out religious and political disputes among the intellectuals? How would Sudan's diversity help to develop interacting composites of the society in the light of emerging class formations and interest groups? What possibilities does Sudan's cultural diversity offer to help achieve national integration instead of conflicts and authoritarian rule?

These questions among many others deserve a special attention because they continue to generate a multiplicity of queries and intellectual disputes. At all costs, a state of differential consensus seems to prevail, to a degree, in the views of Sudanese thinkers in the sense that resolving disputes can only be attainable by increasing liberality of the freedom of thought. However, a detailed account of possible answers for these questions lies beyond the limits of this assessment.

Many cultural features are identified in the writings of Sudanese thinkers. Earlier, Wad Daif-Allah shows that Sudan of the medieval ages was a land of warriors, generosity, courtesy, and nobility. The learned Sudanese acquired a prestigious status, the Shaikhs were dignified, and their followers courageous persons with noble and good manners. Never were the Sudanese people afraid of kings or leaders. Never did they accept any insulting behavior against their personal dignity.

The totality of these virtues accumulated permanent characteristics of the Sudanese people over long centuries of social and cultural interaction. Many anthropological studies confirm these value-orientations in the country's mode of pastoral and nomad life. Related to this, lineal relations and tribal impingements strengthened political alliance, familial ties, and collective behavior amongst the populace.

It has been repeatedly noted that the Sudanese people's ancestry was that of "archers at pupils of the eyes of enemies." Historians have continuously valued the Sudanese warriors who accede to generous words and human treatment. Sudanese people always insist on the exercise of the right to free expression, active participation in decision-making, and freedom.

The Sudanese ancient Nubians fought Abi Sarh, leader of the Egyptian Arab Muslim armies that invaded the Nubian kingdom of the Sudan. As soon as the warring parties realized the need to maintain dignity and tolerance between their religions and cultures, they willingly intermarried to form new generations of Arab and African people. To this day, marriage in Sudan denotes the establishment of a socio-familial institution more than any personal or individual choice.

These old practices with their cultural meanings and ethical implications have not been changed in any significant manner over the passing years. Nor has reciprocity vanished among individuals or groups. Folklore songs and poetry continue to aggrandize these morals as a great social honor.

During the *Mahdiya,* Slatin, the former governor of DarFur who was taken captive by the Mahdist armies, wrote, "I dismounted from my horse's back on hearing the first shot. This meant in Sudan that there was no hope in escaping. Thus, one could only insist on either victory or death" (Slatin, <u>al-Saif wa al-Nar</u>, 1987: 66). Winston Churchill witnessed in the battle of Karari at Omdurman the Sudanese war abilities: Had it not been for the modern arms, the invading army would not have victory. The *Ansar* were lions, never afraid of death, said Winston.

The Sudanese were peoples many of whom strongly believed in witchcraft and/or superstition. Up to this time, high illiteracy continues to handicap large sections of the population. But the country's multi-religious systems of faith, including the Muslim majority, influence the Sudanese epistemology and workaday life. These socio-cultural realities do not support the presumptuous groups that consider Sudan a nation composed of one people with only one language and one religion.

These presumptuous groups expand upon another serious falsification that Sudan is a nation with monotonous ethnic and religious national identification. Because the Sudanese nationals and the whole world continue to realize the significance of cultural, social, and religious diversity in the Sudan, these narrow-minded groups resort to the use of violence to impose their will on the populace.

It is therefore important to allow a greater freedom of thought and expression for the Sudanese writers and thinkers than is available thus far to voice the national sentiments and aspirations of the People of Sudan on the basis of their cultural, religious, and social diversity. All political parties, military groups, and trades unions must appreciate the freedoms of thought and expression as much as they struggle to ensure the civil and political rights' prerequisite of social stability and progression. Moreover, the intellectuals themselves must always show tolerance and appreciation with respect to their different views and schools of thought.

The maintenance and advancement of the people of Sudan depends on the observance of human rights and civil freedoms, without any restriction or hesitation on the part of the Authority. This is a deep contention of the Sudanese masses that have always guided their struggles for civil rights and democratic freedoms. It is the driving force behind the October 1964 and April 1985 uprisings in the modern history of the country.

The worst system of governance will always be a single-party system that rules against Sudanese diversity and striving for liberty. Sudan is a country composed of a pluralist culture that defies all forms of Authority to enforce the will power of people in national decision-making. Each social group is potentially aware of its status and role, although political awareness is the only variable that transforms that potential into the material life. Even the pre-capitalist groups in the remote areas of the country have been gradually absorbed into interests of the core, although they have been abruptly transformed by economic and political marginalization.

Soon after the massive demonstrations of the April Uprising (1985), that subsequently overthrew the May dictatorial regime, many writers succinctly indicated that the masses are much more conscientious than politicians are. They are scrupulous, reliable, wise, and effective in social change than any ruling party may possibly be.

Other intellectuals assert that the masses are often handicapped in their movement by "a bunch of politicians who are good in nothing but corruption. It will take a long time for the masses to stop such hypocrites from destroying their good hopes to achieve national unity. But the genuine intellectuals must stay with the people to salvage Sudan."

Intellectuals, then, include 'both faces of the coin'; they consist of "good nationals" who are concerned for the development of the country, as well as the "evil ones" who, regardless of educational attainment or scientific knowledge, are only interested in exploiting people for cheap personal gain. The masses, after all, glorify the good ones, those who refrain, in self-esteem, from abusing their knowledge to subdue the truth.

We have made an attempt to contrast the views of some Sudanese thinkers. We have closely touched upon their ideas, which were rich and diversified as the Sudanese society is. We have rigorously studied their opinions with a view to scrutinize their world outlook, public experience, and well-thought wisdom along a subtlety of religious ideas, political preferences, and ideological strands.

If around these intelligent practices and meaningful implications a dialogue is peacefully developed with the maximum guarantees possible for freedoms of thought and expression for all people of Sudan, Sudanese intellectuality will be freely exercised to promote the social life. The squabbling of ignorant reactionaries, evil gangs, and those learned thinkers, who wickedly mislead Authority against the will of the people, will finally cease to function.

EPILOGUE

ISLAM AND HUMAN RIGHTS
Islamic Law, Human Rights, and International Law: A Critique[1]

The solutions required to resolving many problems that endanger world peace and development are largely considered in economic and political terms. Stressed in this regard is the view that "a suitable international economic order is very pertinent for the realization of economic, social and cultural rights" (Paul de Waart, 1987:xxiii).

Another approach emphasizes the establishment of a world order based on principles of the Charter of the United Nations and the other recognized international laws. Nonetheless, a third approach is acknowledged in this study with respect to the role of religion, namely Islam, in the efforts made to enhance social justice, equity, and the peace of the world.

Reflecting this particular trend of Islamic thinking, the Republican Brothers' movement of the late Sudanese Islamist Mahmoud Mohamed Taha has been recently reflected in a number of publications seeking to provide international law and human rights with a new Islamic contribution.

In this study, one section will analyze briefly Republican Islamic thought. Another section will discuss the proposed changes to the Islamic Shari'a Law that exists in Muslim countries today. Subsequently, the study will criticize the ideas of the Republican Brothers on international relations and Shari'a Law. The final section presents the conclusions reached in the study.

The origins of Islamic Republican Thought

The Republican thought was instigated in the mid 1940s by Mahmoud Mohamed Taha and is fully developed in The Second Message of Islam[2] that, among many other works, is based on a reformulation of basic dictates of Islamic law, namely, the Qur'an and Sunna. To reconcile divergences of modernity and traditional life in Muslim societies, Taha's thesis accommodates, in actual terms, mystical as well as Marxian and other secular percepts.

The Second Message of Islam is a complex version of Taha's contribution to Islamic contemporary thought. It is an elucidation of his philosophical and mystical thinking, which is hardly understandable without an assessment of Shari'a Law, Sudanese Sufi life, and Taha's own personality. The scope of these topics lies beyond the immediate concerns of this study. However, a few general statements focus on Taha's major ideas.

Taha's mystical teachings on the *'ibadat* (worshipping: faith and practices) have been widely debated among Muslims in the Sudan and the neighboring countries. Many Muslims resisted the ideas of *Sifr al-Salah* (The Book of Prayers) in which Taha propagated the exercise of another version of prayers (the *Silah* prayer) as a special practice of the Prophet. Taha believed the Prophet prayed the *Silah* prayer during his meeting with God at the end of the trip of *al-Mi'raj* to Heavens. The

---

[1] Paper prepared for and presented at the 3rd International Sudan Studies Association Conference, Boston, USA, April 23rd, 1994.
[2] The Second Message of Islam is published in Arabic (1964). 'Abdullahi A. An-Na'im, translated an English version with Syracuse University Press, 1987. Reference is made in this study to the ideas that Mahmoud Mohamed Taha elaborated in many other publications – all in Arabic.

Silah prayer is to be privately pursued by any "knowledgeable Muslim" apart from the traditional prayers of *al-Mi'raj*, which are composed of five daily prayers conferred upon all Muslims on earth.

In his own interpretation of *'ibadat*, Taha believed that the Prophet was praying the *Silah* prayer, which should be pursued in our times as a high spiritual exercise within a new message of Islam. Evolved on this fundamental divergence from the Islamic normal tradition, Taha introduced *Ahmedism* - a new derivative of *Muhammadism* that resembled the Meddinese era of the Prophet - to be implemented in contemporary life. *Ahmedism* pertains to the name of Ahmed, another name of the Prophet, which has been mentioned in the Holly Books before revelation of the Qur'an according to Muslim faith. Seen in the light of Taha's thought, in general, it appears that *Ahmedism* might have been envisaged by Taha for a prolonged mission of the Prophet that would be suitable to contemporary life more than that previously undertaken to the medieval stage of the Meddinese verses.

Orthodox Islamite, as well as a vast majority of Muslims in Sudan, including the Muslim Brotherhood fundamentalist groups, has deemed these and other mystical configurations disruption of Islam. Secularist groups, nevertheless, have also criticized the Republican thought with respect to Taha's views on socialism and other national concerns. Of these groups, it suffices to mention a few words on the communists who advocated the establishment of a socialist state in Sudan. This was rejected by a majority of traditional Muslims who viewed the general premises of the Leninist-Marxist party – class struggle and the role to be played by the working class to enforce policies against owners of capital – as alien to Shari'a Law and practice. The Sudanese communists, however, stressed the relevance of religion, especially Islam, to the provision of moral and spiritual guidance to the good life envisaged in a socialist state[3].

Taha and the communists shared the same view on the Muslim Brotherhood groups as reactionary and harmful to Sudanese value-orientations and religious tolerance. But Taha was critical of the Marxist tenets of communism. On their turn, the communists were strongly opposed to the idea of a religious state as was propagated by Taha as well as Muslim Brotherhood and the other traditional parties.

So fully developed in the *'ibadat* area, Taha's thought in the fields of public law and governance is less developed. A leader of a small political party "The Islamic Republican Party," which did not succeed in the national elections of the Sudan during the early 1950's, Taha laid down the foundations of a new approach in Islamic thinking, public law, and social development[4].

This approach is based on an adoption of the broad orientations of Meccan verses of the Qur'an that emphasize religious liberty and concepts of equality and social justice. The other verses of the Qur'an, i.e., the Meddinese verses, were specifically addressed, in his opinion, to remove the *Jahiliya* (ignorance and violence) of the pre-Islamic society within standards of the time. For the advanced complexities and divergences of the 20th century, Taha proposed a new Shari'a by using *naskh* (abrogation) to replace Meddinese verses with the Meccan ones.

---

[3] For more details, see SCP, Al-Marxiya wa Qadaya al-Thawra al-Sudaniya, Dar al-Wasila, Khartoum, undated.

[4] The foundations of Taha's thesis in social development may be found among many other works in his book Al-Deen wa al-Tanmiya al-Ijtimaiya [Religion and Social Development], Omdurman, 1974. His main Islamic thinking and portions of his ideas on public law are embodied in Al-Thawra al-Thaqaffiya [The Cultural Revolution], Omdurman 1972, and Tariq Muhammad [The Path of Muhammad], Omdurman, Seventh edition, undated, among many other works.

For politics and economic development, Taha seemed to have relied heavily on secular Western thought (both liberal and Marxian) to adopt constitutionality and socialism in his own right. Despite his rejection of capitalism, he expressed many disagreements with Marx on the use of force to assume political power through the determining role of the proletariat "vanguard group" to establish a good life for humankind, albeit he appreciated the rights of the proletariat working class.

A civil engineer, who had studied Western science and schools of thought, in addition to his strict adherence to a life of Sufi contemplation that was normally the tradition in his homeland Rufa'a, Taha was well versed in the ideas of 'evolution' in secular as well as Islamic terms. Elaborated elsewhere (Mahmoud, 1996), Taha's deep knowledge of both sources of thought might explain his liberal reformulation of Shari'a orientations within a broad social, economic, and political framework. For example, Taha recognized the contribution of Karl Marx in political economy and socialism. In the Marxiya (1973:18), he ascertained, "The advantages of capitalism are those of colonialism... The economic order is governed or even created by class struggle... History has almost recorded this for [Marx]."

Nonetheless, Taha criticized Marx in that violence should not be advocated to establish social change. Moreover, the proletariat would not necessarily constitute the vanguard of classes. Rejecting the Marxist political and social system of thought, Taha emphasized the authenticity and divinity of the Qur'an, which contains an infallible source of knowledge on all societal and cosmological processes of this life as well as the other world. A conflict notion of class struggle, however, seemed to have been accommodated in Taha's perception of social change. This view might be felt in his belief that "the struggle is directed by the will of God through anarchy... whereby extravagant groups would act willfully to the detriment of a community that is destined by Allah to vanish... in accordance with the Qur'an" (Taha, Marxiya, 1973:27-28)[5].

Another fundamental difference between Taha and Marx is Taha's emphasis on the role to be played by the individual in society and social change. Since the proletariat was destined by class struggle in the Marxist scheme to destroy the bourgeoisie in order to install a collective state, Taha believed that the well-being of the individual would be seriously jeopardized.

Taha's ideas constitute a complex synthesis of Western evolutionary theories, especially those of Hegel and Marx, Sufi mysticism, and Shari'a sources, the Qur'an and Sunna. He might have been influenced by dialectical evolutionary ideas in some way. Chief among these is Taha's projection of the evolution of Islamic modes and forces of change: "The Bible came out of the Torah... the nation of Muslims would come out of the nation of believers; the Message of Ahmed [another name of the Prophet] would emerge from the Message of Muhammad; and the Brothers would emanate from the Companions... all passing through in the path of proximity to God" (Taha, Tariq, u.d.:5)[6].

Taha also conceived of Shari'a as a doctrine of two contradictory stages: a reactionary Shari'a embodied in the Meddinese verses, and a new revolutionary Shari'a based on the Meccan verses (Taha, Tatweer, 1971:71). The latter stage could be seen through a version of evolutionism in which he professed socialism,

---

[5] The verse is in Sura 17:16: "When We decide to destroy a population, We (first) send a definite order to those among them who are given the good things of this life and yet transgress; so that the word is proved true, against them; then (it is) We destroy them utterly." The Holy Qur'an Text, Translation and Commentary by A. Yusuf 'Ali, Amana Corp., Bretwood, Maryland, 1983, p. 698.
[6] These are only few examples of Hegelian-Marxist influence on Taha's thought. For a detailed discussion of Hegelian and Marxist dialectics, see: Avineri, Shlomo, The Social and Political Thought of Karl Marx, Cambridge University Press, 1968; and Karl Marx, "Contribution to the

equity of man and woman, and adoption of civil liberties as progressive advancements indicated in the verses.

This evolutionism was apparently intertwined with a Sufi mysticism in which ascendancy to a higher degree of spiritual life was envisaged in terms of *Ahmedism*, a new version of *Muhammadism* advocating the Meccan verses to replace the Meddinese dictates, and a strong belief that "Islam embraces all thought and action of the cosmos since nothing, including Marxism, could have been created outside the absolute knowledge of God" (Taha, Marxiya, 1973:6).

What is emphasized for our purposes in this critique is the fact that the Republican thought seems to be a "peculiar" amalgam of secular and religious ideas. The Republican thought might be quite different in many ways from the general configurations of modern Islamists (that aspire to ascertain the validity of Shari'a in accordance with Qur'anic and Sunna interpretations). Varying degrees of minor or major divergence are consequently articulated in the Republican ideas on the inherited Shari'a jurisprudence, which comprises the norms acceptable and exercised by Muslims according to the *madzahib* (schools of Islamic law) all over the Muslim world.

Unlike the majority of Islamic thinkers who would rather criticize orientalist views on Shari'a than Islamic law itself, Taha's major disagreement with Shari'a law was harshly directed to the *madzahib* or the inherited Shari'a jurisprudence. For him, Shari'a "has nothing to give in political matters other than patriarchy. It has no socialism in matters of appropriation. It has no equality between men and women. And on these three elements, democracy, socialism, and the equity of men and women, stand the fundamental rights which constitute the spirit of the

---

Critique of Hegel's Philosophy of Right," in: Tucker, Robert (ed.), The Marx-Engels Reader, New

Qur'anic constitution… that was abrogated by the Meddinese verses, its branches, in the past" (Taha, Thaqafiya, 1972:28).

The Shari'a and Republican Law

Formulated over many centuries by Islamic jurists, the Shari'a Law is strongly rejected by Taha who made of Shari'a personal law, in particular, a special target for his criticisms. Notwithstanding, Taha recognized *hudud* as divine punishments justified, within strict limitations, by the right to retribution and social equilibrium of criminal justice. His disciples, the Republican Brothers, called upon a strong prohibition of polygamy "except in rare cases of barrenness or illness in the wife" (Fluehr-Lobban, 1987:275)[7].

Taha and his disciples stress that their drastic reformulation of Shari'a's traditional heritage is definitely constructed "on the same fundamental sources of Islam and is fully consistent with its essential moral and religious percepts" (An-Na'im, 1990:xiv). This assurance, however, is challenged by the very fact that Taha's ideas on The Second Message of Islam and the path of economic and political development to Muslim societies were primarily based on installation of a socialist state, which no one would correctly consider Islamic heritage or principle so much as it figures out as a Marxist notion of an industrial modern polity.

In public law, Taha's ideas could be seen as a combination of axiomatic constructs of natural law, that emphasize the natural liberty of the individual, as well as positive law which is implied on his acceptance of *hudud* to sustain order and criminal justice in society by law. Furthermore, the philosophical theorization of Taha of a new Shari'a reflecting the ethos of Islam on justice, peace, civil

---

York, 1978.

liberties, and human rights is not "purely" Islamic. An obvious reason is that Taha might have drawn heavily on dialectical thought to hypothesize the Qur'an in terms of antagonistic meanings of the Meddinese verses versus the Meccan ones that could only be reconciled by *naskh* (abrogation). This is a vision of alienation, contradictions, and antithetical synthesis, which is alien to Islamic traditional thought.

Taha, nevertheless, recognized that "there is an interrelationship between the two versions of Shari'a [i.e., a high level Meccan Shari'a of the origin and the Meddinese Shari'a of the branches] that makes some of the postulates of the first Shari'a still valid for use in the time of the Second Message of Islam... For example, the Shari'a of *'ibadat, hudud,* and retribution... [as well as] the remaining Shari'a of transactions in politics, property, and social life for much of it has been exhausted so that it is totally consumed" (Taha, Tatweer, 1971:71).

Taha also recognized the great role of the Islamic Sufi leaders, who had served the first message of Islam among Muslim populations honestly and honorably compared to the fundamentalists who believe in a strict implementation of the Meddinese verses. The latter, in his view, did a great harm to the message of Islam by their political abuses of religion, as well as the Islamic jurists who advocated reactionary ideas and their stands for the use of violence to propagate religious faith (Taha, Thaqafiya, 1972:26).

Taha asserted that the difference between his Second Message of Islam and the ongoing Shari'a is "a matter of degree" (Taha, Tatweer, 1971:71). This is a key concept, in our opinion, for Taha has not shown where the limits could be set between the first Shari'a and the Second Message of Islam. Nor has he clearly

---

[7] Cf. Al-Na'im (1990) on *hudud* and polygamy.

specified in his theoretical praxis the intercepting point between the two proposed versions of Shari'a. That "an interrelationship" could be seen "existing over time," thus making "some of the postulates of the first Shari'a still valid for use in the time of the Second Message" is a vague configuration. The notion of the *Silah* prayer, the idea of *Ahmedism*, and the use of *naskh* to differentiate between his projected modes of Qur'anic verses are equally vague.

Another legitimate question pertains to the assumption that repeated historical requirements might warrant an enforcement of Meddinese verses with respect to the rules of war and peace treaties more than international law, which has always provided an "unmitigated struggle for power" (Matthews, 1980:141). Would it be possible then to use *naskh* once again to abrogate Meccan verses? For how much time, would it be possible to enforce *naskh* should the circumstances speedily change? If, on the other side, *naskh* is legally adopted device for Islamic reform, wouldn't it jeopardize the authenticity of the Qur'an, let alone its divinity as a Holy Book for the Muslim faith? Muslim jurists strongly hold that *naskh* has not been used after the death of the Prophet (al-Fa'ar, 1986:12; al-Saboni, 1981:103-105), although the Caliph 'Umar applied the rules of certain verses differently from the Prophet in the face of new circumstances of Islamic jurisprudence. We will return to this later.

Taha's predictions that the *Jahiliya* of the 20th century would be saved by *Ahmedism* and the Brothers have not actually materialized. A new world-order came about with a new era of power relations after the collapse of the Soviet Union and many other socialist states in Eastern Europe. It would seem, however, that Taha's view that "socialism can not be accomplished unless Marxism is defeated" (Taha, Tanmiya, 1974:32), might have received some focus. But his main thesis on the establishment of a full Message of Islam to succeed the inherited Shari'a was drastically terminated when the deposed dictator of the Sudan, Ja'far Nimeiri, extra-judicially executed him in January 1985. At this point, Khalid al-Mubarak (1992:125-126) asserts that, "The hanging of philosopher Mahmoud M. Taha should be seen in the light of the earlier tolerance of Sufis who flouted many tenets of Islam and committed many objectionable acts."

In a number of recent publications, 'Abdullahi An-Na'im, a leading Republican Brother, endeavors to "develop Taha's general principles into a concrete analysis of their implications for Islamic public law" in the words of John O. Voll (1990:ix in An-Na'im, op.cit.). An-Na'im's book <u>Towards an Islamic Reformation – Civil Liberties, Human Rights, and International Law</u>, in which he diligently professed a Second Message of Islam in public law (his field of specialization), is a major source of information for this critique of the Republican thought in the areas of Shari'a rules and practices in criminal justice, human rights, and international law.

Republican Law and Shari'a Jurists

The criticisms of Shari'a jurisprudence by the Republican Brothers are not coherent in many ways. An-Na'im, for example, rules out any influential contribution by Shari'a "historical" jurists in the fields of public law: The jurists of Shari'a knew no distinction between public and private law. As explained by Joseph Schacht, the distinction made by early Muslim jurists between 'the right of God' and 'the right of human beings' "has nothing to do with the distinction between public and private law" (An-Na'im, 1990:5). This opinion, nonetheless, contrasts sharply with Taha's view on *hudud* as a component of criminal law. Moreover, An-Na'im cautions against the "writings of early and 'classic' pre-modern Muslim scholars on constitutional and political questions... it cannot be assumed that what they produced was necessarily identical or even consistent with Shari'a... They were writing... under extremely unstable political conditions" (Ibid.).

Ironically, An-Na'im wrote and published his own book on "Islamic Reformation" during years of political upheaval and exile! In a footnote, rather than text, he writes "there may have been some Islamic influence in the development of the European Public Law" (Ibid. ft 26:193). In another footnote, he points out that, "Except for a small book by Abu Yusuf (d.798), entitled Kitab al-Kharaj, none of the following jurists addressed constitutional questions... Somewhat specialized treatment of these issues started with al-Baqillani (d.1012), al-Baghdadi (d.1037), and al-Mawardi (d.1058), followed by al-Ghazzali (d.1111), Ibn-Jammaa' (d.1333), Ibn-Taymiyya (d.1328), and Ibn-Khaldun (d.1406)" (Ibid. ft 21:193). Despite this tendency to underestimate the early Islamist scholars, An-Na'im admits that Ibn-Taymiyya's views on relations of the Imam with his subjects are made "in terms not unlike modern theories of social contract" (Ibid. 37).

The contributions of these distinguished jurists of Islamic philosophy, politics, and public law should not be so much reduced if the writer seeks a fair judgment. A careful study of Kitab al-Kharaj, for instance, has shown that the Islamic judge and jurist Abu Yusuf (d.798) touched upon a great deal of the general principles of criminal justice and the treatment of offenders, which have been embodied in the United Nations Standard Minimum Rules for the Treatment of Prisoners in 1955 (Mahmoud, 1992). The contribution of Ibn-Khaldun, as a judge, jurist, and political activist, is renowned as a prominent source of Islamic encyclopedic knowledge while Ibn-Khaldun himself is universally recognized as a prominent founder of sociology. Against those scholars who tend to uproot the Shari'a heritage in order to enforce Islamic reforms, the authenticity of the *madzahib* and schools of thought of early Muslims (such as 'Ali Ibn Abi Talib and Ibn 'Abbas) is highly valued by the majority of Muslims whose support of Islamic changes of the Shari'a law could only be gained in due respect to this heritage rather than a "drastic revolutionary" approach to do away with it.

Another serious tendency of An-Na'im to relegate Shari'a jurists and jurisprudence to Western modernity, as opposed to many other Islamic modernists who emphasize areas of agreement and compatibility between Islamic Shari'a and modernity, is magnified in his views on the default of Muslims to comply with the percepts of both Islam and modern life. He strongly accuses "the vast majority of Muslims throughout the world (to be) living at a superficial level of both Islam and modern civilization. Although they claim adherence to Islam and exhibit apparent commitment to its ritualistic formalities, most contemporary Muslims fail to appreciate and live up to its moral and spiritual essence. Moreover, although they have grown accustomed to enjoying the benefits of modern technology and claim adherence to modern institutions, the majority of Muslim peoples have little appreciation of the values and ways of thinking that underlie and sustain that technology and those institutions" (An-Na'im, 1990: 186).

Related to this attenuating statement, he holds that "although the majority of Sudanese are nominally Muslims, their normal behavior hardly conforms to the religious dictates of Islam" (Ibid.132). Contrasting this view, many Sudanese scholars believe that the Sudan has experienced a tolerant path of Islamic faith, which is significantly different from the experience of many other Muslim societies. Khalid al-Mubarak (1992:122-123), for example, correctly notes "the heritage of the Sufis [in Sudan] is a distinct and effective tradition that has left an indelible mark on the people... Even a drunk man was tolerated by the Sufis when he joined in their events."

It is appropriate to affirm at this particular point that "the vast majority of Muslims throughout the world," especially those in Sudan, belong in actual fact to the largely impoverished population of the world that has been continually deprived of economic, political, and cultural rights due to injustices and the absence of freedoms and modern technology. Unfortunately, An-Na'im's condemnation of such a *Jahiliya* (ignorance) among Muslims of the world today casts doubt on the religiosity of Muslims and their moral life, as was earlier presumed by many orientalist Islamists in the past decades of colonial times.

This elitist point of view, which flagrantly challenges the faith of "the vast majority of Muslim peoples throughout the world," is a sheer violation of the very Qur'anic teachings that the Republican Brothers claim to adopt. It is a violation of the right of Muslims to individual liberty and responsibility in matters of faith and religious behavior. Mohammed Allal Sinaceur (1987:207) explains succinctly that in Islam: "there is no reciprocity of consciences. No one replaces anyone else. There is no parallel to the Christian fellowship based on reparative compassion. If one fails in a ritual duty, human rights are infringed, but as rights of God. This makes responsibility something extremely personal, except in precise cases, such as the duties of [maintaining] solidarity, exerting authority, taking up arms, and devoting oneself to scientific research. 'No burdened soul', says the Koran [Qur'an] (6:164), 'shall bear the burden of another.'"

In another citation of orientalist skepticism about the Muslim faith, An-Na'im (1990:197, ft. 42) adopts Ignaz Goldziher's view that "Just as the pagan Arab adhered to the *Sunna* of his ancestors, so was the Muslim community enjoined to uphold and follow the new *Sunna*." This derogatory opinion is simply unacceptable since the Arab ancestral traditions cannot be equitable to the *Sunna* of the Prophet, which was revealed to him by God. Of all the traditions that comprised the Arab pre-Islamic heritage, the Prophet only approved that which complied with the Qur'an. The Arab *Jahiliya* was not devoid of philosophical and intellectual activities. Nugud (1992:20) has recently argued, "The consciousness of this period was prepared to receive the idea of monotheism through a process of mental suffering and anxiety... When the Qur'an was revealed, they had already been involved in dispute and dialogue on religious faith."

Based on Schacht's judgment of Muslim consciousness, An-Na'im, furthermore, agrees that "Because all the divergent and sometimes conflicting views [of Shari'a] are regarded equally valid and legitimate, any Muslim has the choice of taking whatever is acceptable to his or her individual conscience" (An-Na'im, 1990:32). Here, Sinaceur (1987:206-207) explains, "In Islamic society, the human personality has significance. It is tantamount neither to 'one' nor to 'all and sundry.' What religion consists in is to proclaim openly words of truth. And the believer is entitled to understand the Book of God and the Sunna without help of an intermediary. From this stems the tendency, a tendency that can turn to individualism, to contrast what is written with what is affirmed by authority, under the pretext of tendering good advice, as its duty." Ironically, Mahmoud Mohamed Taha, who was not trained as a professional jurist, developed his writings and Second Message of Islam solely on his individual knowledge of Islam.

One fails, in fact, to appreciate the imperative behind criticisms of the disagreements between Shari'a jurists since such divergence figures out as a characteristic of modern jurisprudence in public law, as well as instruments of human rights and international law. Shestack (1989:71), for example, mentions many problems of this sort in definitions and areas of jurisdiction and other serious questions about what normative judgments should be applied or not with respect to immunities, principles, or rights.

The tendency of the Republican thought to describe Muslims living in *Jahiliya*, "a severe state of confusion and crisis," in the words of An-Na'im (1990:67), is originated in Taha's elitist worldview on the Muslim community, as was earlier explained. This view, nonetheless, could have been justified by the prevailing state of political repression and economic recession in most of the existing Muslim states in domestic and global terms. Adversely, the Republican writers hold Shari'a a scapegoat for these faltering conditions, or a possible source of terrorism against non-Muslims. Kurshid Ahmed (1983: cited in An-Na'im, op. cit. ft 18, p. 193) has eloquently characterized the situation in this well known reality: "the current cycle of [Islamic] resurgence... is not inherently antagonistic to the West, but rather is hostile to whatever or whoever is perceived to be the cause of frustration and oppression, be it internal or external."

Recently, a few western scholars demonstrated on the basis of sociological and anthropological investigation that classical Islamic civilization has undoubtedly encouraged *Ijtihad* (new interpretation), scientific inquiry, and cross-fertilization with the other European and Asiatic civilizations. Admitting that there has been a strong realization of the need for innovation and modernity in the Muslim world, Fluehr-Lobban (1987) confirms the techniques applied by Shari'a Courts in Egypt and Sudan, among many other Muslim countries, to ensure a gradual progressive incorporation of modern rules into Islamic jurisprudence through judicial circulars. Ann Mayer (1988:108) refers to "a fearless, searching inquiry into the defects of the existing Islamic sciences and methodologies and an attempt to construct Islamic knowledge on a modern, scientifically sound basis... to integrate the modern sciences within the Islamic tradition."

These modern endeavors, added to many other attempts, utilize a "gradual approach" instead of a "revolutionary drastic approach" that is advocated by both the Republican Brothers and the Muslim Brotherhood despite their ideological differences. An-Na'im's criticisms of Islamic modernists will be assessed shortly. Of special interest is the calling of Republican Brothers to the intensive use of *naskh* or abrogation of Meddinese verses, which are seen in their thesis as branches replacing the Meccan verses of origin. Because *naskh* is a pivotal center of the Republican Islamic law, our critique is turned now to its validity in the context of a legitimate interpretation of the Qur'an, the most fundamental source of Islamic law.

The Rule of Naskh in Islamic Law

The principle of *naskh* means "abrogation of the legal efficacy of certain verses of the Qur'an in favor of other verses" (An-Na'im, 1990:20). An-Na'im assumes that *naskh* is accepted by "the vast majority of *Sunni* jurists and schools of thought and is clearly at the foundation of many principles and rules of Shari'a, especially in the public field." Of these jurists and schools of thought he does not mention any specific names. In fact, both medieval jurists, such as Ibn Kathir (d. 774 H) and modern Islamists, including A. Yusuf Ali, ascertained the fact that *naskh* is "a sign of God's infinite power that His creation should take so many forms and shapes not only in the material world but in the world of man's thought and expression" (Ali, 1983:46). Mukhtasar Ibn Kathir, an authenticated book of the Islamic jurist Ibn Kathir, ascertained that the occurrence of *naskh* was part of the revelation of the Qur'an, which took place only during the life of the Prophet.

An-Na'im (Ibid. 21) adds that: "As a matter of Shari'a, an abrogated or repealed verse(s) of the Qur'an was to remain abrogated to maintain consistency... positive law [was] developed on the basis of a subsequent revelation of the Medina period abrogating apparently inconsistent revelations of the earlier Mecca period." Here, An-Na'im admits, however, that Shari'a law is public law. This view must be compared to his earlier view in the same source that "The jurists of Shari'a knew no distinction between public and private law" (Ibid. 5). He contends that it is possible "to reconsider the process of abrogation [by equally enacting the] verses that have been previously abrogated as the new basis of Islamic law and to that end deem previously enacted verses to be abrogated from the legal point of view... to resolve problems raised by the modern application of the public law of Shari'a."

Some of the objections against the use of *naskh* were earlier mentioned in this study. Other objections might be summarized in terms of philosophical and religious aspects, in addition to legal and jurisprudence problems. A major objection to an application of the proposed shift from Meddinese verses to Meccan ones is that the totality of the Qur'an cannot be interpreted as separate parts in legal terms. The Lord says in Sura al-i-Imran: "No one knows its hidden meanings except God." The full text of the verse (3:7) reads: "He it is Who sent down to thee the Book: In it are verses basic or fundamental (of established meaning); they are the foundation of the Book: others are allegorical. But those in whose hearts is perversity follow the part thereof that is allegorical, seeking discord, and searching for its hidden meanings. But no one knows its hidden meanings except God. And those who are firmly grounded in knowledge say: "We believe in the Book; the whole of it is from our Lord" and none will grasp the Message except the men of understanding."

Taha was well aware of this divine aspect of the Qur'an, for he did confirm that the knowledge of the Prophet, being directly revealed from God, was not conveyed as a whole to the early Muslims. This implies that the Lord (who is all-knowing) and the Prophet (with the knowledge received from the Lord) comprise a special category of divine knowledge of interpretation of the Qur'an that is not attainable to the other beings. For Taha, nonetheless, a new knowledge would have to be acquired through the advent of *Ahmedism* in the 20th century to replace Muhammadism of the Medina era – a tenet of Taha's thought for which he has been constantly rejected by the majority of Muslims who irrevocably believe in Muhammad, the sole messenger of Islam, and who believe that Ahmed is merely another name of Muhammad.

It is because of this fundamental basis of Islamic faith that the interpretations of the Qur'an, that had been explained by the Prophet to the Companions, were meticulously learned and preserved by the minds and hearts of the early jurists such as 'Ali and Ibn 'Abbas. The same interpretations have been carefully safeguarded against change by the succeeding jurists Ibn Kathir, Zamakhshari, al-Nasafi, al-Tabari, etc., of the medieval times as well as the modern jurists: A. Yusuf 'Ali, Mohamed 'Abdu, Mohamed Farid, Mahmoud Shaltut, etc. All these interpretations are almost typical, irrespective of time.

Since the late 1960s, a new trend has been developed by Mustafa Mahmoud and Shaikh Sh'arawi Jum'a of Egypt to explain the occurrence of modern scientific phenomena in the light of some verses of the Qur'an, for example, the verses on genetics and those on the environment such as the formulation and fall of rains, plantation, etc. The verses of *Mu-minun* Sura (23:12-14) are translated as follows: "Man We did create from a quintessence (of clay). Then We placed him as (a drop of) sperm in a place of rest, firmly fixed; Then We made the sperm into a dot of congealed blood; then of that clot We made a (foetus) lump; then We developed out of it another creature. So blessed be God, the best to create." Also, verse 5 of the *Hajj* Sura that describes the stages of man's physical growth in accurate biological terms.

Naskh, the way Republican Brothers claim, has not been implemented since the death of the Prophet. Rather, the guided Companions and the early jurists developed the Shari'a as canonical rules based on the Qur'an and the Sunna. In a well-reported Hadith by al-Shaf'ie, Mohyi al-Deen Abi Zakaria Yahya Ibn Sharaf al-Nawawi[8], the Prophet asked all Muslims to abide by his Sunna and that of the guided Companions. An-Na'im (1990:58) documents the "ambiguity" of the use of *naskh* during the early centuries of Islam. It is astonishing, however, that he refers to *naskh* at the same time as a tradition that was "recognized by the jurists and constituted the cornerstone of their conception of Shari'a." Linked to this assumption, he mentioned the use of Caliph 'Umar to *naskh* as a legitimate Islamic procedure.

Actually, the Second Caliph 'Umar Ibn al-Khatab abrogated the use of the *hadd* (God's prescribed penalty) of theft during the year of the Ramada – a year of drought and hunger. 'Umar's abrogation of the *hadd* was a temporal measure taken in response to a social disaster with due respect to the juridical premises of the *hadd* that do not allow imputation of a hand of a thief in the case of need. 'Umar also converted the share of spoils of war to *al-Mu'alafa Qulubuhum* (uncertain believers who were virtually incorporated in the general layers of the believers by the time that 'Umar assumed the Caliphate) into another humanitarian aid for the poor, irrespective of their religion. Unlike the Republican Brothers' intention to reconstruct Qur'anic meanings with *naskh*, 'Umar's experience of *naskh* was carefully restricted to the treatment of temporal situations rather than a constant reformulation of Qur'anic structural meanings.

Taha considered *naskh* an essential requirement of his philosophical thesis to establish a Second Message of Islam. N*askh* further became a prerequisite to Taha's projection of *Ahmedism*, a stage of achieving a new era of Islam. To enact the rule of *naskh*, *Ahmedism* must come first to guide the Brothers. It appears, however, that An-Na'im believes in the enforcement of the rule, regardless of its philosophical or mystical implications. This decision, nonetheless, seems to have generated some confusion in An-Na'im's shift from Taha's advocacy of mystical evolution and a natural law of individualism to another approach strictly confined to a "revolutionary" positive law. Taha's firm projection of *Ahmedism* – besides his acceptance of key elements of Marxism and socialism side-by-side with his submission to the application of *hudud* – sharply contrasts with An-Na'im's emphasis on Western constitutionality and liberalism and his decline to fully accept *hudud* and polygamy like the other Brothers.

In legal terms, *naskh* poses a serious problem with respect to the extent to which it could be used to abrogate Meddinese verses. Muslims have consistently believed that both Meccan and Meddinese verses are "integral." They are not separated in meanings or context from each other, although they may address in one verse of another different situations or problems. For example, An-Na'im (1990:54) observes that, "the substance of the message of Mecca emphasized the fundamental values of justice and the quality and inherent dignity of all human beings... The Qur'an during the Mecca period always addresses the whole of humanity, using phrases such as "O, children of Adam" and "O, humankind". By the same token, nonetheless, An-Na'im seems to have ignored the fact that Meddinese verses stressed the significance and relevance of the same values throughout the life of the Prophet in Medina. Moreover, his translations and interpretations of the Qur'an are sometimes inaccurate.

---

[8] See for this *Hadith* and other instructions of the Prophet, al-Nawawi's volume: Riyadh al-

Although An-Na'im (1990:xv) assures that he has "consulted Abdullah Yusuf 'Ali, The Holy Qur'an Text, Translation and Commentary, but sought to simplify the language while retaining the exact meaning of the text to the best of [his] ability," he has not referred to 'Ali in the translations of verses (4:90), (8:39), and (60-61) on page 146 of his book. He does omit from the translation of verses (2:193) the word "justice" which together with "faith" encompasses the meaning of *Deen* (Islam) in the context of the verse. Another verse, (22:39), mentions, in name, the commemoration of God in "monasteries, churches, synagogues, and mosques." These are inaccurately changed to "temples of worship and property." Other inaccuracies are discussed in text.

Both Meccan and Meddinese verses of the Qur'an include rules and principles of the "good life" of the moral society of Islam. Consider, for instance, *Hajj* (22:1, 5, 27, 34, 38, 49, 73, etc.). These verses are addressed to the humankind as a whole. Similarly, Meccan verses, for example *An'am* (6:150, 151), *A'raf* (7:31-33), *Nahl* (16:90-91, 101, 114, 115, 119, 125, 128), *al-Isra* (17: 23-37), *Lukman* (31: 14-19), etc. include detailed rules, prohibitions, and principles of proper behavior and social relations for Muslims.

The Meddinese *Baqara* Sura, which the Prophet called a "Zenith of the Book," encompasses both types of value-orientations, providing fundamental principles of justice to the inherent dignity of all human beings. This is clear in *Baqara* verses 21, 188, 190, 195, 264 and 272 on honesty in commercial relations, non-aggression, charity, and religious freedoms. Many phrases of the Meddinese verses are often universal or cosmological in meaning just, as Meccan verses tend to be. Even in those verses, which are specifically addressed to issues such as

---

Saliheen min Kalam Sayid al-Mursaleen, 3rd edition, al-Shamarli, Cairo, undated.

punishment of an offense, the verses contain certain recitations of God that are self-explanatory to the general objectives and meanings of the verses. They alert the reader to His all-encompassing wisdom and absolute knowledge to which Muslims willingly submit.

The Republican Brothers believe that there are many injustices in the application of Shar'ia on Muslim women. Linked to this, An-Na'im (1990:55) writes that *qawama* (guardianship and authority) of men over women "was taken by the founding jurists as authority for a whole variety of rules of public law." Thereafter, he mentions examples of discrimination on grounds of gender in family and private law: "A Muslim man may be married to up to four wives at the same time but a Muslim woman can only be married to one man at a time" (Ibid. 176). Furthermore, "If either form of guardianship, of a husband over his wife or of a Muslim over a non-Muslim, is repudiated, there would be no justification for prohibiting marriage between a Muslim woman and a non-Muslim man. The evolutionary principles of [Taha] would repudiate both types of guardianship" (Ibid. 181).

The Qur'an does allow for the *qawama* of men unto women in a marriage relation of adjusted rights and duties to be shared in good understanding, love, and mercy between all members of the family. These beautiful meanings are clearly expressed in *Baqara* and Rom Sura. 'Ali (1983:73-74) translates from *Baqara* Sura: "[Wives] are your garments and ye are their garments." 'Ali (Ibid. 1056) also translates verse 21 of *Rom* Sura as follows: "He created for you mates from among yourself, that ye may dwell in tranquility with them, and has put love and mercy between your (hearts): Verily in that are Signs for those who reflect." Women, moreover, are granted legal rights to run their own business, pursue educational attainment, and exercise political activities. With more understanding of Shar'ia jurisprudence, high female educational attainment and participation in the modern labor market, as well as excessive politicization of the women's movement with men's support, a greater improvement than is being accomplished thus far could be established in Muslim societies to ensure women's rights fully.

The process of change has to go through political and economic achievement rather than mystical orientations. Muslim women have a role to play in this respect. In her prominent work on Islamic Law and Society in The Sudan, Carolyn Fluehr-Lobban (1987:92) referred, as a whole, to the Sudanese Muslim women of Northern Sudan with whom she conducted intensive interviews in Khartoum. The interviews did not necessarily refer to supporters of the National Islamic Front, Muslim Brotherhood, or Republican Brothers. Fluehr-Lobban documented the fact that the Sudanese Muslim women "presented a strong exterior with a certain toughness of mind and spirit combined with a core that is, like most Sudanese, filled with dignity and generosity." Fluehr-Lobban has been highly critical of "the Western perception of social reality and its peculiar view of the poor conditions of the Muslim women" (Ibid. 92).

An-Na'im (1990:54-55) interprets the notion of *qawama* with respect to "the guardianship and superior status of men over women, thereby sanctioning further discrimination against women whenever the Qur'an was not explicit on the matter." This interpretation is quite different from an authoritative interpretation by A. Yusuf 'Ali (1983:190) who defines a *qawama* person in terms of "one who stands firm in another's business, protects his interests and looks after his affairs; or it may be standing firm in his own business, managing affairs with a steady purpose." 'Ali translates the verse of *qawama* as follows: "Men are the protectors and maintainers of women, because God has given the one more (strength) than the other, and because they support them from their means." The differences between the two interpretations are clear:

An-Na'im emphasizes meanings of "superiority and authority" by virtue of "the advantage" of men "over" women. Ali stresses the "protection and maintenance" of men to women for God has given "the one more than the other" etc. Interestingly, An-Na'im (Ibid.) correctly notes that the Qur'an "was not explicit on the matter." This nicely coincides with Ali's interpretation. God has not specified "the one" responsible for *qawama* in gender terms. Whoever provides, protects, and maintains the other shares full responsibility in the *qawama*. This further means that *qawama* is not a male issue; it is a non-gender responsibility.

Of profound significance, the Qur'an prohibits the marriage of a Muslim woman to a non-Muslim man on the basis of faith, which is unfortunately ignored in the proposed Republican law for the emancipation of women. Here Farrag (1990:141) explains that, "if a Muslim marries a Jewish or a Christian woman, he is marrying a wife whose belief he can respect and in the founders of whose religions he believes... with the result she will also practice her faith in an atmosphere of respect proceeding from the doctrines of her husband. A Muslim woman is not entitled to marry a husband who has no faith in Islam or its Prophet... [It] is forbidden for a Muslim man to marry a polytheist or an animist, since he will not be able to respect that in which he has faith."

The relevant verse in the Qur'an is that of *Baqara* (2:221): "You shall not allow a non-believer to marry a Muslim woman till he believes [in Islam]." Is it plausible to apply *naskh* to an explicit rule of Islamic faith? The more those readers realize the integrity of Qur'anic verses and their inalienable inter-relatedness, the more obvious it becomes that the principle of *naskh* is practically irrelevant to a viable reformation of Islamic law.

An-Na'im reference to polygamy as an example of discrimination covers the permission of a man to marry up to four wives at the same time, but a Muslim woman can be married to one man at a time. One wonders at this particular point if An-Na'im really calls for "equity and justice" between Muslim men and women such that a woman could be married up to four men at the same time, as is guaranteed to men! This kind of polygamy is certainly prohibited in Islam in order to preserve a vital principle of genealogy, i.e., to observe the dignity of women as birth-givers, and to maintain the rights and well being of children.

The grounds rationalizing polygamy of a Muslim man are based on individual and societal needs that is evident in the cases of demographic imbalances in the sex-ratio, whereby the number of women in marriageable age might well exceed the number of men, or where other humanitarian instances warrant marriage of a husband to a widow suffering destitution with orphans, as is originally indicated in the Qur'an. Earlier mentioned, even the Republican Brothers recognize the need for polygamy in the case of "barrenness or illness in the wife" (Fluehr-Lobban, 1987:275). Otherwise, the Shari'a jurists prohibit polygamy, which in any rate, is restricted by several provisions of the Qur'an including a command to maintain only one wife "for fear of injustice."[9]

This discussion brings us to another critique of An-Na'im's proposition to use the rule of *naskh* to abrogate the use of force on the part of Muslims. An-Na'im lays out his proposition in immense hostility and harsh criticisms to both traditional and modernist Islamists who uphold the use of force whenever it becomes

---

[9] *Nisaa* Sura, verses 3 and 129.

necessary to do so. In particular, An-Na'im (1990:64) criticizes Ahmed Hassan's (1970) conclusion that: "If Muslims everywhere are weak, they may tolerate the aggression of the non-Muslims temporarily. But simultaneously they are duty-bound to make preparations and make themselves powerful. Secondly, when they grow powerful they are required to live in a state of preparedness and to shatter the power of the enemies of Islam." An-Na'im believes, however, that Hassan's view is "opportunistic and unprincipled... a conclusion that is incredibly naïve"

Despite An-Na'im's concern with peaceful relations per his criticisms, Hassan's interpretation could be legitimately based on Qur'anic texts that explicitly rule out An-Na'im's criticisms. The Qur'an explicitly requires Muslims to be peaceful and non-aggressive as well as being strong and prepared for enemies. Sura Anfal (8:61) reads: "Against them make ready your strength to the utmost of your power, including steeds of war, to strike terror into (the hearts of) the enemies, of God and your enemies, and others besides, whom ye may not know, but whom God doth known. Whatever ye shall spend in the Cause of God, shall be repaid unto you, and ye shall not be treated unjustly. But if the enemy incline towards peace, do thou (also) incline towards peace, and trust in God: for He is One that hearth and do knowth (all things)."[10] *Jihad* [holy war] is not confined only to the force of arms. An-Na'im (1990:145) correctly notes, "The term and its derivatives refer to self-exertion."

Furthermore, Hassan's proposal is practically reflective of the ongoing realities of armament, military organization, and geopolitical concerns and power relations between governments of the world today – a situation which essentially requires a balanced relation of security and peace. A. Yusuf Ali (1983:430) explains that, "the immediate occasion of (the) injunction of preparedness to the enemy was the

---

[10] See The Holy Qur'an, op. cit., p. 430.

weakness of cavalry of war in the early fights of Islam. But the general meaning follows: "In every fight, physical, moral, or spiritual, arm yourself with the best weapons and the best arms against your enemy, so as to instill wholesome respect into him for you and the Cause you stand for."

This important commentary suggests that within a prevailing mode of mutual respect for justice and peace, the use of physical force can be replaced with a higher level of fighting in intellectual, moral, and spiritual terms. Unless a global-regional balance of power relation is justly assumed between all nations, Muslims and non-Muslims alike, a world peace and order will not be effectively enforced. We will elaborate on these issues in our discussion of the Republican perspectives on human rights and international law in the subsequent sections of this critique.

Another critique focuses on An-Na'im's (1990:65) misinterpretation of the Muslim code of behavior, which is dramatically labeled in his words "a duty to attack non-Muslims... a fundamental principle of Shari'a, irrespective of 'aggression" by the non-Muslims side, or their being 'enemies of Islam'." It is striking how An-Na'im could actually postulate a picture of Muslim society, one of aggression and violence, based on the Prophet's *Hadith* that "Whoever from among Muslims sees an indecency... must change it by his hand; if he cannot, he must do so by his tongue; if he cannot, he must do so by his heart." An-Na'im (1990:156) claims that, "these sources should now be interpreted as indicating nonviolent action, which is consistent with the rule of law."

As a matter of fact, the Qur'an is eminently composed of teachings of *'ibadat* that should be exercised in contemplation, brotherhood, humanitarian affairs, and peaceful co-existence between Muslims and non-Muslims. The Qur'an includes many verses on these specific meanings. Interpreted by 'Ali (1983:862), for example, verse (22:39) highlights the fact that "the little Muslim community [of Medina] was not only fighting for its own existence against the Meccan Quraish, but for the very existence of faith in the One True God... It affected not the faith of one peculiar people. The principle involved was that of all worship, Jewish or Christian as well as Muslim, and of all foundations built for pious uses." The verse is translated as: "Did not God check one set of people by means of another, there would surely have been pulled down monasteries, churches, synagogues, and mosques in which the name of God is commemorated."

Apart from wars and the other historical conflicts that came about in their own right as objective events between Islamic nations or empires and non-Muslim entities, the whole civilization of Islam has been primarily based on values of the Qur'an and those of the Sunna. The *Hadith* of the Prophet is awfully misinterpreted or at least misplaced in the text and context of An-Na'im interpretation. The *Hadith* might not have been used to legitimize aggression by misguided Muslims so much as it has been a constant source of inspiration for orderly relations and keeping of peace. Combating criminality is a public duty in national as well as international law. Here, it is suspected, however, that the inimical relations that shaped the polemics on Islamic affairs between Republican Brothers and the Muslim Brotherhood group at the University of Khartoum during the 1970s throughout the 1980s might have inspired the idea that a state of aggression [is] prevalent among Muslims "throughout the world."

Before closing this section on Shari'a and Republican law, it is interesting to note that Taha "maintained that *naskh* was an essentially logical and necessary process of implementing the appropriate texts and postponing the implementation of others until the right circumstances for their implementation should arise" (An-Na'im, 1990:56). Even if an "up-side-down" replacement of Meddinese verses

214

would be envisaged to enforce Meccan verses alone, what if "right circumstances... arise" once again for the enforcement of Meddinese verses, for example in the case of anarchy and its economic, social, and political contingencies?

Using a utopian perspective, An-Na'im does not clearly appreciate the realistic conditions that warrant a use of force for border control and internal public safety. At the same time, he values the "orientalist" criticisms of the Islamic jurists who support the use of force in the case of anarchy. These inconsistencies are evident in An-Na'im's discussion of al-Mawardi's justification of the "usurpation of power in the provinces by force, on grounds of necessity, though admitting that such usurpation was contrary to Shari'a" [which emphasizes justice and peace] (An-Na'im, 1990:5). Here, An-Na'im comments that: "Muslim scholars working at the time of the decline of the Abbasid dynasty... were primarily concerned with maintaining the unity and security of the Muslims under extremely unstable political conditions."

An-Na'im (1990:5) further mentions that Gibb (1955) depicted al-Mawardi's emphasis on the "best interest of the Muslim community at the time... breaking down to the whole super structure of the juristic system." This evaluation seems to have been silently admitted by An-Na'im. In fact, al-Mawardi's formulation might be well appreciated by modern political scientists. For one, Ramsey Clark (1993:133) suggests the creation of an UN Armament, Arms Limitation and Military Control Agency to "provide standards and supervision... to achieve a size and arms capacity no greater than that required for order control and internal public safety [for each nation]." Clark's statement clearly sanctions the use of force, whenever appropriate, with the most restricted limitations of international law on the matter. The suggestion is quite consonant with the Islamic orientations discussed in this critique.

The United Nations Security Council might have realized the same principle, to some extent, in sanctioning the use of force to establish peace and order in the anarchic situation of Somalia. Article 4 of the International Covenant on Civil and Political Rights recognizes instances of applying the rule of derogation from the obligation of the States Parties under the Covenant "in time of public emergency which threatens the life of nation and the existence of which is officially proclaimed." Clearly, the principle is admissible under international law, albeit within strict limitations on the use of force. A comparison between the safeguards of Shari'a vis-à-vis modern international law could be pursued in this particular concern. But this certainly lies beyond the scope of this critique.

Shari'a Law and Human Rights
Under this section on Shari'a and international human rights norms, two important points need to be clarified: 1) the real nature and relevance of Shari'a to law, whether positive or natural; and 2) the extent to which Shari'a could be implemented in a modern system of public law, namely constitutional law and criminal law.

For a counter argument to An-Na'im's assertions on the irrelevance of "historical Shari'a" to modern law, and his strong criticisms of Shari'a shortcomings in terms of a viable system of developed "positive law", it is appropriate to recall Sinaceur's interpretation of two major features of the Islamic conscience that govern its conception of human rights: "First, the Islamic conscience seems to be from the outset a legal conscience, since neither the division between law and individual conscience, nor the opposition between positive law and natural law, has any place in it; and since each individual can draw, without the intervention of any magesterium, on the law established by Islam. Second, Islam from the outset makes responsibility something essentially personal, inasmuch as no duty can be fulfilled by substitution, even inspired by reparative compassion."

These views were nearly emphasized by Taha in his stress on the individual, the ultimate focus of Islamic concerns. Related to this, Taha (al-Tanmiya, op. cit. 32-46) believed that individualism is capable of removing the contradiction between science (including, in his opinion, socialism without which there would be no social development) and the religion of Islam.

Islamic law is essentially composed of a set of rules that lay out the path for a moral system of individual obligations towards the Lord, in the first place. Other obligations pertain to the individual himself as well as the other individuals and groups. The rules are organized in a hierarchical preference such that a God-fearing individual would be able, with or without external mechanism of positive law, to regulate his mind and soul in accordance with the Qur'an and Sunna. This is a high level of spiritual and moral commitments that is implied by the Prophet's *Hadith* on al-Jihad al-Akber (the greatest struggle) of a Muslim individual. Most Sufi groups aspire in their spiritual and material life to an attainment of the maximum degree possible of al-Jihad al-Akber, which covers both *'ibadat* and *mu'amalat* (worshipping and transactions). A Muslim is entitled a right to adjudicate; but God rewards him if he pardons the offender instead of having him punished by law. Both positive and natural laws are intertwined within a higher law of morality.

Faruki (cited in An-Na'im, 1990:78) explains in the area of legislation, "often the shari'a states a principle simpliciter and leaves it to human beings to work out the legal details and regulations that flow from the principle. Or shari'a may specifically release to the sphere of human reason and understanding the setting up of regulations in certain matters... the very existence of different schools of Islamic law shows that a great deal of Islamic law is interpretative and derivative from shari'a in nature... for [which] legislative temporal authority should be identifiable, which authority would be in pari materia with the legislative branch of the constitutional state of contemporary political science."

A fundamental principle that underlies the establishment of *madzahib*, seems to have been based on the extent to which Muslims might freely submit to a public authority that would be conferred on the *'ulama* (learnt scholars or leaders of religious sects) for the observance and/or enforcement of Shari'a. This has been the case in Sudan and many other Muslim countries since the medieval ages. In other words, the preference of Muslims has often been highly selective and individualistic in issues of governance and political conformity rather than submissive to a consolidating power or a political group, including Muslim Brotherhood or the Republican Brothers. This inclination to natural liberties might explain further the commitment of a large minority of Muslims to Sufi groups, which is evident in most contemporary African and Asian societies.

The genesis of this intrinsic logic of Islamic individualism is traceable to the first state of Medina, which under the leadership of the Prophet resembled a highly refined mode of spiritual and moral life more than a legal or constitutional entity, although it was a formal political entity as well. Mohamed Mahmoud (1991:18) sums up the situation in these words: "The State established by the Prophet [in Medina] embodied an alliance between different groups aware of their distinctions and antagonistic interests. The personality of the Prophet was a balancing force to these contradicting elements, and did curb their contradictions.

This, nevertheless, did not eradicate the ongoing competition between forces aspiring to power amongst the Medina population, as soon as the Prophet passed to the other world. Tribal affiliations maintained a base of linearity in which the power structure had been earlier entrenched... The sources of Islamic history reflected these facts. The Prophet had not nominated a successor or a specific method of selecting a successor. The Qur'an did not include a special rule to assist the Muslims to decide on the mater, other than general guidelines. The issue of succession was determined in the light of a power balance between the *Ansar* (the Helpers of the Medina residents) and the *Muhagireen* (the Migrants from Mecca)."

In the area of constitutional law, Taha did not elaborate a full theory of a modern state within a Second Message of Islam, although he did mention the need to develop a modern Sudanese polity unto a "melting pot" of the tribal, linguistic, and cultural diversity of the country. Having strongly criticized the lacking of "historical" Shari'a to a developed constitutional law, An-Na'im (1990:ft 25:208) resorts to the experience of Abu Bakr, the first Caliph of the Prophet, who "emphasized his accountability to the Muslim community and made obedience to him conditional upon his conformity to the law of God in administering the affairs of the state... Although this early and authoritative precedent may offer possibilities for the political and legal accountability of the government to the general population, it has not been developed as such under Shar'ia." Moreover, Abu Bakr's statement "does not explain how the Caliph's conformity with the law of God may be determined. Another question is how to hold the Caliph accountable and to whom," comments An-Na'im (Ibid.).

The Republicans' literature on Shari'a constitutional law is rather tautological for the very fact that Shari'a is not a function of a political system of government so much as it stands as a system of spiritual guidance. Shari'a provides a viable source of canonical rules that are meant, in essence, to regulate the social and religious life of Muslims. The implementation of Shari'a, nonetheless, is not necessarily channeled through a political authority or a religious state because the commitment of a Muslim to Shari'a rules is an individual responsibility in the first place.

It is well documented in Islamic history that the Medina Muslim community managed to establish a religious polity under the direct supervision of the Prophet on whose death the early Muslims were strongly disagreed as well as on the political issues of the state. The modern times of Muslim testify to the same fact that Shari'a is a fundamental source of legislation rather than a temporal political authority. This is understandable in legal terms so that legislation would include all of the rules required to enable Muslims to practice their social and spiritual rights, in accordance with Shari'a. It goes without saying that the other non-Muslim citizens of the state would have to be granted the same rights according to their own faith within such a political formulation.

Muslims have always been entitled in different historical contexts to select the most appropriate views of Shari'a schools of thought and action to govern their social and religious life. Islamic Shari'a courts have actively observed the Islamic jurisprudence of these aspects in Muslim societies (Fluehr-Loban, 1987). Shari'a judges and jurists have always participated in the promotion of Shari'a *madzahib* to accommodate modern views and situations. To preserve the purity of Shari'a and its spiritual functions in a Muslim society, Shari'a must not be used or abused in the worldly conflicts that usually characterize a political striving for power between citizens of a state.

Because the Republican Brothers aspire to install a religious state, An-Na'im views on constitutionality are inconsistent. On the one hand, he excludes "the secularist approach in the Muslim context from the renewal-reform tradition because secularism is <u>not</u> an <u>Islamic</u> response to the challenges facing Muslim societies" (1990:48). But he strongly adopts a modern system of "western constitutionalism… to be appreciated as a contribution to the totality of human experience and knowledge from which the Muslims and other peoples may adopt and adapt as they deem fit in light of their own religions and cultural traditions" (Ibid. 70). Western constitutionality of course is secularist system of a worldly government.

Elsewhere, An-Na'im (1992:98) appears to have shifted his attention from a concentration on the Second Message of Islam to acknowledge the need to adopt secular views openly. In his opinion, "human rights advocates [in Sudan] should seek to achieve a sufficient degree of reform of Shari'a in order to remove all principles and rules inconsistent with international standards of human rights or openly call for the establishment of a secular state" (Ibid.). Notwithstanding, it will certainly jeopardize the legitimacy of human rights activists to propagate ideas of justice, peace, and equity among Muslims without due respect to the strong teachings and dictates of Islam in these issues. In practical terms, therefore, both secular and Islamic ideas could be logically used to strengthen human rights in a Muslim society. The experience of Sudanese progressive organizations, including the Sudanese Women's Union whose membership is largely composed of Muslims, testifies to this fact (Fluehr-Lobban, 1987).

The choice of Muslims to be governed by a particular form of a national government conforms to the political experiences and level of development attained by the popular movement of the nation states in which they participate with the other non-Muslim groups. It is within this political conformity, that a correct version of Shari'a might be properly implemented for social and religious objectives, in peace. The fact that the atrocious practices of fanatic regimes, such as the June 1989's military coup of Sudan, have been indiscriminately exercised against opposition groups, irrespective of their religious beliefs or familial linkages with the ruling party, testify further to this need.

The Republican writers could certainly help to advance the cause of human rights in Muslim countries if they confirm the contribution of Shari'a jurists as well as modern Islamists in these humanitarian fields, instead of their strong inclination to underestimate the significant heritage of Shari'a, indiscriminately.

To discuss the extent to which Shari'a might be implemented within a modern system of international criminal law, the remaining part of this section compares the methodology and techniques of both Shari'a jurists and Republican Brothers.

Humanitarian principles to ensure a decent treatment to members of the humankind, human rights might be enjoying a close relation with Qur'anic and Sunna teachings. In fact, human rights are not a new phenomenon in the Muslim World. Riffat Hassan (1982:55) has succinctly written that, "The Qur'an – which to me as to other Muslims is the repository of par excellence of divine wisdom – gives its readers an infinite worldview embracing every aspect of life. Consequently, it contains references to more 'rights' than can be enumerated here."

Hassan (1982:55-62) further mentions the rights to life, respect, justice, freedom, privacy protection from slander of backbiting and ridicule, and the right to the "good life" as fundamental human rights of human kind in the Qur'an. Other important rights include rights to a secure place of residence; a means of living; protection of one's personal possessions; seeking knowledge; developing one's aesthetic sensibilities and enjoying the bounties created by God; protection of one's covenants; moving freely; seeking asylum if one is living under oppression; social and judicial autonomy for minorities; and the right to protection of one's holy places.

Many Western writers have increasingly recognized the deep entrenchment of human rights in the Third World religions and cultural traditions. James W. Nickel (1987:62) confirms, "Human brotherhood, human dignity, and the duties of justice and generosity are emphasized by these societies." Nickel states that, "The Islamic world generally finds the idea of human rights compatible with its religious traditions, particularly because the Koran [Qur'an] emphasizes duties of respect, justice, and mercy... Further, Muslims have long traditions of religious and social tolerance – at least for other monotheists." Nickel then makes the point that "as elsewhere, these values are often contradicted by a reality of oppression, cruelty, corruption, and gross inequality [especially] by military governments [which] often impose economic austerity on the populace... and repress those with liberal and leftist views."

True, dictatorial regimes comprise a determining factor in the atrocities committed in the name of religious, national, or other ideological concerns. A fundamentalist party, the National Islamic Front (NIF) of the Sudan was not able to implement a highly politicized version of Shari'a punishments without a military dictatorial regime during the years 1983 and 1989 to the present time. An-Na'im's criticisms of the application of Shari'a Penal Code in Sudan have been largely voiced by many secularists, as well as Islamists – although on different ideological and political premises than those of the Republican Brothers.

Moreover, An-Na'im (1992:127-131) lately emphasized the fact that "human rights violations are likely to be massive... when a military regime seeks to impose and maintain a totalitarian ideological state regardless of its particular type of orientation." This signifies, in our opinion, another important shift from *his* thesis on "historical Shari'a" [as a source of human rights violations] to a closer appreciation of the direct causes of human rights violations in contemporary life, namely, dictatorships and totalitarian regimes. The availability of a democratic system of government is a fundamental safeguard to immune society from oppression. Democratic rule, rather than any vague configuration of a sacred government, is a real guarantee for Muslim practices as well as the other non-Muslim social and religious activities.

Nickel (1987:66) also speaks about a "conflict between human rights norms and Islamic beliefs and practice... in such matters as full equality for women, full religious freedoms and political equality for unbelievers, and, in the most conservative states the use of some punishments such as the amputation of a hand for theft." To comment on this aspect, a discussion on Islamic criminal law is now made about the Republican thought which apparently upholds similar views on "historical Shari'a."

Shari'a Justice and Republican Law
In an upright statement, An-Na'im (1990:ft 40:216) affirms that, "in Jewish law, which is believed by Jews to be divine, jurists were able to restrict the practical application of the specified capital punishment for some fifty offenses through extremely strict rules of evidence and procedure." In another place, An-Na'im (1992:ft. 84:219) affirms restrictions made by Shari'a early jurists, for example Ibn 'Abbas, Abu Hanifa, and Ibn Hanbal regarding alternative punishments "in accordance with the degree of harm inflicted by the aggressor upon his victim."

Notwithstanding, An-Na'im (1992:101) posits the Shari'a criminal justice as discriminatory to gender and religion: "Numerous problems of substantive law, evidence, and procedure are raised by the prospects of implementing this branch of Shari'a." Later, however, he refers to "sophisticated and detailed principles of criminal responsibility on homicide... developed by the founding jurists."

Earlier criticized, the inconsistencies of the Republicans' evaluation of Shari'a criminal justice are sometimes produced by a confusion of Shari'a natural law with concepts of modern positive law. As an example, a discussion is readily made on the Republicans' opinion on the implementation of *hudud*. Although An-Na'im does not clearly reject such implementation, he suggests "purely religious rationalization of *hudud* is insufficient justification for including these offenses and their punishments in the criminal law of a modern nation-state" (Ibid.114-115).

A possible reaction to An-Na'im's statement may be available in a number of authoritative references on *hudud*. 'Awad (1991:16), for one, explains, "The principle and rules of *ta'zir* (discretionary punishments) are the origin of Islamic penology. The *hudud* are exceptional punishments whose implementation is extremely restricted by a sophisticated system of evidence. Islamic jurists confirm that both *hudud* and retribution are based on a genuine rule of pardon, rather than prosecution. Hence, any *hadd* could be pardoned unless the offender himself or any other Muslim reports it to the authority. The authority is not entitled to mitigation of a *hadd* penalty if it is proven through prescribed Islamic rules of evidence that the offense has been actually committed by the offender. The early Muslims rarely applied arrest or pre-trial incarceration on offenders. Instead, they extensively used as a system of pardoning, reconciliation, and *diya* for compensation."

'Awad explains that, "although *hudud* could be waived for a lack of concrete evidence, the rights of individuals involved in the offense are subject to prosecution. If an accused is a juvenile, or a lunatic, or if he has committed the offense without intention or under intimidation, he shall not be charged for it" (Ibid. 27). Furthermore, Matloob (1986:221) mentions, "the Prophet always informed the offenders, who had reported the commission of a *hadd* to him, about the punishment of the *hadd*. Moreover, he would insistently urge them to repent so that they might escape the imposition of the penalty." 'Awad also explains that an accused person shall not be put under oath in a *hadd* or retribution crimes. In the case of adultery, women are exempted from testimony.

In conclusion, *hudud* are strongly related to religious concerns rather than the usual objectives of punishment in modern public law. It follows that implementation of *hudud* in a modern public society should advocate the same Sunna of the Prophet. This implies that the implementation of *hudud* should be enforced within a system of evidence so purified in faith, where the least suspicion about a witness of a *hadd* would automatically discharge the whole case. This model of the Medina early Muslims could only be pursued in our life today as a personal commitment on the part of the offender and the *hadd* witnesses. The most appropriate authority to deal with such cases would probably be a Shari'a High Court, whose decision must be subjected to approval of the Supreme Court. Should that occur, the national laws as well as international law must recognize it as a religious right for Muslims *per se*.

In addition to many human rights organizations, including Islamic associations, the Sudanese Bar Association strongly holds that *hudud* implementation must be conditionally based on availability of a suitable living standard in the Sudanese society, which has been seriously wracked in social and economic terms by dictatorial rule. Equally important, the need of the Sudan to establish a coherent national unity for all its Muslim and non-Muslim nationals would be firmly maintained on the basis of a secular system of government rather than a political religious authority.

An-Na'im (1990:ft 54:217) asserts that in Shari'a Law "no general principles of joint liability were developed to apply to all categories of offenses or to criminal responsibility in general." He also criticizes the recommendation of some jurists to use force for the purpose of extracting confessions from individuals of repeatedly bad character." An-Na'im (1990:105) affirms, "The early Muslim scholars and jurists did not distinguish between the religious, ethical, and legal aspects of criminal law enforcement. Shari'a is extremely rudimentary and informal... Given the lack of reliable specialized historical information, it is difficult to provide a detailed survey of the actual administration of criminal justice in Muslim history."

This very statement, nevertheless, defeats the viability of An-Na'im's assertions to a large extent: many Islamist scholars find that the rules of criminal responsibility, prohibition of torture, and "sophisticated and detailed principles of criminal responsibility on homicide," theft, adultery, etc., have been carefully formulated in "historical" Shari'a.

Matloob (1986:215) elucidates the fact that Islamic law has set forth many principles to ensure justice, being a major Islamic value, in the treatment of offenders. Some of these include "definition of crime by law, criminal responsibility of the individual person, presumption of innocence until proven guilty, and equality of individuals before the law." These principles and rules have been lately incorporated in modern laws such as Articles 7, 11 (1 and 2), and 12 of the Universal Declaration of Human Rights.

Other principles include the fundamental rule of interpreting doubt to the advantage of the accused, interrogation of the accused by the plaintiff directly, the right of the accused to be silent in police interrogation or court examination provided that such silence shall not be used against the accused in *hudud*, etc. Matloob (Ibid. 216) sums up the knowledgeable system of Shari'a criminal act, criminal responsibility, *qasd* or '*amd* (criminal intention), complicity, joint liability, use of force in self-defense, coercion, necessity, and recidivism. "All these and many other rules are deeply rooted in Islamic Law. They only need to be technically reformulated in the language of contemporary criminal law," ascertains Matloob. This statement implies that Shari'a heritage can be used a source of criminal law in modern jurisprudence in connection with the cultural and religious commitments of Muslims. In this writer's opinion the proposed "technical reformulation" of Shari'a law should be scrutinized by international human rights comparative studies.[11]

Torture is very strictly prohibited in Shari'a law. An accused person shall not be compelled in any way or subjected to any cruel, inhuman, or degrading treatment. Proceedings of trial are based on principles of individual responsibility in prosecution, trial, and sentence. The Shari'a recognizes the impact of circumstantial evidence on the commission of a crime whereby a judge may, on his discretion, treat the case in due consideration to circumstances of mental

---

[11] This writer has repeatedly proposed the preparation of an Encyclopedia of Islamic Criminal Justice to the United Nations (1983), Sudan Government (1984), and the Endowment for Democracy (2001). Encyclopedia should discuss the similarities and differences between Islamic Shari'a Law and international human rights norms in the light of current State experiences, as in the case of Sudan, Nigeria, and other Muslim countries. Having earlier prepared the Sudanese Encyclopedia of Criminal Justice (in print), research on the Encyclopedia of Islamic Criminal Justice will begin in January 2003.

illness, compulsion, intimidation, etc. (Matloob, 1986:230-240). Elsewhere, al-'Awaa (1986:249) affirms that the rule of supremacy of certainty over doubt (or that doubt is an advantage to the accused in modern jurisprudence) was elaborated and frequently applied by the Muslim jurists.

The modernist Islamists, of whom many have been cited above, do not reject the use of modern non-Islamic jurisprudence inasmuch as it complies with the fundamental principles and rules of Shari'a. In adopting this approach, legal, religious, and socio-cultural concerns are increasingly recognized, without an ultra-legal approach which might abrupt the development of Shari'a in the final analysis. Muslim penologists and criminologists realize those significant aspects of the Shari'a law have been incorporated into the colonial heritage of criminal law. For example, the Sudan Penal Codes of 1925, 1974, and 1983 were based on both Anglo-Saxon Law and the Indian Law that originated in Islamic Shari'a Law. Equally important, Abu Zaid (1990:41-42) reaffirms in a study of criminal procedure in Arab legislation that modern Muslim laws of criminal procedure and evidence draw heavily upon Islamic Shari'a and Western laws.

An-Na'im believes that Shari'a embodies discriminatory texts of race, religion, and gender: that should be abrogated before a real reformation is actually enforced. Earlier stressed, the abrogation of Qur'anic verses creates more problems than it might unlikely resolve. The other approaches advocated by Muslim modernists, individuals or governments, seem to have been more practical in the experiences of Morocco, Tunisia, Southern Yemen, Egypt, and Sudan (before the 1983 imposition of Shari'a penalties by the notorious September Laws of the defunct Nimeiri rule, which was further adopted by the NIF existing government). The rights of women, in Shari'a Law as well as modern status, in marriage or divorce, child custody, employment, and labor conditions witnessed a remarkable progress in many Muslim countries. Once more awareness is raised among the public through progressive political parties and human rights groups, educational programs, and participation of the mass media and the press, more legislative enactment would be encouraged in an evolutionary way rather than a revolutionary method of action.

Slavery is not an Islamic institution. The Shari'a is certainly advanced in the methods applied to seal off this non-human practice from Muslim societies. The Qur'anic rule of treating prisoners of war (the main source of slavery) is to free them in "generosity or by ransom" according to the verse 47:4. That Muslims maintained slavery, according to An-Na'im's (1990:174) insistent view, is not a function of Shari'a so much as it could be seen in the light of the political and economic conditions of these times. Slavery has been recently reported in Sudan and Mauritania in relation to economic and political injustices more than a direct result of Islamic Shari'a Law. In Sudan, slavery is a direct consequence of the escalating civil war, especially in the western and southern areas of the country, due to military struggles and inter-ethnic feuds between the indigenous population, the central government, and the Sudanese People's Liberation Army (SPLA).

Africa Watch (1990:151-161) documents the fact that "slavery, hostage-taking, and pawning are illegal under Sudanese law [which includes Shari'a provisions into it]. Customary law in western and southern Sudan recognizes the state of hostage and client/pawn though the precise meaning of these states remains unclear... There has been no systematic attempt to enforce Sudanese law against slavery... the SPLA may be taking captives and civilians in occupied areas in ways that can degenerate into slavery. There are also accounts of the treatment of captives that suggest a situation that has already degenerated into de facto slavery."

Islam and International relations

Broadly speaking, a universality of international law is generally accepted, although serious divergences underlie the existing state of international human rights between Western powers and Muslim societies. In this situation, there are misconceptions about Islamic Shari'a vis-à-vis instruments of international law on the use of force, status of non-Muslims, and the limits of Islamic jurisdiction over Muslims beyond the boundaries of the nation state. To clarify these aspects, the general characteristics of Islamic international law will be briefly discussed in comparison with modern international law.

Despite the fact that "a restricted core of values and criteria universally accepted by the States [including Muslim countries] is gradually emerging" (Cassese, 1990:64), "whether the government of sovereign states, especially super states are in a good position to promote human rights is far from self-evident. Given the way the world works, human rights considerations are generally subordinated to wider geo-political concerns, even by the most enlightened of governments" (Egeland, 1988:1). Nickel (1987:62-63) remarks, "One finds the most favorable public attitudes toward human rights in the developed non-communist West... this does not mean that these governments have never tried to manipulate public opinion or suppress dissent. And while showing some respect for the rights of their citizens, they have often supported extremely repressive regimes abroad when that was thought to be in their interests."

The suspicions of Third World scholars are reverberated in this statement: "What concerns Black and Third World people is not just the war but the new order, the new imperium, which is emerging from the ending of the cold war... The ending of the cold war has left the United States the sole super power in the world. The contestation between the West and the East is over, and the West is free to range over the South, marauding it as it will" (Sivanandan, 1991:85).

Aside from the long-standing dispute on the hierarchy of the economic, social, and cultural rights versus political and civil rights between socialist countries and the Third World on one side, and the Liberal Western countries on the other, there are many misconceptions of Islamic principles, rules of diplomacy, and balance of power relations. The Muslim wars and conquests during the medieval times, apart from the most recent 'Uthman [also Ottoman] era are often cited as a substantive reflection of "Shari'a international law" in terms of an expansionist intervention in non-Muslim territories by aggression or violence. Nothing is far from the truth. The 'Uthman conquests are hardly comparable to the early Muslim wars. For example, in the Sudan (1821 and the aftermath) tens of thousands of the Sudanese people were massacred in retaliation of the death of Ismail Pasha, son of Mohamed 'Ali the *Wali* [viceroy] of Egypt.

The fact that Muslim wars were made in self-defense of their faith is seldom mentioned. The aggression of the decaying empires of Rome and Persia against the newly established Islamic society is almost forgotten. The civilized warfare of the early Muslim armies and their humanitarian stands are ignored. It is imperative to recall these succinct statements in the matter by A. Yusuf 'Ali (1983:414): "A righteous war is a community affair, and any accessions resulting from it belong to God or the community or Cause... Certain equitable principles of division should be laid down to check human greed and selfishness... These principles are followed in the best modern practice of civilized nations."

'Ali (Ibid. 413) nullifies the persistent allegation by orientalists that Islam was spread by the use of force: "As Kingsley remarks in <u>Hypatia</u>, the Egyptian church 'ended as a mere chaos of idolatrous sects, persecuting each other for metaphysical propositions...' The social conditions produced an amount of discontent, for which the only redress came only with the advent of Islam. It was for this reason that the Copts and the inhabitants of Egypt generally welcomed the forces of Islam... in 639 A.D. ... What happened in Egypt happened generally in Western Asia."

Knowing that the medieval evolution and development of the rules of governance have been a function of power relations and violent struggles between imperial and regional powers, including Islamic Caliphates and empires, it is important to emphasize that, whenever applied, Islamic Shari'a Law provided many safeguards in terms of human rights and humanitarian affairs. This occurred on the basis of "established methods of peaceful intercourse and settlement of disputes through diplomacy and arbitration" [of the Shari'a], An-Na'im (1990:158) correctly recognizes.

Despite the general atrocities of war, the early Muslims managed to observe the Qur'an and Sunna in conquests of the medieval ages firmly. One example is that the *Baqt* Agreement between the Muslim army of Egypt and the Christian Nubians of Sudan was seen by many historians to have been concluded in a mutual exchange of trade and peaceful relations for centuries (Adams, 1977). The heritage of Shari'a in diplomacy, war and peace, and other aspects of international relations cannot be simply viewed as one of conflicting norms and serious divergence with modern international law. Rather, the principles and values of the inherited Shari'a might be scrutinized to consolidate international law and the other forms of religious or worldly rules.

Compared to the atrocities of medieval wars that occurred against Muslims and Jews in Europe, as well as Western colonial conquests in Africa and the New World, in addition to the two World Wars, the Muslim wars were closely governed by a progressive system of negotiations, peace treaties, and observance of the environment and humanitarian affairs. This is clearly stated in relation to verse 2:190 of the Qur'an: "Fight in the cause of God those who fight you but do not transgress limits; for God loveth not transgressors." This means in the words of 'Ali (1983:75) that: "War is only permissible in self-defense, and under well-defined limits. When undertaken, it must be pushed with vigour, but not relentlessly, but only to restore peace and freedom or the worship of God. In any case strict limits must not be transgressed: women, children, old and infirm men should not be molested, nor trees and crops cut down, nor peace withheld when the enemy comes to terms."

In modern jurisprudence, Buchheit (1978:37) confirms that, "the international community must not give states carte blanche to enforce security measures in any manner they please... The best rule therefore would seem to be this: where the claimant group has not been driven to utilize violence as a justifiable means of self-defence against an oppressive State... then the State may exercise its prerogative of attempting to suppress the secession without the resulting disturbance becoming a factor in this calculation of current disruption. However, should a governing State in this position engage in a savage campaign needlessly causing injury to the lives, property, and human dignity of the insurgents... then the fact of this excessive brutality, above that excusable as reasonably necessary to counter the secession will enter the calculation."

The procedure suggested by Buchheit, as was mentioned above, had been actively pursued by Muslims since the early times of Islam to deal with armed conflicts within a Muslim society in varying degrees of rural, tribal, and urban settings. Arab countries have also suggested it in an attempt to prevent the Gulf War between Iraq and its Arab neighbors. 'Ali (1983:1405) explains that, "if one party is determined to be the aggressor, the whole force of the collective community [of Islam] is brought to bear on it. The essential condition of course is that there should be perfect fairness and justice and respect for the highest principles: for Islam takes account of every just and legitimate interest without separating spiritual from temporal matters. The League of Nations fails because these essentials are absent."

Robert D. Matthews (1980:141) writes, "Although states do often resolve their differences short of the use of violence, international politics do take place in the constant shadow of war. States are therefore compelled by the very circumstances in which they find themselves to show a concern for their security and are generally prepared to allocate scarce sources to obtain it... Without an accepted mechanism to reconcile conflicting interests, each of the actors in the international system is left to protect and further its own interests... violence can and does occur... international policies do take place in the constant shadow of war." Furthermore, Alson (1992:8-9) asserts that, "the International Court of Justice remained a relatively marginal actor in terms of the UN's overall human rights endeavours... The Security Council has a long history of refusing to consider itself as an organ for the promotion of respect for human rights, except in so far as a given situation constitutes a threat to international peace and security."

In a world order dominated by a supremacy of power politics, especially after the Gulf War, "the major powers as well as those lower in the hierarchy of power, especially countries aspiring to regional hegemony [are involved in a new arms race] seen as an essential prerequisite for winning a respectable place in the new 'world order'" (Marek Thee, 1991:12-13). As a consequence of this, Thee demonstrates that, "All major powers, including China and smaller countries seem to have drawn the conclusion that they too can and need to acquire modern weapons to withstand the challenges of contemporary international relations, in peace and war."

Seen in the light of these facts, it is unfortunate that An-Na'im (1990) has been overly concerned with a tendency to "condemn" the Shari'a heritage, even in conditions that might justify the use of force in self-defense. It is important to observe peace and order in international relations by all nations, Muslims and non-Muslims. The Encyclopedia of Human Rights (Lawson, 1991:357-358) refers to the Declaration on Principles of International Law concerning Friendly Relations and Co-operation among States in accordance with the Charter of the United Nations.

Based on the Declaration, this writer believes that more understanding is needed to appreciate the convergence between principles of international law, which in fact are greatly consonant with religious orientations, and Islamic Law. In this respect, Islamic principles might be stressed in international law to consolidate the United Nations Declaration on Principles of International Law that: States shall refrain in their international relations from the threat or use of force against the territorial integrity or political independence of any State; settle their international disputes by peaceful means; not intervene in matters within the domestic jurisdiction of any State; observe the principles of equal rights and self-determination of peoples and the principle of sovereign equality of States; and fulfill in good faith the obligations assumed by them in accordance with the UN Charter.

In "An Agenda for Peace: Preventive Diplomacy, Peace-Making and Peace-Keeping," the Secretary-General of the United Nations issued a significant report pursuant to the statement adopted by the Summit Meeting of the Security Council on 31 January 1992. The Secretary-General (1992:754) holds that "Under Article 42 of the Charter, the Security Council has the authority to take military action to maintain or restore international peace and order. While such action shall only be taken when all peaceful means have failed, the option of taking it is essential to the credibility of the United Nations as a guarantor of international security... I recommend that the Council consider the utilization of peace-enforcement units in clearly defined circumstances... Such units from member States... would have to be more heavily armed than peace-keeping forces."

Explored earlier in previous sections of this critique, the Qur'an provides workable solutions in situations of peace as well as those of war. The implication of this fact is that the Meddinese verses are as needed in modern life as the Meccan ones are. Recently, prominent African personalities concluded that, "progress in resolving the numerous conflicts in Africa depends on the Organization of African Unity (OAU) reviewing its principle of 'non-interference' in internal affairs. The former OAU Secretary General Salim Ahmed Salim noted that the OAU's narrow interpretation of sovereignty had made it stand by in apparent helplessness as many of these conflicts have torn countries apart."

Two main comments remain to be discussed in this section. The first comment deals with the fact that, except for the regional wars that have been ongoing between the Muslim countries of Iran, Iraq, and the Gulf States, or with non-Muslim countries in the Bosnian war with Serbia, the vast majority of Muslim States have been strongly committed to international law and world peace.

Second, the 30 Years War between Israel and Arab countries is not a function of Shari'a application. Rather, it has been a war of hatred and politico-economic injustices for whose redress the genuine principles of Shari' on justice and peace could be properly addressed in juxtaposition with international law.

Peace negotiations should be strongly supported between the warring parties such that a just settlement should be firmly enforced. A significant component of the settlement is to ensure a permanent balance of power between Israel and the Arab countries in terms of equity of armament and military might through an agreement of arms reduction and commitment to the Declaration of Peace and the other international instruments. This, practically, is a factual ingredient of peace in that disturbed part of the Middle East. Equitable military power relations would likely culminate in a firm peace keeping agreement between Arabs and Israel, whose major concerns are based on regional security and economic co-operation. This would further pave the way to achieve a peaceful settlement to the cause of the Palestinians as well.

In the case of the civil war of Sudan, the application of a harsh version of Shari'a punishments in 1983, regardless of the humanitarian aspects of Shari'a, contributed to escalation of the war. The new Penal Code of 1991, which has been issued under the dictatorial rule of the NIF, protects crime doing by the authorities by section 11 and section 15. The latter states that, "killing in the course of performing duty is not a crime." This is definitely a non-Islamic law, which is meant to abuse Shari'a for political purposes. The sections inserted in the Code cannot justify, for instance, the torture of Dr. 'Ali Fadl to death or the extra-judicial execution of many other civilians or army officers in 1990 and the aftermath.

The main aspects of civil strife in Sudan are deeply rooted in political, economic, and socio-cultural conflict between the ethnocentric and the political and economic monopolies of the country's central governments and Sudan's regions including the South. The solution of civil war is therefore political in nature and essence. Bearing in mind the existing rule of the NIF, which has evidently made of the Sudanese State a terrorist regime, the imposition of a religious state on the Sudan, is quite alien to this objective approach.

The Comprehensive Political Settlement of the National Democratic Alliance (NDA), Sudan's largest opposition entity, requires the government to create the climate conducive to confidence building between the warring parties, establish a transitional government for democracy rule, and ensure national participation in decision making. This should culminate in the setting up of an All-Sudanese Constitutional conference with the close participation of the United Nations, IGAD, the US, Egypt, and other concerned parties. Towards the achievement of this end, the IGAD/US-supported Machikos Peace Protocol (Nairobi, 2002) constituted a significant step provided that the NDA and all the other Sudanese opposition groups participate fully in the peace negotiation, which thus far included only the SPLM/SPLA and Sudan Government.

Conclusions

The striving for peace and development in the national, regional, and international arenas is greatly varied with respect to secular and religious approaches. Unger (1987:42) notes a crucial fact seems to indicate that "society did not cease to have a certain structure: a system of powers and rights that constantly regenerated a practical plan of division and hierarchy and expressed an enacted vision of the right and possible forms of human association. But this order had been repeatedly disturbed. Its repeated shaking had laid the basis for a special kind of insight."

Motivated by this ambivalent situation, the Republican Brothers group of the Sudan sought to introduce a Second Message of Islam through which Shari'a Law would be replaced by a new revolutionary public law abrogating certain texts of the Holy Qur'an in order that Islam would be compatible with modern human rights and recognized international law. In so doing, the Republican thinkers claimed a strong adherence to the "totality" of the Qur'an and Sunna, the fundamental sources of Shari'a Law.

The critique makes an attempt to unmask the Marxist as well as liberal origins of the Republican thought, in addition to its mystical and spiritual orientation. In the area of public law, the proposed Republican law appeared to have been confused between principles of natural law and rules of positive law. Relegating Shari'a, however, to secularist standards and evaluations in terms of Western constitutionality and criminal justice is not an appropriate method to undertake Islamic reforms in contemporary Muslim societies. Nor does it provide a fair perspective into the contributions of Islamic jurists in the fields of private, public, and international law.

In contrast to the Republican method, Islamic modernist scholars and jurists adopted practical techniques to advance the cause of implementing modern principles of human rights and international law in national legislation, with due respect to the rich heritage of Islamic jurisprudence. Significant changes have been enforced in the areas of marriage guardianship, divorce, child custody, etc. using judicial circulars and other devices rather than *naskh* – a drastic revolutionary approach proposed by the Republican Brothers.

The need for a progressive implementation of Qur'anic texts is well established in Muslim societies today. Towards the achievement of this goal, it is expedient to study the historical context in which each verse of the Qur'an was revealed to the Prophet, accurately. Nonetheless, the use of *naskh* to abrogate certain verses of the Qur'an is not serviceable to this effect. The authenticity of the Holy Book of Islam is a divine aspect of Muslim faith. Although the Qur'an includes fundamental teachings on justice and the observance of human rights and freedoms that are recognized by international law, it is primarily a Book of Faith and worshipping. This, however, does not rule out the possibility of finding different interpretations among Muslim scholars for the same verse over time, in response to social change and problems of development.

An-Na'im's interesting book <u>Towards an Islamic Reformation</u> includes penetrating insights into the complex depths of the divinity and continuity of Islamic law, albeit in controversial judgments and categorical evaluations. This critique suggests that a greater contribution of Islamic jurisprudence in the critical areas of human rights and international law could be accomplished if Shari'a heritage, a viable source of juristic precedence, is equally emphasized in the process. This suggestion is best understandable in the light of the existing state of human rights and international law, which is rampant with divergence and escape clauses despite their universality and significant convergence.

The great Islamic thinker A Yusuf 'Ali (1983:143) explains that Islam was revealed to the Prophet Muhammad, peace and prayers upon him, to make of Muslims an "*Ummat* [nation] justly balanced," as has been made by God, "that [they] might be witnesses over the nations." This is a role of peace, justice, and order that must be played by the Muslim *Ummat*. The essence of Islam is to avoid all extravagancies on either side. It is a sober practical religion." Finally, "there are paradoxes in life: apparent loss may be real gain; apparent cruelty may be real mercy; returning good for evil may really be justice and not generosity. God's wisdom transcends all human calculation," says 'Ali (1983:143,747).

NOTES ON WOMEN'S RIGHTS IN ISLAM
M.E. Mahmoud

The call for the peaceful co-existence of religions is a significant strategy to increase scholarly involvement of Muslims in the international effort to expand the realization of international human rights norms.

Equally important, the Sudanese secularists or religious believers, the Copts, Christian sectors, all African religion worshippers, and all Muslim groups are equally responsible to promote a fruitful dialogue with the women to insure human rights and freedoms for all citizens regardless of sex, race, or religious beliefs. The emphasis laid on scholarly dialogue is extremely important in light of the attempts to ridicule Muslims or insult the sacredness of Islam with irresponsible epithets. Related to the cause of democracy and women's rights in Sudan, this wrongful approach will only generate hostility and will cripple the corrective movement the Sudanese mostly need to surpass the NIF's terrorist rule, which has ruthlessly destroyed the peaceful coexistence of religions in the multi-religious nation of Sudan.

Yusif 'Ali wrote in his <u>Translation and Commentary of the Holy Qur'an</u>: "The principles of inheritance law are laid down in broad outline in the Qur'an: the precise details have been worked out on the basis of the Apostle's practice and that of his Companions, and by interpretation and analogy. Muslim jurists have collected a vast amount of learning on this subject, and this body of law is enough by itself to form the subject of life long study."

There is no doubt that of all the monotheistic religions, Islam produced more rights to women than the *Jahiliya* or the world civilizations and situations that existed in the early centuries of Islam. Compared to the Greek, Roman, Persian, and Arab societies, Islam excelled as a great civilization as it granted the women the right to inheritance, child custody, choice of the spouse, participation in societal affairs, among many other important rights. The Holy Qur'an taught, "Mankind is made of one Soul."

The Prophet Muhammad taught, "Women are the "*shaq-a-yiq*" [equal sisters] of men." Many Muslim thinkers, jurists, or activists understood these teachings. However, they adopted ultra-fundamentalist views that deprived the Muslim women of the rights and meanings of the Qur'an, and the *Hadith*. Other Muslims adopted a nominal recognition of women's rights that was further undermined with a strong ideology of male-dominated gender expectation.

Recently, more Muslims began to appreciate the spirit of the Qur'an and the Hadith that emphasize the sisterly status and role of women and men on equal basis. After all, the most virtue that God wants mankind to practice is to worship God. This means the individual's God-fearing belief and activity, not the State's or political party's legislation or religiosity. Still, several schools of Islam, Christianity, or Jewish religious groups, in addition to African spiritual parties are not consistently supportive of women's status or role as an equal sex with the men.

Francis Deng, Talal Asad, Harold Barclay have earlier documented the low status of women in specific Sudanese Arab or African groups (See <u>Historical Dictionary of The Sudan</u>, Lobban, Jr., et al for detailed bibliography). In <u>Islamic Law and Society in The Sudan</u>, for example, Fluehr-Lobban (1987) documented the fact that Copts Orthodox Christian women or men are not allowed to divorce even if substantial reasons warrant the divorce and the further protection of their rights.

This note is meant to touch upon broad aspects of the subject, rather than a detailed study that professional jurists are certainly more competent to tackle than my general information and personal ideas might possibly do. The issue is very important because, like all other principles of Islam, it immediately arouses lively matters that are worthy of a serious discussion more than any simplistic propaganda or hasty evaluation. Reference is made to the concepts of "Islam and Muslims" rather than the terminology of "Islamism and/or Islamic." For this writer, Islam is the faith, the belief, and the religion whose source is the Holy Qur'an and Muhammad's authenticated Hadith. Muslims are all those who believe in Islam, irrespective of political stand, economic status, or any other criteria.

The Holy Qur'an realized the right of women to inheritance. Under Islam, women acquired an advanced status of inheritance that constitutes a significant basis to promote women's rights in the course of time. Recalling the pre-Islam women's state of affairs in many societies, the women have been deprived of the right to inheritance along with many other personal rights. Still today, the males worldwide are the ones who act with tremendous control over inheritance rights, save for a few cases of disputable wills that often end with fewer rights for the women than Islam firmly provided for them in the Holy Qur'an.

The recognition of women's rights in Islam is more humane than the dehumanizing denial of women's rights by the European-based Greek-Roman system, the Chinese "Yang" tradition, the Arab *Jahiliya*, or even the present time systems that the UN and human rights reports bitterly criticize. Still, many prejudiced persons launch poorly grounded attacks against Islam mainly because they fail to understand the promotional contributions of Islam to women's rights, as well as the other positive aspects of Islam.

Islam irrevocably assured the right of women to run their own businesses, own land, and take up public functions. Contrary to this historic advancement, European powers expropriated the right of African women to own land or to manage business. This policy seriously undermined the high status of the African women in South Africa and other colonies, as Fatima Ahmed Ibrahim, Nawal al-Sa'dawi, Ayisha Imam, Ifi Amadiume, and many other women writers affirmed. The national law, however, that applied the Qur'an rules of inheritance in Muslim societies, was a real savior for the Muslim women from such expropriation.

During the dark years of colonial rule, Islam unlike European laws, the Arab *Jahiliya* culture, or Asian customs, granted the right of women to act as independent persons. In the case of Sudan, for example, the British administration was not able to change the law of inheritance in Shari'a courts. A great many Sudanese Muslim women have been fully entitled to inherit, obtain dowry, own land, lead political demonstrations in the street, and run their own financial affairs way over the European women whose males were colonizing the country!

In Islam, women, more than men, are granted rights of protection and provision by the men, fathers or husbands. Men, however, are granted twice as much as a female gets in inheritance. Thus far, this rule has been used obviously to help males to perform the role of *Qawama* (provision for, care, and protection of the women and family). Although the *Qawama* principle appears gender-based, if a man fails to perform the *Qawama* duties, the woman is entitled to a legal divorce if she so desires.

The male gender-based dominating status is more prevalent in Western industrial societies, as well as the Third World agrarian countries or Bedouin communities, than it might be attributed to Islam. When a woman performs the role of *Qawama*, as is happening today in many instances, society must recognize the fact that she would be actually playing the role of a full guardian, rather than simply or temporarily replacing a male's status. This is an intriguing point for women's organizations to seriously consider the promotion of women's rights in Islam as independent humans.

Without a clear analysis of all these facts, it is unfair to throw a negative judgment at the system of inheritance in Islam. It is not enough to refer only to one part of the comprehensive and uniquely detailed verse of inheritance in Al-Nisaa. "To the male, a portion [is due] equal to that of two females" is not an absolute rule that is automatically applicable in all circumstances. A careful reading of the rules of inheritance indicates that in multiple cases the female might inherit more shares than a male might gain in other conditions. Verse 11 says, "If [they were] only daughters, two or more, their share is two-thirds of the inheritance; if only one, her share is a half."

Verse 11 of al-Nisaa Sura was revealed when the widow of Sa'ad ibn al-Rabi' came to the Prophet with her two orphan daughters complaining about Sa'ad's brother who seized all Sa'ad's property for himself. She was further aggrieved that her daughters would not be married without available property. The Prophet asked her to wait until a revelation would dictate how the case would be settled. After the revelation came, the Prophet asked Sa'ad's brother to give two thirds of Sa'ad's property to the two daughters, one eighth of the property to their mother, and only the remainder for Sa'ad's brother (Sayed Sabiq, Fiqh al-Sunna, Volume 3:424).

According to the inheritance rules of the verse, there are 12 individuals entitled to inheritance. These include 4 males, that is to say the father, the grandfather(s), the mother's brother, and the husband. The inheritance includes 8 women: the wife, the daughter, sister, half a sister whether born by one mother or to one father, a brother's daughter, and the grandmother(s). In the case of a person who dies "leaving a sister, but no child, [the sister] shall have half the inheritance. If (such a deceased was) a woman who left no child, her brother takes her inheritance." Here women and men are treated with equal shares.

"If there are two sisters, they shall have two-thirds of the inheritance (between them)." Here the sister women obtain more than all relatives of the deceased person even if they were all males "If there are brothers and sisters, (they share), the male having twice the share of the female" (*Al-Nisaa*, verse 176). Here, the *Qawama* rule is applied conferring provision, care, and protection responsibilities upon the male with respect to the female. By extension, a divorced woman who is not yet married is eligible to inheritance rights.

Other than these rules, Islam permits two additional avenues to realize the women's inheritance rights. One avenue includes the Will of a dying or dead person who may possibly allocate up to one third of the total property to a woman or a man. If the bequeathed property is more than one third of the total property, the heirs of the dead person must approve the Will before it would be implemented. Moreover, a Muslim who wishes to give a gift to his daughter or wife would find it possible to use the *Hibba* (gift) system, in addition to the prescribed rules of inheritance, to insure more rights to the women by discretionary power.

It is true that with the large entry of women into the labor market, the enjoyment of inheritance rights on the basis of the *Qawama* principle might encounter a negative dependency of women on the men. Nonetheless, until the largest majority of women would be able to exercise full enjoyment of equal rights with men as a legitimate goal, the ongoing struggle for the realization of the women's international human rights should utilize the rules of inheritance in Islam being recognizable guarantees for the women's rights.

The women must be encouraged to set themselves free from dependency on men. Education, work, income, active involvement in the community and State affairs, and advanced relations in marriage, the family, and the work place must be founded on mutual respect, equal pay for the same work, and human communication. The success of women in achieving these objectives is possible if all sources of encouragement are utilized. Islam, international human rights norms, and local cultures are all significant resources.

In the meantime, if the women decide to release the Muslim men from the Qawama requirements of protection and provision for the women and families, many positive "principles," rather than "rules," of women's inheritance in Islam will continue to influence the alternative or would-be system of inheritance. Why? Islam guarantees established rights for the widows, orphans, and the other helpless females. These rights should be insured and promoted, not reduced, as male-dominated societies consistently tend to impose today.

Based on these facts, it is far from the truth that women's rights in Islam are a source of antagonizing or restricting the women's struggle to acquire contemporary rights. Most important, male-dominated authority abuses the women's rights, as actual events indicate in Sudan and other countries. It is the failure of Muslims and Muslim critics to make fair assessment of women's rights in Islam that is jeopardizing the women's movement and rights, rather than Islam or the rights that Islam offers for the women.

This writer strongly rejects the exaggerated portrayal of Muslim women as women "enslaved" by Islam. Ibn Warraq and the other critics are advised to differentiate between the promotional nature of women's rights in Islam on one hand, and the Muslims' negative performance towards *Ijtihad* and social progression, which is the biggest violator of Islam in actual reality, on the other.

Speaking about the women's independence, I have to salute *the Suq al-Tawaqi* of Omdurman, the women's market that was located in the middle of the Omdurman market. It was a market of hundreds of women who were trading in a variety of goods including Chinese needles, turbans and local *tawaqi* (hats), as well as dates and fruits brought about by businesswomen from all over the country. Suq al-Tawaqi was a great manifestation of the Sudanese women's independence, especially the participation of elderly women. It was a unique tourist center as well.

Many mothers or grandmothers would send their children to sell home-woven products in the *Suq* (market), which was a direct source of financial resources. Seasonal businesswomen from the neighboring villages, or from the far northern provinces (for example, this writer's grandmother, Khadim-Allah and his aunt, Abdda of the Bawqa village) would sell local products to the *Suq* from time to time. The Suq al-Tawaqi women were pious Muslims with many of them pilgrims and firm Sufis. The Khartoum governor in the Nimeiri's rule destroyed the al-Tawaqi unique market a few years before the April Uprising 1985. That was a destructive action that grossly violated the women's rights.

The potential of women to participate in and to lead a public life is quite evident in Muslim communities. Women of the Sudanese Women's Union, members of the Algerian liberation movement, the Egyptian activists Huda Sha'rawi and Nawal al-Sa'dawi, and thousands of teachers, nurses, and other professional groups throughout the Muslim world exemplified this fact. It is the ignorance and/or mischievous behavior of men, whether Muslim or non-Muslim, which actually restrict or wittingly trivialize the sources of women's rights, whether Islam, international norms, or the two.

Many women in the rural side of the country have not benefited from the right of inheritance in Islam or even the other rights of education, participation in political life, and economic enterprise, etc. Asad studies on the Kababish, for example, documented the fact that Kababish Muslim males believe that wealth is strictly "male's affairs." So, there is no need for a woman to have wealth at all. Equally, Sudanese urban Muslims are not adequately interested in women's rights.

Many Sudanese groups share with the Kababish the same gender discrimination views that confiscate the women's civil status. Hundreds of cases in the Shari'a courts testify to the selfishness of the "Muslim educated" males who struggle with well-paid lawyers to expropriate the vital rights that Islam granted for the women to obtain fair shares of inheritance, maintenance, or child custody. Hence, there is an urgent need to educate Muslim societies about these rights with a view to enhance equality and social justice in accordance with international norms.

Compared to the inheritance status of women in the world systems that perpetuated great injustices before and after the advent of Islam, the right of women to inheritance in Islam is closer to egalitarianism than many other systems that only care for the male's status. This is why women's activists, for example the renowned leader Fatima Ahmed Ibrahim, appreciate the rights of women in Islam and call for their legal and social observance as a necessary step to promote the women's rights.

Ibrahim's strategy was practically workable in the Sudanese society whose Muslims constituted 80 percent or more of the total population and whose women were largely illiterate in the rural side of the country, in addition to the high number of women whose rights have been curtailed in the city. Despite meager facilities of the women's movement, a persistent state of male domination, and persecution practices by succeeding non-democratic regimes, the Women's Union did a good job educating the women and sensitizing society to women's rights in the last century.

In this century, however, a comprehensive analysis with detailed statistics is required to assess the social, economic, and political trend of change in the women's status. This social change assessment is crucial in light of the fact that the NIF government has negatively rubbed the women from significant rights and accomplishments for more than a decade. The NIF destroyed dear accomplishments of the women's movement.

The NIF curtailed the women's right to free movement in and outside the country, the right to work, and the right to compete for high status public service positions, etc. Although a distinguished woman of the caliber of Dr. Souad al-Fatih al-Badawi is appointed a presidential advisor, she failed as a conservative NIF leader to support the International Agreement on the Eradication of All Forms of Discrimination against women. Elaborated discussions indicated in the Darb al-Intifadah List in the International Internet (2001) that the Women's Union and the new women's organizations in the war-affected areas and rural Sudan must be encouraged to increase the slow progression of the women's rights.

Organizational and, most important, doctrinal challenges are part of the women's progressive agenda, as views by Sondra Hale and Nazik Hamad clearly revealed in the Intifadah List's discussion. Men's support is important. The tasks of planning and decision making to promote the women's rights with a full-scale secular campaign in companionship with the Women's Union's struggles that adequately recognize the contributions of Islam are equally needed. The two strategies, however, entail undeniable discrepancy in strategy and tactics, which needs further analysis and discussion.

Commentary on the Sudanese Women's Union

Fatima Ibrahim was the first elected woman parliamentarian in the Arab and African Region in the 1960s. She is a prominent opposition leader of the Islamic Front's rule of the Sudan and a distinguished international women's leader and human rights' activist. She has been repeatedly elected President of the Sudanese Women's Union and the winner of the United Nations' Human Rights Prize. Ibrahim is currently Chairperson of the United Kingdom-based Sudanese Committee for the Defense of Women and Youth against Human Rights Violation, in addition to other important Diaspora activities.

Throughout this commentary, this writer affirms that his views are not representative of Fatima Ibrahim, the Sudanese Women's Union, or the other concerned parties. The commentary is expressive of this writer's opinion as indicated in text, which might be agreeable or not to Fatima, the Women's Union, or the other women or women's organizations that this writer highly appreciate and respect without exception.

The first observation about Fatima's thought is that the Women's Union concentrated on the Muslim women. The Union did not pay equal attention to the non-Muslim women's population. These include the Christians and the believers in African religions of whom the Dinka women, for example, according to the scholarly research of Dr. Francis Deng, are not equally treated with men under the patriarchal system that is largely practiced among many other Sudanese population groups as well.

The situation of the Muslim woman in Sudan has remarkably improved in the last 50 years or so due to the educational attainment, women's entry in the modern labor force, and women's rights movement that succeeded in the political arena to a great extent. The SWU has definitely struggled more than any other group all over the Sudan – female or male – throughout the last half of the 20th century to raise the awareness of women about women's rights. The Union accomplished significant achievements that Fatima Ibrahim eloquently summarized in the work earlier discussed in the Epilogue on the women's rights in Islam. To acknowledge these facts whenever women's rights are mentioned is a fair credit to the SWU and its devoted leadership.

The challenge facing the SWU with respect to the social, cultural, and family rights that the state and society still deny and resist, nonetheless, is enormous. Under the existing NIF's rule (1989 to the present), the SWU has been facing the serious collapse of the 1960s-1970s achievements for which the Union struggled long decades to accomplish. Grave concerns include the NIF rejection of Sudan's obligation to rectify international women's rights, chief of which is the International Agreement on the Eradication of All Forms of Discrimination against the Women (CEDAW) and the other important international instruments.

The collapse of women's rights under the NIF terrorist rule equally includes the dismissal of thousands of skilled women from the state bureaucracy and the private sector. It also includes the persecution of a large number of poor migrant women, especially from the war-affected areas in the South and the western and eastern Sudan. These migrant women struggle in the informal sector to sustain their lives and the lives of their families with no assistance from state or society. Some of them sell the Sudanese popular diet, the *marrisa* (native beer) and other foods for the working poor in the industrial areas of the towns.

The police/metropolitan brutality against these women and their children or other family members increased under sexist assault by the NIF administrators who continue to destroy the Sudanese tolerant life with unprecedented abuse of religion and state powers. The women are in dire need of protection from the NIF authorities that mercilessly persecute them as "a religious duty."

The Islam that Fatima explained in her writing is the same faith that the 25+ million Muslim Sudanese venerate with the billion other Muslims all over the world. Huge differences, nonetheless, exist between the SWU use of Islam in community work for the promotion of women's rights and the authoritative Muslim groups that include the NIF, Muslim Brotherhood, Ansar Sunna, and the other orthodox Muslims. The emphasis Fatima placed on the ethos of Islam - a faith of justice, wisdom, and peace - is never shared or enforced by the NIF ruling groups or the other Muslim conservative organizations.

For sure, both parties are aware of the spiritual and social significance and the ideological influence of Islam in Sudanese society. Each party, however, interprets the same holy sources of Islam in accordance with their own political and ideological interests. The SWU affirms the rights of women in Islam and struggles for more. The NIF banned the SWU and further imposed in the Sudanese nation a terrorist version of theocratic rule based on outdated medieval experiences of Muslims that restricted women's rights to a great extent. The rights curtailed include the right of women to choose a spouse, travel abroad without guardian, practice a profession of their choice in the public or private sectors, among other restrictions of individual rights and public freedoms.

The SWU's stand with Islam is not comparable to the Muslim Brotherhood or the Ansar al-Sunna non-progressive thought. The Islam that Fatima and the SWU defend and want to be clearly understood and appreciated is the same popular Sufi

Islam that millions of the Muslim people of Sudan have been experiencing since old times. This is because Islam respects the individual's choice and public freedoms, and it rejects state meddling in people's personal faith.

With this shared appreciation of the spirituality and social impact of Islam on the Muslim women of Sudan, the SWU moved for 50 years or more with women struggling for their rights and the promotion of women's status in all aspects of the contemporary life. The SWU struggled for the realization of the ILO labor rights, CEDAW, and the other international human rights norms. The Union forged ahead successfully through a grassroots community-based movement that deservedly awarded the SWU the United Nations' Human Rights Prize in 1993.

Contrariwise, the theocratic law that the NIF leaders made and continue to manipulate against the Muslim and non-Muslim people is a harsh version of Shari'a law. Many medieval and also contemporary conservative jurists interpreted and enforced that version with state powers to lower the women's status as a major component of male-domination.

Based on the fact that Sudan is a predominantly Bedouin and peasantry society, Fatima (May 2002) wrote the following interesting information on the positive response of main Bedouin and peasants' traditional leaders to the SWU's ideas to liberate the rural women: "Have you read the message that Mr. Babu Nimr, the al-Missairiya Chief, addressed to the SWU... in his memories, which Dr. Fancis Deng translated to English? In that message, Babu wrote these words: 'Tell Fatima Ahmed Ibrahim that I granted the women of my tribe equal education to the men's education.' This message is a crown on the Union's head because it ascertains the acceptability of the Union's struggles and plan of action by the chief of a nationally and politically significant tribe. Similar to Chief Babu's support of the Union was the position of Umda Saroor al-Saflawi who awarded me a golden medal when I won election of the Constituent Assembly. Also, Umda Madibu, the Chief of the Rizaygat tribe who honored me with an invitation to meet with him when he visited the Capitol a little while before the military coup of the National Islamic Front."

The SWU's President concludes in the following evaluation of the SWU's strategies and struggle methodology: "This means that the Union's ways to achieve the equality of women with men have been acceptable to the '*umdas* (local administrators) and chiefs of the Sudanese tribal groups. This is a great success that ascertains the possibility of achieving the Sudanese women's equality were we able to remove the NIF military rule to put a final stop on the occurrence of military coup in our country, for good."

As far as social scientific research is concerned, Fatima's evaluation is particularly significant. A social change agent, the Union: (1) maintained mutual respect with the targeted population by acknowledging the cultural setting of rural Sudan and inculcating programs of change through this mutual cooperation; (2) collaborated with the local community and its leadership with a view to expand union activities; and (3) anchored the Union's promotional activity within the realities of the rural Sudanese underdeveloped structures.

This is a methodology that is highly appreciated by many anthropologists and the other scholarly experts in the areas of social change and development administration. In political terms, the SWU's methodology indicates the experienced methodology of the socialist groups that emphasized the appreciation of the culture and value system of society before an attempt was made to influence people's minds with new thought or action plans.

The SWU is required to increase the good work initiated and expanded for decades among the Muslim women. The mission is now more critical than ever before because the NIF rulers (1989 to the present time) distorted the meanings of the Sudanese Sufi Islam popular religion to become a discriminatory domain of the state. Equally important, the SWU must pay full attention to the non-Muslim women population whose rights have been largely ignored by state and society for long centuries.

Commentary on M. I. Nugud's Renewal of Women's Rights

This writer recalls Mohamed Ibrahim Nugud's work, Renewing the Program (Mahmoud, 2001). Nugud, the Secretary general of the Sudanese Communist Party (SCP), encourages intellectual women to study Islam to develop appropriate guidelines for the Muslim women. Nugud suggested such "academic work" would promote the women's rights. Nugud, however, did not specify the SWU in his call. And yet, this writer notes the Nugud's call connects with the efforts of Fatima and the SWU to establish a corrective movement to stop the NIF ruling abusers of Islam and their supporters from the ill practices and misconceptions of religion that negatively affect the women's rights.

In Fatima's thought, she came with a clear interpretation of Islam as a religion of peace, justice, and equality. Fatima, however, did not relate the success of women's movement with academic endeavors. Rather, she requires workaday popular activity with the poor women in particular – as the SWU has been consistently practicing – to pull up the women's status.

Nugud's handling of the Sudanese women's rights and issues reflects the SCP's half-century's concern with the women's movement. Soon after its inception, the SCP largely acknowledged and helped to develop the Sudanese Women's Union as an independent organization, not a party entity; a national activity established to defend the rights and to raise the political awareness of all women of the country. In the light of Nugud's deep concerns with religion and '*Aqida* (faith), that are best approached as community and individual preferences – rather than State affairs - the Renewal's ideas on women's rights and issues deserve a critical look.

First, Nugud calls for the activation of women's participation in societal affairs (State + society). He stresses in several places of his SCP Renewal Program the role of women as the "center of the family." Second, Nugud calls for the realization of women's rights in accordance with women's own struggles and organizations. This is a SCP old tradition that contributed a great deal to advance the women's movement of the Sudan. Although this writer doesn't know the size of SCP women's membership today, it is a great credit that SCP was a pioneering party in women's political leadership. The party, however, did not increase the women's movement in recent decades as the concern obviously went to the males.

Third, Nugud strongly criticizes the "*Harim*" mentality (that antagonizes women's enlightenment, economic and administrative participation, and political activity), the "*Takfeer*" (atonement) practices, and the other reactionary or backward policies and impositions by NIF or the other similar groups upon the women of the Arab and/or Muslim societies. Here, Nugud further holds that the women's rights must be developed as areas of scholarly social and political fields of interest, "not as issues of the religion's area."

In this writer's opinion, Nugud's classification observes the distinction between religion as faith (that is the most important fact about all religions) and the political and social contents that religious teachings might involve in the course of protecting or increasing faith. Nugud, however, stresses, "Women's rights should be applied *'dona masas bi usul al-aqida al-Islamiya'* (with full observation of the origins of Islamic Faith), as well as Christianity, or the generous African beliefs."

However, the "origins" of faith, whether Islamic, Christian, or African always raised serious theoretical and political problems when taken to State affairs. That is one main reason why human rights' societies separate between State affairs and all issues of *'Aqida* [faith]. Reflecting on the thoughts of Nugud to apply the fundamental issue of women's rights "with full observation of origins of *'Aqida*," a few questions might help to explain major aspects of such problems:

What school of Islamic thought would SCP adopt in the Nugud's Renewal Program to guarantee "full observation of *'Aqida*" while secularly struggling for the full recognition and realization of individual freedoms and the women's international rights? What if available interpretations fell short of the International Agreement on the Eradication of All Forms of Discrimination against Women? Would SCP then promote a specialized reconciliatory cadre to mold party's secularism with religious *'Aqida*?

What if scholarly theoretical and political work recommends the adoption of orientation or interpretation contradictory to the consensus of conservative groups that have continuously interpreted the "origins of faith" to favor male-domination? What if schools of thought disagree on the meanings or interpretation of origins of faith? What does it mean that the women's rights (Muslim or otherwise) "must be discussed in only political and social contents, not in the religion area? Perhaps, Nugud's needs to prepare an Explanatory Note or Exemplary Research on this part of his renewal to clarify the differences between the party's secular agenda (religion is not a State affair, but a community/individual concern) and Nugud's emphasis on *'Aqida* as a conditional reference of women's rights.

Earlier, 'Abd al-Khaliq's Program adopted a firm commitment to women's rights. 'Abd al-Khaliq wrote in his Program: "The National Democratic State must guarantee the Sudanese women full equality with men." This sharp statement is fully consonant with the Copenhagen Agreement, i.e., the International Agreement on the Eradication of All Forms of Discrimination against Women. This international agreement was later rectified in the 1980s after his extra-judicial execution in July 1971. 'Abd al-Khaliq statement appears at loggerheads with the conditional clause of Nugud's Renewal that, like the Charter of the National Democratic Alliance (NDA), subjects women's rights to the condition of Faith: "*dona masas bi al-adian* [religions]," as NDA partners wrote or "*dona masas bi al-Aqida*," as Nugud affirmed.

The NDA's and Nugud's conditional clauses remind readers of the 1995's Memorandum of the Sudanese Women's Forum (SWF) led by Zeinab Osman al-Hussain to the NDA Council's meeting in Asmara. The Memo expressed the protest of the Sudanese women, Muslim or non-Muslim, who spoke at that time for the Sudanese Women's Union, DUP, SPLM/SPLA, Umma, USAP, Nuba Mountains Abroad, and the Ramadan Martyrs' Family League. Many human rights groups and activists, including SHRO-Cairo, strongly supported the women's memo.

The women's political representatives required the NDA to guarantee full legal protection to the women's rights without limitation or condition. The women and the human rights organizations asked the NDA to recognize the International Agreement on women's rights. Equally important, they required Sudan Government to rectify the agreement without any reservation. The NDA did not timely respond to the SWF while the Sudan Government continues to reject the International Agreement.

Nugud's conditional clause is not supportive of the women's pressure on the government to recognize the agreement. Furthermore, Nugud's Renewal makes no mention of the International Agreement. The proposed commitment to the "*'Aqida*" clause in Nugud's Renewal colors the SCP handling of the women's issues and rights with a dogmatic mode - the very domain that Nugud cautions the SCP to avoid in theoretical as well as political terms in other parts of his project.

Is this the liberal transformation Nugud's Renewal seems to drive, or is it a most unfortunate reconciliatory trend with Sudan conservative majority groups? Even if Nugud might have been tactically providing for the party under the traumatic conditions of the NIF reactionary conservatism that is still plaguing Sudan, the tactic seems dangerous enough to warrant a corrective reply.

Apart from the Muslim or Christian fundamentalists, there are many groups that interpret religion teachings on the women's rights with contradictory views that deliberately confuse society's awareness about the women's rights. Many of these Muslim or Christian groups do not support the International Agreement on the Eradication of all Forms of Discrimination against Women. These groups exerted a great pressure on the sessions of the United Nations Conference on Population and Development (Cairo, 1994) to prevent the Conference from supporting the women's rights.

The Al-Azhar, the Vatican, Turkey, Iran, and many other conservative entities from all over the globe rejected most of the Conference proposals that supported the women's right to abortion, serious revisions of gender relations versus male-domination, the right to family planning, etc. To reject or reduce these strong demands of the world's women, the participant men who were in control of States and other power institutions were able to alter the main document of the Conference with drastic changes. '*Aqida* was the favorite and most influential factor that the men used and abused to roll back the women's struggles to enhance equality and justice in the social life. The same tactics were used in the Beijing Conference on Women's Rights later on.

The linkage of women's rights with *'Aqida* (faith) would continue to open the door for all kinds of interpretation that are not necessarily favorable to the women's rights or concerns. This exercise would continue to influence in a negative way the recognition of women's rights. It would certainly jeopardize the full realization of women's rights as stipulated by international law or the women's movement to insure full equality between men and women, political rights, cultural freedoms, etc.

Another example is that a great many Muslim writers condone polygamy with no assurance of the Qur'anic conditions or preferences that virtually cause polygamy to give way to monogamous marriages, if carefully interpreted. The women's right to choose a spouse without guardian pressure is another right that is not recognized by many parents or family heads who might be ideologically oriented to act contrarily to the interests of the women.

These are Civil Society concerns that should be dealt with on firm grounds of mutual respect, regardless of sex or race. State legislation must protect the right of women to run their lives without fear, persecution, sexism, discrimination, or racism. State legislation must not involve the State in *'Aqida* as a condition for women's rights.

The fact that conservative managers govern Muslim societies with unfair male-oriented legislation has consistently restricted the full realization of the women's fundamental rights. Instead, women are humiliated with betrothals and arranged marriages, divorced without rights, and subjected to persecution and humiliation for nothing but gender differentiation and the male-domination. The most recent case of the Egyptian human rights activist, Dr. Nawal al-Sa'dawi that has been judicially prosecuted to separate her from her husband based on a *Hisba* case, is a good reminder. Al-Sa'dawi's alleged crime was referred to her open critique of kissing the *black stone* of the Holy Ka'ba as unnecessary procedure based on a different religious interpretation from her prosecutor's.

Nugud's Renewal, however, includes positive suggestions. For example, he calls for "specialized studies on women issues by a devoted male and female cadre with the highest scientific and academic credentials and abilities of scientific research and production that is not exhausted by the workaday activities of masses' work to conduct the research."

Early in mid 1980s, the State application of Shari'a Law by the Nimeiri junta incited spontaneous as well as official public debates that strongly abhorred the September Laws that manifested an authoritative version of State intrusion in the matters of faith. Since then, the Sudanese public acquired a greater sensitivity and political awareness about the serious aspects of State's "religiosity," which manifests the State managers' economic, ideological, and political benefits rather than any ethical or moral orientation.

Nugud's proposal raises a serious question on whether SCP is calling for State religiosity, which is an extended version of the religious State that is watchful of women's rights in accordance with religious *'Aqida*. If that is the case, Nugud's Renewal as a program of progressive group should be asked to separate in the clearest terms possible between the "secular State" and "State religiosity" or "the religious State."

There are Muslim thinkers like Egypt's former Chancellor al-Ashmawi who made significant discussions on Islam and contemporary life. The socialist leader 'Abd al-Khaliq Mahgoub ascertained women's equality with men. The Islamic thinker Mahmoud Mohamed Taha emphasized women's equality with men on the basis of his Second Message of Islam. Perhaps the community studies that Nugud proposes in Renewal would strengthen the public awareness on religion as an individual value system rather than State legislation or law enforcement.

Based on this discussion, this writer feels that: (1) Nugud's Renewal needs to be sharply rephrased to endorse with no reservation the Copenhagen Agreement on women's rights, which is the contemporary minimum standard of women's rights and issues in our world today. (2) The "full observation of *'Aqida*" would not go hand in hand with the women's needs or struggles in the diverse nation of Sudan where religion is often abused or misinterpreted to favor male domination and gender relations. (3) The concern for *'Aqida* must be handled as a personal community issue for women or for men to decide for themselves, without any party pressure, State religiosity, or legal commitment.

A Note on Western Feminism

In general, the women's movements share common characteristics and objectives all over the world, in spite of the obvious differences of the environment and culture by region or continent.

In the west, American women were remarkably led by African American women, for example Harriet Tubman and Sojourner Truth (1850s) who as African women suffered racism and enslavement besides the gender discrimination that they publicly suffered with the mainstream white women.

In the 1950's, American women campaigned vigorously for women suffrage. The women's movement included traditional groups that preferred to work within the legal media institutional structure of the state and many reformist groups such as the National Organization for Women (NOW) that concentrated on equal pay for equal work, equal employment opportunities, and many other important rights.

Also related to the civil rights era of the 1960's and the 1970's, more women's radical or revolutionary groups focused on the emancipation of women from male domination, especially with respect to the sexuality of women, reproduction rights including the right to abortion, and lesbian rights. The two trends of the American women's movement contributed marvelously to the women's feminist independence from male-domination.

Still, while African American women demand greater emphasis on the eradication of racism to allow the Black male to find a better life in America than thus far attained, the white feminist movement emphasizes the psychological and sexuality liberation of women as a foundation to attain the other rights. The disagreement between women's groups in America is not clearly reflected in the Sudanese scenery.

The Kampala Women's Conference indicated that the newly established women associations are highly interested in structural political and economic change to stop civil war to insure the good life for the displaced population and the victims of war. This very emphasis dominated the conference discussions despite the fact that many women wanted to discuss personal status issues being an important reference to gender relations (see Iihsan al-Gaddal's report in The Sudanese Human Rights Quarterly, Issue 12, 2002, shro-cairo.org)

There is increasing awareness of women's sexuality rights in society besides the hardships of Diaspora life and the impact of western feminist thought abroad. It is apparent the main interest of the SWU is centered on the collectivity concerns of family life (maternity, personal status, etc), labor rights (unions), education, and health, more than the typical concerns of western feminists. These concentrate on the ability of a woman to manifest in her own right her personal determination, utilize talents, ascertain individual will, and exercise whatever plans a woman might have including sexual permissiveness with full freedom, as white males fully enjoy in western industrialized societies.

The rejection of white feminists to the domains that restrict this emancipation is not a consequential repercussion. It is a necessity and a concrete part of women's feminism that is based on the complete rejection of male domination, conservative religious and social thought and practices, and patriarchy as the major sources of women's suppression. The feminist movement, therefore, is seen as a threat to mainstream values in America, as it is seen as a social threat to the stability of family life and the struggle for male-female equality for collective goals in Muslim societies.

The sharp contrast in the area of interest between feminist western thought and the communal basic needs approach of the SWU has already started to grow, one way or another, in the main body of the Sudanese women's movement. The significance of both areas of interest, however, seems to compliment one another. And yet, the SWU and the emerging women's groups have not yet adopted a cooperative policy in this direction in any clear way.

The Sudanese Women's Union and Western Feminism

The Sudanese Women's Union (SWU), apparently the biggest and most politically experienced woman organization of all Sudanese women's groups as well as many other known women's organizations in the world, emphasize the attainment of women's political, economic, cultural, and family rights more than women's lesbian or sexuality rights. These latter rights, however, should not be sidelined or ignored in any human rights debate, this writer firmly believes.

The potential conflict between the Women's Union, which adheres closely to mainstream politics and Muslim society, and the newly established organizations, despite the meager information available for the public and researchers about them, is not small. It is growing in response to the structural forces of change, the information revolution including the Internet, and the negative impact of globalization that so far increased the deprivation of poor workers and farmers, especially the feminization of poverty among women and children all over the world.

The conflict is highly escalated under the terrorist ruling regime of the NIF that displaced unto Diaspora millions of the Sudanese men and women in very difficult conditions. The political strategies that the SWU maintained for half a century in unrelenting confrontation with reactionary regimes to be able to survive to promote the women's rights in a society largely poor and economically and politically backward are not increasingly questioned and criticized by new formulations of women's emancipation groups. The Muslim Brotherhood women's groups equally challenge the SWU's strategies. The Brotherhood has been coordinating with the NIF state and security apparatus to isolate the SWU or silence it for good, exactly as they did in the late 1950s and the early 1960s through the 1970s and mid 1980s in close collaboration with the Abboud and Nimeiri dictatorships.

The SWU is motivated to struggle for its very existence versus two challenging groups of the women's movement: (1) the radical groups that adopt western feminism, apparently, to expand among the educated elite, especially in the Diaspora and the newly established women's organizations in rural Sudan; and (2) the conservative, government-supported, Muslim Brotherhood groups and other conservative elements, the traditional rivalry of the SWU's since the late 1950s.

Observers notice that the public openly knows not a single Sudanese lesbian group because they, the lesbian Sudanese, have not clearly announced a lesbian organization to this day, although individual cases might occasionally articulate from time to time. The Muslim Brotherhood group and the radical women's groups attack the SWU. The Muslim Brotherhood group never hesitates to call on the authorities to harass the Union any time with whatever means they find available, as Fatima Ibrahim documented since the early 1950s in her book Hasadona fi Ishreen 'Ama.

The mainstream for the SWU is currently suppressed with state power by the Muslim Brotherhood elements. However, the conflict between the SWU and the feminist elements has been most recently polarized when the SWU issued a statement (UK, May 2002) emphasizing grave concerns for protecting the Sudanese mainstream from "western feminism invasion."

The SWU's struggle to stabilize and to increase women's rights is extremely difficult in the light of the ongoing state persecution and the organized hostility by both Muslim Brotherhood and radical groups. In her most recent works, the SWU

President emphasized raising community work and popular struggle among poor women inside the country and the SWU sympathizers in the Diaspora, as the SWU successfully struggled for since the early 1950s. Whether this same strategy would inevitably attract the main sections of the Sudanese workingwomen to join the SWU in and outside the country remains to be seen.

It is true that large sections of the Muslim community might not accept any corrective movement of the NIF and other conservative or even radical misconceptions of Islam through western feminist thought or Muslim Brotherhood indoctrination. The popular Sufi Islam society might only respond favorably to a corrective movement of the NIF terrorist and reactionary rule that provides a clear understanding of "the real Islam," in the words of Fatima a religion consonant with public freedoms, peace, democracy, and social justice.

The Women's Union is required to increase the good co-operation between its forces and the women's movement, especially the new organizations that successfully work for the same goals of women's promotion in their own right. Of these newly established groups, the Women's Kampala Conference (March 2002) emphasized the significant role that southern, Nuba Mountains, and Diaspora organizations played to promote women's status despite the situation of war.

The women's groups need to enlighten themselves with international human rights norms. The women need to appreciate the humanitarian method and the political struggle that made of the Sudanese Women's Union a school of women's advancement worldwide, hence the highest esteem of winning the United Nations Human Rights Prize in 1993.

ON THE PROGRAM
'Abd al-Khaliq Mahgoub (June 1971)

(*) We define specifically our aims of reviewing the Program:

a) We do not want to design objectives in a mechanical way, i.e., the process of sorting out what is being achieved of the ongoing Program and the evaluation of what remains to be achieved is dialectical and inter-related.

b) We conceptualize our aims for the stage of the National Democratic Revolution at a time the concepts and aims of this stage are laid out by the petty-bourgeoisie strata. Some of these conceptions and the aims in question are wrongful and false. Therefore, our Program will be presented in a high level of both ideological and practical context.

c) The conception of the horizons, features, and fundamental issues of socialism from a communist point of view is different from the petty-bourgeoisie thought.

d) The Program will attract in this way the Democratic Forces to the communist point of view in this stage and the struggles of these forces for the achievement of the aims, as specified in the Program. The SCP conception in a deeper course of [implementing] the Marxist-Leninist [thought] includes the attraction of large social forces towards the Socialist Horizon. Thus, the process we are up to using constitutes the gist of our revolutionary thinking and experiences. It tests our abilities to apply the communist method on the reality of the Sudanese Revolution.

(*) We begin by specifying the main issue of the Democratic Revolution, the issue from which all the other issues of this revolution branch out. I think the cause of the Economic Revolution (development) is that link.

The main strategic enemy of our National Democratic Revolution is neo-colonialism and the semi-feudal bourgeoisie alliance at home. The main target of the National Democratic Revolution is to strengthen and develop national sovereignty. [The achievement of this target, however,] is impossible without economic advancement and the installation of an industrial-agricultural society.

a) With that installation, Sudan will be free of the danger of neo-colonialism domination. Sudan's international economic relations will be utilized for the benefit of the Sudanese People and the enforcement of Sudan sovereignty.

b) With this installation, the internal forces that in the service of colonialism destroyed our national sovereignty, the Economic Revolution and the avenues it takes, the forms it creates, and the social forces it develops are issues that are not restricted to the economic development alone. These [issues] constitute the decisive factors [of the final result]: either national sovereignty or neo-colonialism domination.

- The Economic Revolution of our under-developed society does not deal only with technical issues of the economy (technology) within the limits of developing production forces (the basis of society). The success of the Economic Revolution requires a confrontation with the issues of political, social, and economic change.

The increase in productivity rates of the advanced industrial societies nowadays is made on a technical basis (technology, etc. This increase doesn't mean that the economic crisis of the capitalist society is not any more centered on its capitalist social system. In the world today and in the less-developed nations, there is no way available to increase development rates such that the masses would be saved the suffering of poverty and pauperization. There is no way without facing the issues of social, political, and economic change (social structure), and also dealing directly with the super-structure of society.

- In order to develop the forces of production (the Economic Revolution) it is a must to:

(*) Liquidate all production relations that inhibit development.

(*) Establish a political authority that consists of the social forces beneficiary to that Revolution.

 (*) Establish intellectual, legal, and philosophical institutions in congruence with this social change, etc.

[A careful treatment of] the absence of the Economic Revolution, henceforth, is the most critical approach to tackle the fundamental issues of this stage.

THE DEMOCRATIC ECONOMIC REVOLUTION

We start with a corrective conception to the dimensions of this Revolution from the economic side, the regular measures and figures of economic development in our world today. The Democratic Revolution economically requires the growth of production forces up to the level that makes the transformation of production relations of the next stage (Socialism) an off-spring of the urgent objective needs of development, in accordance with the individual needs and the will-power of the working classes. The industrial-agricultural revolution had to spend centuries to score that level. With the conscious determination of the working classes, this period of time was reduced in the Soviet Union (The New Economic Policy). (This of course doesn't mean that the New Economic Policy placed the Soviet Union at that time at the same level of the production forces of capitalist countries. But I meant to say that the policy of the National Democratic Revolution achieved sufficient growth to enter into the stage of socialist installation).

The Economic Revolution - as such - aims to build an advanced industrial and agricultural Sudanese society. This questions the theory of attaining possible progression to move towards socialism through a society that limits its industrial activity to the production of consumption commodities (Chapter II). We believe that the task of building up heavy industries (Chapter I) is a determining matter for the upbringing of society as it moves into the real context of the Economic Revolution.

I. Dealing with the Problem of Economic Surplus

This is a social-economic problem. We know that it is possible for the under-developed countries to invest almost 12% of its Gross National Product in productive investment (or in industry and agriculture). This, however, will not be accomplished without investing in the "potential" economic surplus.

The development of this surplus requires a revolution in the national production relations such that the exploitative social classes would be eradicated (with consideration to the political aspects). The robbery of this surplus by foreign capital must be completely stopped. The State must play its role as an economic agent to develop the country according to the demands of planning, financial and tax policies necessary to utilize the potential surplus, etc.

Let us find the surplus within the economic formations of our country. What are these forms? Where is the potential economic surplus in them?

(*) *In Agriculture*

1. The capitalist agriculture of the Northern Province, especially the gardens (of Kassala, DarFur, Khartoum) and the seasonal mechanized agriculture.
2. Semi-feudal-capitalist agriculture in the large-scale schemes of the Northern Province [region].
3. The small-scale production of the Nile banks.
4. The state capitalist agriculture that includes the cotton schemes of al-Gezira, al-Managil, the White Nile, and the Blue Nile (agricultural Reform Schemes).
   These four branches could be amalgamated under the cash economy's agricultural umbrella or what we call in our country the Modern Agricultural Sector.
5. The animal husbandry-agricultural formation: This is the subsistence economy sector that doesn't fall under control of the cash-commodity economy. [It consists of]: (a) Mixed animal husbandry-agricultural formation, and (b) Animal husbandry.

Among all these formations the semi-feudal ownership should be confiscated whenever it exists (cattle of the animal husbandry sector and the animal agricultural sector). The other semi-feudal relations must be abandoned.

a. This is a source to grip the potential economic surplus of agriculture. As it is not a target now for the Sudanese Revolution to eradicate capitalism, it must not take measures to monopolize the economic surplus that is controlled by that class. Instead, [the Revolution] should resort to:

. Impose different taxes on these classes to transfer part of their economic surplus to the State. This needs application of the so-called progressive taxes and a flexible tax collection department over-penetrating the whole Sudanese society.

c. Curb the capitalist exploitation of the schemes that already suffered from capitalist development, especially after the [Sudanese] October Revolution [1964]. In the Gezira Scheme, for example, the State must control all agricultural machines to provide tractor services to the farmers with class-oriented prices. Small farmers would receive these services with prices much less than those paid by the middle-class farmers or the rich farmers. This should equally include the irrigation services of the Northern Province as well as tractor services in the mechanized agricultural regions, etc.

d. On the Capitalist Industry: This comprises the small capitalist workshops (crafts) that spread all over Sudan and the factories that eventually surfaced with the initiation of the capitalist boost (The Ten-Years' Plan).

e. Class-taxation policies and price-control by the State play a decisive role to transfer part of the economic surplus to the State for industrial and agricultural investment.

On Distribution and Services

All distribution, in addition to a sizable portion of services (transport, restaurants, etc.), is vested in the hands of different capitalist strata.
[Suggested policy] is the same as in (d).

Foreign Capital

Here we mean western capital or the so-called "Arab" capital. What concerns us are the stands undertaken and the measures that do not generate a considerable economic surplus outside the country that, in turn, increase poverty and decrease the economic development projects. It is important to re-invest part of the profits, according to the development schemes, and to spend part of the earned profits inside the country with local currency to energize the Sudanese economy (Industrial Investment Act).

Between Consumption and Investment

The potential economic surplus that must be transferred to investment depends on the proportion accruing of the difference between total consumption and investment. This also is a social, political, and economic issue.

(*) We have to observe:

a. The fact that food in Sudan is abundant. The first step for the Economic Revolution is to care for this sector (agriculture and animals) to provide for [needs] of the working people, especially the city population and the working class that is responsible for the installation of an industrial society. In the present time, the working masses in Sudan live in famine or on the verge of it (less than 2200 calories per day). This is not conducive to economic activity. It is essential that the State guarantees via economic activity special price policies (not price censor that is difficult to apply in a country with a partial [informal] market as Sudan is, but sufficient price to the producer and reduced sale price for the working masses). This insures an adequate share of these important food materials with suitable prices to raise the income of these masses.

b. Specifying the [optimum] level of the basic needs of citizens will help to design an importation policy guided by class-specific economic principles. This means a sharp reduction of luxury commodities and the incorporation of those that have already become necessary commodities. The ongoing policy on the basis of the basic year (1951) is outdated. The awareness of the working masses increased with struggle as well as benefits and aspirations. The [suggested] procedure would decrease the consumption rate of the National Income and increase investment. It will equally supply all necessary materials of the imported commodities.

c. [To eliminate] unproductive expenditure, especially the spending on State bureaucracy:-

- Close the gap that exists between State ranks by evaluating jobs on the basis of a viable economic criterion.
- Change the education curriculum to include technical and vocational education in all stages to direct the graduates toward production centers, reduce unproductive employment, and stop unplanned migration to the city - thus developing the village - in addition to the firm application of construction plans and the absorption of trained personnel.
- Consolidate the exercise of democracy so that the masses would be able to defend the Homeland with their organized initiatives. This will save the huge expenditure that is now spent for the security forces, especially the army.
- Re-structure the State apparatus on a democratic basis and appropriate participation of the masses in State affairs. This will reduce the costs and weaken the position of the bureaucracy that usually increases State spending.

(*) Adopt a flexible and realistic investment policy in the different fields of the services that:

1. Provide for the basic needs of the masses.
2. Cater to the new needs that develop out of the successful achievement of development projects.
3. Advance with an unlimited rate to the advantage of every citizen while observing the population increase, on condition that the proportion of productive investments increases in the Gross National Product.

4. Consider the services that influence production (roads, water for the settlement of nomadic groups, etc.). This should be economically utilized (selecting the right sectors to modernize transports, launching an organized campaign instead of the random or disjointed effort to eradicate thirst, and spreading water-wells as economic units), etc.

The policy of expanding services (that was corruption by political parties in the past and a false idea of social change in the present time) without striking any balance in production [relations] does not serve the Economic Revolution or our political conditions. It caused in the final analysis a complete stoppage of the necessary services (as was the situation following the failure of the Ten Years Plan up to now).

(II) The Organization and Development of Production Forces

(*) The economic and social processes that deal with the development of the potential economic surplus are concerned with the task of transferring production investment to promote the production forces in the direction of accomplishing the Democratic Revolution through a non-capitalist path of development. All this prepares the objective terms to bring about the socialist social relations (The Socialist Revolution). This orientation, therefore, involves a social, political, and economic process that is both comprehensive and complex.

(*) The success of these processes rests in the handling of the problems encountered in each economic formation, individually and efficiently, such that the final overall result would lead to the comprehensive revolutionary democratic change of the society.

(*) The build-up of heavy industry demands in the first place the setting-up of the industries of energy and minerals, trained personnel, and the availability of the infrastructures of these industries. The efficiency of these factors will create a viable developing industry that is capable of providing proper consumption commodities. This will be achieved by solving the problem of industrialization and consumption, [i.e.] the problem of economic development, with consideration to the proportional increase of the masses' living standards. (The experience of our country in the area of making consumption industries "Chapter 2" without the infrastructure in question ascertains the fact that this type of industrial production is performed at the expense of the masses as it reduces the real input of the masses).

Because this industrial sector is strategic for the total processes of economic development, and it represents the industrial sector as a whole, the State must take responsibility for installing it in a comprehensive and absolute manner. This of course is a difficult mission. However, our international trade relations, particularly with the socialist countries, will relieve the difficulties if we apply an alternative policy that allows a perfect, slow, and gradual activity.

The earlier policy with regard to consumption industries failed since it was first implemented within the Ten Years' Plan:

(a) It did not liberate our national economy from dependency.

(b) It did not lead to the production of cheap-cost consumption materials to help promoting the living standard of the masses. The masses were burdened with the high profits the capitalists reaped (The Act for distinctive industries and their protection).

(c) Due to the escalated increase in the price of industrial commodities and the global reduction of the price of primary agricultural commodities, we continue to suffer the high cost of these industries, etc.

(*) [We have to] enforce a complete change in the current magnitude of Chapter 2's Industries that only established a few workshops for light industry. (A) These industries must move in a new direction that aims to place the agricultural industries (agriculture, animal husbandry and fishery, woods, etc.) in the front [line of industry].

1 - This grants a better marketing to our products, and it will develop our National Income to face out the problems of economic wealth.

2 - It will provide in-depth broader training to the workers and technicians, the backbone of industry.

3 - It will help to solve the problem of diversifying the Sudanese economy, especially in the cotton cultivation.

(*) To avoid [transferring] to this New Industrial-Agricultural Sector the negativity of agricultural growth, as inherited from colonialism and the succeeding rule of reaction classes (here we mean the cultivation of cotton in a large scale while neglecting the other agricultural sectors):

1 - Intensify the capitalist investments of the sector.

2 - Distribute the industry on a geographical basis with consideration to the economic and social requisites. (The developing tribal groups and nationalities and the existence of a workers' class all over the Homeland will decisively work out the issues of the revolutionary social development in this stage and the next stages, etc.).

(B) Orient the consumption industries to produce the commodities that would be considered necessary within the framework of the renewed living standards. This means that the production capacity of these commodities consistently widens in light of the enlarging social needs as the more developed production forces and productivity rates become.

- "Chapter 2" on industrialization with its two branches will act as an arena of State activity and the middle-range capitalism. But the capitalist production will be directed by the State and supervised by State price policies and class-specific taxation.

Before all, we face at this point: (1) Weaknesses related to the enlightened Sudanese middle-range capitalism that is interested in industrial production. (2) The parasitic nature of this class that obviously articulates in the concentration on the distribution sector, estate, and a few services (transportation, restaurants and recreation shops, etc.).

It is expedient for the National Democratic State to adopt a dual policy to be able to move this class into industrial production [by means of]: a) Attraction policy based on flexible cash-generating planning, etc., and (b) State intervention whereby the State enters the unproductive traditional areas of this class (proper housing policy, expanding State role in transport and internal trade, etc.) to force it to move to the industrial activity.

(C) In our under-developed country with its scattered markets, there is a spread of many crafts. The capitalists who supply these industries with raw materials largely exploit the owners and workers (and sometimes they exploit them in the marketing of the products), in addition to State escalated taxes on the raw materials, trade licenses, etc. All this subjects the working and consuming masses to exploitation. This sector plays a significant role particularly in the Sudanese village economics.

(*) The State must assist the sector [by measures] to:

a) Facilitate borrowing with easy terms.

b) Reduce taxation on raw materials and trade licenses in a radical way.

c) Direct these groups to organize in production and marketing cooperatives.

III. The Agricultural Animal Husbandry

This is the [major] entry of the Industrial Revolution of our country because in the agricultural and animal husbandry sectors lies our national wealth from which the economic surplus is extracted and must be re-invested in the installation of the New Industrial-Agricultural Society. The success of this sector evidently determines the endurance of the Revolution.

(*) Enforcing a radical transformation in the subsistence economy of this sector such that the production relations will be renewed to achieve a high living standard to the working masses and a surplus adding to the national surplus for investment.

(*) Strengthening the cash-crop policies in this sector in various forms. Chief of these policies is the State role in the distribution process to supply the working groups of this side of our national economy with different industrial and consumption commodities and to purchase their animal and agricultural products. The [effective] presence of the State will remove the impact of the parasitic brokers who control part of the economic surplus and the price of products. This is equally a social necessity to help unite the nationalities and tribes and to disseminate the spirit of cooperation between these groups (most of the brokers nowadays are related to the Arab Nationalism that gave rise to prejudices and hostility at times).

(*) Increasing the animal wealth, incorporating it in the cash-crop economy by the Nomad's Settlement, and modernizing the mode of production:

A – Providing for water-wells and distributing them in an economic way to act as production centers. Changing the map of the dispersed population by the abundance of population settlement and production locus around the wells. This includes the provision for (1) Drinking water 2) rains for the cultivation of animal food, (3) natural graze under scientific supervision, (4) forage stores, (5) light industries and crafts, especially for animal products, meat and milk, etc, and (6) the services that up-grade the living standards of the working masses and develop their wealth.

B) Eradicating the harmful tribal habits that inhibit incorporation of the animal wealth in the cash-crop economy (between Southern tribes, Nuba Mountains, etc., where the animal wealth is maintained as a symbol of social esteem and pride):

1. By organized intellectual work among these groups so that transformation occurs through the masses' spontaneous acceptance of the New Society and its values.

2. By the lively example that the groups involved in the New Settlement Life [practically] offer.

3. By up-scaling the level of necessary commodities (the consumption level of the masses). This appears contradictory with our aim to extract economic surplus for development. The contradiction is apparent and is temporary. Most of these groups satisfy their basic needs less than the minimum acceptable standard (less than 2300 calories per day). They depend sometimes on natural products (fishery and forests in the South). They rarely come in contact with the market (cash-commodity). The promoted and broad exercise of the new habits would convince the masses to abandon the old habits in order to utilize their animal wealth and agricultural products (if available) in the circle of cash-crop transactions.

285

(C) Insurrecting a wide movement of awareness to organize these masses in the production and marketing cooperatives in which the State plays a role of encouragement and guidance (This is a result of the severe under-development of our country). The State has to encourage the masses with the spirit of work and discipline as important practices that are necessary for the promotion of production forces. The State:

- Assists the cooperatives with different bank loans.
- Reduces the price of industrial machines as needed to develop and modernize the production.
- Adopts in all these measures a class-oriented policy that aims to up-grade the life of the poor and small producers to the level of the middle-range producer. This enhancement will not only lead to the advancement of production forces. It will also create the objective conditions to establish collective farms and build the socialist society.
- Enforces the Technological Revolution as a large-scale process that incites the presence of specialists and experts.

(*) The Revolution in the Modern Agricultural Sector with its four components as earlier mentioned refers to:

1. A change of production relations in a way compatible with the existing stage of democracy to open the path for the growth of production forces.
2. A class-oriented policy to raise the status of the small or poor farmers to the status of middle-range farmers.
3. New formations developed with the socialist mode to become a firm basis of the socialist transformation of our country.
4. Increase in the productivity of the land and the worker. This needs revolutionizing the machines, fertilizers, etc. It also means diversifying the Sudanese economy, reducing the agricultural manpower, and turning it to the industry.

These objectives will achieve:

a. Up-scaling the living standards of the working masses, hence insuring the existence of a market for the industrial products.

b. Making a large surplus for investment in the Sudanese new advanced industrial and agricultural society.

c. Providing the industry with the necessary manpower.

d. Curbing the capitalist growth by developing a new basis for the next socialist development. This guarantees the achievement of the Democratic Revolution's aims. It means entry into the stage of socialist installation.

(*) [In the case of] confiscating the semi-feudal capitalist lands of the Northern Province [region, or districts] to replace them with farmer production cooperatives, the redistribution [of land] must satisfy the needs of the poor small farmers. The State must take the same steps as earlier mentioned to make success of this New Economic Formation by applying bank loans, reducing taxes, prioritizing transport and shipping, optimizing the prices of machines and fertilizers, etc. This formation will increase the dynamics of the non-capitalist agricultural development and is the nucleus of the Socialist Revolution. It is the framework of training the masses to exercise the democratic economic administration.

(*) In the same direction, through persuasion, revolutionary work and experience, the small farmer production of the Nile banks will be part of the agricultural cooperatives.

(*) Necessary measures should be undertaken to curb the capitalist rush that was boosted in the State capitalist agriculture with the collapse of the [Sudanese] October Revolution 1964. The State must:

1 – Provide services for the agricultural machinery.

2 – Adopt a class-specific tax policy to up-scale the status of the small poor farmers.

3 – Check over the abuses of distributing land allocations [al-hawashat] and redistribute the outcome among the poor farmers.

4 – Re-organize the State-farmer's partnership. (a) Specify a production average to fix the existing partnership. (b) Locate the State-farmer's shareholding of the production average on a class basis that aims to increase the small farmer's share. (c) Make a graded system to gradually increase the farmer's total share over State share on condition that the small farmer's returns consistently exceed those of the middle-range or rich farmers, and (d) Improve the labor conditions of the farm workers, including specific minimum wages.

(*) Review the laws of the Mechanized Agriculture's Corporation to insure stoppage of the dominating capitalist growth of this sector.

a. Convert part of the schemes to State farms.

b. Place the other section, especially the regional schemes of the indigenous population (Nuba Mountains), into possession of the production cooperatives of local inhabitants with the necessary aid.

(*) The New Agricultural Formations

The growth of the production forces of agriculture does not rely only on the necessary agricultural social and economic reform measures. It presupposes expansion of the cultivated land. The non-production arable land constitutes a high percentage of land in our country. What is important is to observe the fact that in utilizing this land: (1) Most of it is a public property. This should help to make new production relations and agricultural formations. (2) The land needs an advanced system of irrigation with high capitalist investment.

(*) These factors determine as an economic requisite the establishment of State farming a new pattern to reinforce the non-capitalist Democratic Revolution. State farming creates vital tissues to facilitate the next Socialist Installation. Additionally, this new pattern offers more economic surpluses to strengthen the position of the State in the processes of economic development. The Managil-Gezira Scheme formula that was founded by the capitalist state is not the only pattern of the Agricultural Revolution of our country. We must not remain captive of this pattern. State farming is more progressive in social, political, and economic terms.

(*) The production and marketing cooperative is a new economic and social formation that operates with guaranteed State guidance and intervention - at times - to develop the organizational structure and to strengthen the spirit of discipline and work. In this area, there is an urgent need for the political action and persuasion of the masses. The experience of cooperatives in the past was limited and disfigured. It led to the control of capitalist elements and more exploitation of the working farmers.

The final result of this revolutionary operation that will convert our existing under-developed society into an advanced industrial and agricultural one aims to: (1) Develop the production forces to secure national independence and continuously improve the living standard of the working masses. (2) Complete eradication of the production relations that handicap the restructuring of our society on a revolutionary democratic basis chief of which are the semi-feudal relations, tribal lineage relations, and subsistence production relations, and (3) Curb the spontaneous capitalist evolution and insure State and cooperative leadership of the national economy. All this will create the objective conditions for our country to move into a socialist industrial and agricultural society.

(IV) Main Elements in the Installation of Advanced Industrial-agricultural Society

The National Democratic State plays a significant economic role to achieve the previous tasks. As top agenda, Planning acts as a prominent means to boost the potential economic surplus and direct investments towards the realization of the final social, political, and economic objectives for the advancement of this stage.

A) With the application of Scientific Planning according to objective conditions, the State directs the course of investment and controls the distribution of the economic surplus in between the production and services sectors. This [distribution] will insure a large evolution of the production forces besides the promotion of the masses' living standards.

B) The State develops society according to a variety of economic plans. Each plan comprises a complete program for social, political, and economic work at a specified period of time.

C) Planning invests in the enthusiasm of the revolutionary masses that are aware of the stage objective and their own input. This enthusiasm is an important economic factor in the ongoing conditions of our country. This New Consciousness is also a means of exercising democratic censorship on production, participating in the specification of Plan objectives, and liquidating the bureaucratic administration that is an obstacle to the reduction of production costs.

(*) The State designates the financial monetary policy to achieve these economic plans. Thus, the State transforms the Annual Budget to a flexible tool to:

a) Extract the necessary surpluses for production and services investment.

b) Change the Annual Budget always according to the growth of the Gross National Product (GNP). The Annual Budget's dependency on the direct and indirect tax must be reduced annually as these taxes are a burden from which the working masses most suffered. These taxes further express the state of exploitation and backwardness that must be eradicated. The Annual Budget must excessively depend on the external surplus of the State productive and commercial activities.

c) The State puts forward a monetary policy to serve the purposes of development planning. Full consideration must be shown to avoid the inflation that hurts the lives of the struggling masses.

d) Taxation should be directed in a class-specific way in the service of the social, political, and economic objectives of Economic Development.

e) The State directs the external trade (importation) with priority to the importation of capital commodities and adequate importation of the best-quality basic consumption commodities.

(*) Economic and trade relations play an important part to help achieve the Economic Revolution in our under-developed country with respect to the importation of industrial capital commodities, technical expertise, etc.

(a) Our Revolution is national and democratic and aims to establish an industrial and agricultural society in a non-capitalist path [of development]. The success of this Revolution means it has to move on to reach out to the horizons of the Socialist Revolution and the contemporary realities of the world today. We rely mainly in our economic relations on the international socialist society, especially the Soviet Union as the most advanced partner of that society.

(b) Economic cooperation that involves the countries of the National Liberation Movement must be enhanced. This cooperation for sure will be mostly based on Trade, as all these countries are under-developed. They cannot help us with industrial capital commodities or advanced technology.

(c) We should understand the situation, as it exists concerning the capital received from capitalist sources (western capital, private institutions or State's, or the other international agencies - the World Bank and its agencies, the Arab Oil-Producing capital), etc.

(A) These capitalists are not a reliable source for the execution of the major revolutionary tasks we are pursuing. They decide for themselves the areas of investment most of the time. Still, they refuse to contribute to heavy industry. They emphasize the right to decide freely on the disposal of their capital principal and profits.

(B) They play a major role spearheading the neo-colonialism objectives to stop the socialist transformation of underdeveloped countries, strengthening the capitalist elements, and using all twisted ways [for that purpose].

(C) For these reasons, we must pursue all forms of international cooperation to develop our nation.

Fully aware of the social and political nature of these capitalist sources:

(1) We, accept whatever is not contradictory with our national sovereignty and the aims of our national democratic development with the guarantee of fair compensation in the case of implementing procedures that develop our country in a non-capitalist way.

(2) The Sudanese Democratic State specifies the areas of capitalist investment to the capitalist sources.

(3) [The State] reinvests part of the profits within the framework of the [State] Economic Plan, and

(4) {The State] guarantees the training of Sudanese cadre in institutions of the capitalist source.

THE DEMOCRATIC CULTURAL REVOLUTION

(*) The advanced agricultural economy does not spontaneously develop a comprehensive cultural democratic revolution. This revolution comes with consciousness and planning. It comes via the lively experiments and emulation of the other experiences of mankind in the field. In truth, this revolution also represents a social and economic factor that must be utilized to achieve its construction. It is not reasonable to reconstruct our society in agricultural and economic terms in the midst of the illiteracy that is surrounding it in the present time. It is impossible to build socialism without awareness and a comprehensive and specialized science. Thus our Cultural Revolution is based on the following concepts and elements:

(1) The complete eradication of illiteracy in the country by:

A) The effort of popular democratic organizations including youth unions, students, women, and intellectuals of the regular professions, workers' intellectuals in labor union, etc. This will increase the enthusiasm for the new social values. It will respect the free democratic initiatives of these groups. With that, the organizations will become an effective powerful force in the field. The revolution will spread in expanding cycles, one after another, starting with the circle of production centers, industrial, agricultural, animal husbandry, etc.

B) The expansion in the foundation of regular education, including the schools' moving with the Bedouin nomads until they settle.

(2) Changing the curriculum of regular education such that:

A) The pupils can learn all types of knowledge in our country's education system with the aim of developing the new specialized intellectual in a comprehensive manner.

B) Students in all stages of education must acquire practical fieldwork (industrial and agricultural) to be incorporated in the village life. Hence, they will contribute to the development of production forces and the political and social input of the agricultural sector. Thus, we avoid their split from the village [life] and the unplanned migration to city for employment, etc.

C) Encouraging scientific aptitudes in education will help to establish and train a competent cadre to lead the Economic and Cultural Revolution.

D) The cross-fertilization of human thought in interaction with the progressive trends that believed in the future of humanity and the abilities and dignity of mankind [will be largely advanced]. In addition, the new cultural renaissance of our country that aims to resurrect the new Sudanese who is free of fear and estrangement will not succeed and flourish unless it depends on this progressive and humanitarian perspective.

The enlightening scientific thought is representative of this perspective. It is the spring that supplies the perspective with the elements of life and vibrancy. With scientific thought, the Sudanese will be free of the fear of nature and the ignorance that stamped the Sudanese life and took it prey for social exploitation. It is under this false consciousness that the *Al-Fuqara*'s [pious healers] institution grew in the northern part of our country and became a means of robbery and exploitation. The African magic maintained its influence in the Homeland's south and in dispersed parts of its west.

The Sudanese who is free of these factors, free of fear, and is part of the world of knowledge where humans are centered as the most generous being, will build the advanced industrial and agricultural society. The liberation of the working masses from this fear and the social institutions of this fear will not be completed with legislation and compulsion. The liberation will come about with the dissemination of workaday awareness, with the Cultural Revolution that springs out of the roots of society and shakes it from bottom to top with a loud movement. It is the victory of the democratic determination, the awareness and consciousness of the Masses. Consciousness is based on the freedom to choose and to come closer to the truth. Compulsion, legislation, and the curtailment of choice are not part of the means of knowing the truth.

(3) The new Sudanese who is open to the Cultural Democratic Renaissance will develop the needs for integration, unity, projection, and the enjoyment of the pleasures of life. With fine arts, humanity finds the source of beautifying its existence to move away from animal life to the effective life of humanity. Our People have continued to make their arts throughout their civilization progression. Arts developed at times but went down at other times according to the social, political, and economic circumstances that encompassed the processes of artistic creativity. This connecting thread, nonetheless, continues to penetrate deep inside the life networks of our People. It has bonded the Arab and African civilizations that produced the popular arts' production that is wrought by the laypersons and is received by the Masses in their workaday life. (This includes sculpture, dancing, songs, music, etc.)

The movement of the Sudanese intellectuals who are influenced by the incoming European beauty norms since the days of the colonial rule and the aftermath were not able to delve deeply into the depths of popular arts to re-establish them to meet the contemporary needs of our People. Developing their own laws [of evolution], the tools of each movement were acting separately from one another.

The Democratic Revolution in our country will take up the responsibility of rising up this new art to continue developing all that is humanitarian and progressive in the popular artistic creativity, that is to give rise to the heritage in the conditions of constructing the new society. These conditions pertain to the deterministic global conflict between the cultural trends that believe in mankind and the trends of reaction that degrade the status of mankind to that of an animal with no future but a predatory life.

This resurrection will only materialize in accordance with freedom and democracy and a stance undertaken by the National Democratic State to assist and encourage, not to coerce or to suppress. The critics of the subject or the object of artistic work are the competent critics and the conscious public. With the insurance of freedom to the works of art, hundreds of creative artists will emerge from among the Masses, and millions of the Masses will receive in a creative way the artistic product.

The State must provide for the material conditions of this arts' renaissance (theaters, studios). The State must provide the opportunities for knowing all international arts. The good ones will survive to develop the knowledge of our People. The bad ones will wither away.

(4) Scientific Thought is the fertile soil to grow the tree of the Cultural Democratic Revolution in our country. It requires the availability of freedom and democracy in our society. It represents the most serious component of scientific institutions, universities, research centers, etc. The science that pursues the truth and exercises freedoms cannot be attained in a climate devoid of freedom.

The National Democratic State is founded on science. It does not develop, sustain, or succeed in the process of taking our society into socialism if it depends on the falsification of the social or natural sciences. It will develop when it depends on the discovery of facts that transcend to a decisive power in the fields of social revolution and the leadership of the Sudanese Society to socialism through the most secured ways. [The facts] will become a powerful force in the fields of natural sciences to increase the ability of our People to control nature and to utilize it for prosperity of the working masses.

- Based on all this, the National Democratic State guarantees the freedom of scientific research to all our society, especially in universities and research centers. The State provides the conditions necessary to spread freedom and democracy in these institutions. With this concept and framework, the independence of universities and research centers will be deeply entrenched.

  - The freedom to impart and to exchange information will be insured for these institutions so that they will be aware of the new sets of knowledge of the global order.

(5) The Sudanese intellectuals of the known regular professions will play a prominent role to widely spread the Cultural Democratic Revolution. They are able to play this role because the traditions and experiences of the revolutionary struggles of our country placed the majority of this social stratum in the lines of the Sudanese revolutionary democracy. This started with the students' movement that directly developed after World War II and the revolutionary democratic organizations (democrats and communists) it produced.

Through this Cultural Revolution, the intellectuals of the Sudanese working class will effectively emerge as a known group, together with the struggling Masses. These modern specialized intellectuals will interact with the older strata of the intellectuals. They will unite with them to achieve the objectives of the Cultural Revolution to continuously enlarge the new circle of the working class and intellectuals of the struggling masses. Hence becomes the process of culture and thought in our society, one deeply rooted in our society's cells.

(6) Because this Cultural Revolution is 'democratic' with the full meaning of the word, it is important to correct all our concepts, stands, and the backward traditions of our society that reflect the ensuing results of the societies of exploitation and coercion under which we suffered for centuries. The most dangerous of these concepts and positions is what relates to women and the national and tribal groups.

The National Democratic State must guarantee the Sudanese women full equality with men. This legal equality must be converted [the text, here, is incomplete in the original document] for the revolutionary evolution of production relations, and to promote the values and orientations amidst the forces of advanced agricultural production.

Concerning the national and tribal groups that are lingering behind with respect to the Cultural Democratic Revolution:

(*) The free growth of the cultures of these groups must be practically encouraged.

(*) There will be no effective growth of these cultures unless the languages and dialects of these groups are focused upon and the National Democratic State seriously develops these tools and uses them in education (according to educational experiments in the field) and in the comprehensive cultural renaissance.

(*) These cultures must be part of the organic elements of the Sudanese Culture.

DEMOCRATIZATION MEANS A COMPREHENSIVE CHANGE OF LIFE
IN OUR COUNTRY

The Revolution will not reach the socialist horizon of our country without completing the tasks of the National Democratic Revolution, democracy in production relations, the political rights of working masses, and the political system. The experiences of all successful social change revolutions in this century starting with the Great October Revolution in Russia and the post WWII revolutions in Europe, Asia, and Latin America informed us that the only bridge to cross over to socialism is that of democracy. The other experiments indicated that when a section of the petty-bourgeoisie, that defaults in satisfying the historical prerequisite of changing society via comprehensive and sustained democracy, endeavors to lead the movement of social change, there would be a complete failure to take society to the doors of socialism.

(*) The Democratic Revolution begins with the eradication of the old version of production relations that handicapped the development of production forces in this stage and is an obstacle to the independent uprising of the working masses. These old and backward relations are practiced in the production relations that reflect the deep penetration of classical colonialism as well as neo-colonialism in our national economy, the semi-feudal relations of the animal husbandry and agricultural production, and production relations of the subsistence economy. ([This revolutionary process should] curtail the growth of capitalist relations such that capitalism would not develop to a mastering system, i.e., [the process has to] keep the capitalist growth within the limits of middle capitalism according to State planning policy).

(*) This Democratic Revolution dictates the growth of new production relations, according to achievements of the Economic Revolution with continuous observance to the advancement of democratic relations that molds in the final analysis the Democratic Revolution and opens the path for socialist development. The weakening of capitalist relations must be closely observed (although capitalism might have grown up during the process of eradicating the old production relations and the working out of new relations). This will take place through the growth of [the New] State production relations, production cooperatives, etc.

(*) The conscious implementation of democracy in production centers requires the establishment of production councils with legislation, participation of the working masses in the administration of economic and administrative units, etc. Effective participation must be ensured in accordance with the free democratic desire of the working masses and their class organizations (unions, associations, revolutionary committees, cooperatives, etc.).

- This is an investment in raising the rate of productivity and increasing the Gross National Product. It involves training and practice of the working masses to establish the material foundation of the People's Authority, and to help the masses' march in the path of integrity and vigilance (prohibiting estrangement).

- It prevents the growth of the bureaucracy that separates the executive productive instrument from the masses.

(*) The National Democratic Order is based on the expansion of all the benefits for whose attainment the People struggled and some of which they had already acquired. The succeeding dictatorships that governed our country sometimes expropriated all of these benefits or partially confiscated them in other times. The right of the working masses to political, economic and cultural association, publication and information, etc., must be fully guaranteed. The National Democratic Revolution provides the objective conditions for the working masses to convert legal rights into practical enforceable rights. The Revolution provides for the material elements and constitutional legislation. (Arming the working masses constitutes an advanced material element in this process).

The Sudanese Revolutionary Democracy adopted a position in this serious cause that is particularly vital to the future of our Homeland by:
(a) Understanding the development of the Democratic Revolution throughout the political history of national movements, in a critical and analytical way.
(b) Appreciating the final result of the evolution of the Sudanese People's Movement and its experiences in this regard.
- Bourgeois Democracy made a great leap in the history of nations, exerting the effort to enjoy self-rule and paying dearly as it unfettered the chains of many feudal systems. But the Bourgeois Revolution did not liberate mankind to move from the arena of needs to the arena of freedom. That occurred because it brought about a democracy based only on the freedom to own and the division of society into haves and have-nots on the basis of private property. This aborted the movement of freedom and democracy. [Democracy] was only incarcerated in the framework of legal rights and equality, thus devoid of the real context of rights: equality and democracy. These [values] were announced [only] as legal rights not as practicable rights. At this point, the evolution and advancement of mankind up the ladder of social progression continued the struggle to take uprooting changes in the Bourgeois Democracy from legality to effective law enforcement.

Socialist Democracy represents this very transformation because the liquidation of the capitalist private ownership brings about the necessary material conditions to exercise political rights. By placing the authority in the majority domain of the working masses, the Rule of People will be realized, and the optimum conditions to stop the perpetuated estrangement of this majority will cease to occur.

Moving society to a high social stage doesn't negate at length the legal rights that the national movement accomplished during the Bourgeois Democratic Revolution. It doesn't mean a liquidation of the political rights of the masses.

- The experiences of our People in this concern inspire us with rich lessons. The semi-feudal bourgeoisie that controlled the means of production managed to manipulate all institutions of mis-guidance, lethargy, and sorcery, especially among the farmers. It made of the political rights, for the most part, nothing but a legal promulgation.

In spite of this, the Sudanese revolutionary democracy and its social forces that maintained advanced political consciousness succeeded in the process of exercising these rights to enhance the Revolution in our country. The unions of working classes changed the life of workers, economically and politically. These were the farmers' movement and the rise of their unions in the 1950s, the progressive and communist Press, the positive impact of the SCP [realized] legitimacy in the October Revolution, student movement organizations, the Sudanese Youth Union, the Sudanese Women Union, professionals associations, etc.

In the first months of May 1969, following the fall of the semi-feudal bourgeoisie rule, the struggling masses sustained the new authority with their enthusiasm and the exercise of political rights in the midst of the most serious reactionary counterrevolution. This happened despite the incomplete application of the political rights of the struggling masses. (The continuous confiscation of SCP legitimacy by the Republican Order No. 2), dissolution of the Revolution

Protection Committees that sprang out of the revolutionary spontaneity of the masses, the non-taking of measures to change production relations to guarantee the enforcement of political rights, etc. The attack was further launched with the November 16th, 1970 measures against activities of the democratic masses. Political freedoms were prohibited. The result was that the voices of reactionary forces were loudly heard all over the country as they acquired the right to organization (National Committees, Village Committees, etc.).

The Sudanese revolutionary democracy expressed sound understanding and conception of the effective rights of the masses through their long struggle vis-à-vis the reactionary persecution of the nation (especially the six years of the reactionary military rule 1958-1964). The masses have analytically evaluated the social and economic factors that handicapped their [movement] and the exercise of political rights and freedoms. These forces raised after the October Revolution 1964 the motto of "Revolutionary Democracy" that figured out as a critique of the bourgeoisie democratic system of rule, the distorting form of the democracy applied after defeat of the Revolution. It was a dialectical critique based on objective rationality.

The major events our country witnessed when the forces of reaction dared to confiscate the right of the working classes to political assembly by outlawing the communist party of these classes (late 1965) made the climax of a political process with significant implications. What did the repercussions of these events that overwhelmed the whole regime and led finally to its demise indicate?

The [exercise of] political rights, as experienced through the masses' awareness of the targets of the Democratic Revolution in our country, is a weapon in the service of these masses with no use to the forces of reaction that receive it with hostility and act to destroy it. Hence, the revolutionary processes of social change and the democratic change started to overlap in our country, especially in the course of these events.

(*) The semi-feudal bourgeoisie alliance failed to establish a stable political system while these political rights were exercised. (The Islamic Constitution Bill embodied the Program of these forces that was clearly inimical to the political rights - a document of political bankruptcy, etc.).

Based on our critical analysis of the experiences of national movements and the rich experiments of the movement of the Sudanese People, the National Democratic Revolution will achieve the necessary conditions to transform political rights from a legal promulgation to an effective exercise of the struggling masses. These rights represent the main tool of rising up the political activity of the masses so that we'll have millions of politicians aware of the development of the creative and superior abilities of the Revolution.

We also move on [in our struggle] according to our understanding of the Revolution as the highest level of popular creativity and spontaneous achievement. We do not accept the concept of patronage over the masses' movement. The guarantee for the continuity and growth of the National Democratic Revolution is the vigilance of the masses and the growth of popular activity not that it stands aloof to show admiration or disenchantment. It is the millions that make history, not a few individuals whatever competence or miracles they might have. Democracy and revolutionary change are thus correlated and are inseparable.

(*) The political rights of the struggling masses under the National Democratic

Rule include the right to political assembly. We offer with our experiences and studies organizational forms for the struggling groups as they realize aims of the Revolution. But the masses while liberating themselves from the times of negligence, spontaneously move and create forms of organization that are a thousand times greater than any political program could possibly conceptualize.

The struggling masses, therefore, have the right to political expression based on their own interests, the right to create economic and political organizations expressive of their sentiments, and to protect and reinforce the National Democratic Revolution of our nation. This applies, in particular, to the working groups of the sectors of agriculture and animal husbandry on whose vigilance hinges the whole destiny of the National Democratic Revolution.

The communist workers' part of the Sudanese revolutionary democracy is not prejudiced to the creative establishment of the means of change and organization that the struggling masses form throughout the process of revolutionary change. The reason is that these masses do not anticipate any predestined future other than socialism. They do not yearn for any future but the future of socialism.

The strata and classes that fear the entry of the Democratic Revolution unto its final stage are afraid of the march to socialism. They are the ones who are horrified of the exercise of the Sudanese working classes' political right to organize their Marxist-Leninist party. It is a class organization that is independent economically and politically. It is the instrument of organizing the best children of the struggling People to decisively lead the Democratic Revolution and to build the socialist society.

The struggling masses of the farmers are allies of the workers class in the Democratic Revolution to achieve the next installation of the socialist society.

The alliance is built on free choice and contention, with democracy. At the same time, the workers class is the only of its sort that would increase members via different stages of the National Democratic Revolution. It is the only party to which the majority will gradually move on, the more our country steps forward to establish the advanced industrial and agricultural society, and then to install the socialist society. It is hence the true democratic class because it is not afraid of the future, but is part of the movement of history that continuously moves forward.

(*) The National Democratic Rule will use all its means and powers to destroy resistance of the forces and strata of reaction to stop any attempt from their part to return to the centers of power and influence. The National Democratic Rule, therefore, represents the wide democracy of the struggling masses, the dictatorship that suppresses resistance of the strata and forces of reaction. This implementation springs from:

a) The legitimate right to defend the Revolution and progression in the face of the forces of backwardness and reaction.

b) Our understanding and the experiences of our People in the various forms of "democracy." This understanding and these experiences ascertain that there is not any "general" or "absolute" democracy.

-   Democracy was always class-specific. Earlier, the "parliamentary democracy" was practiced. But it carried nothing except the dictatorship of the semi feudal-bourgeoisie alliance. Nowadays [June 1971], a "revolutionary" democracy is enforced; that is nothing but the dictatorship of the petty-bourgeois military strata, etc. The National Democratic Rule carries its own context and is expressive of the total class interests it bears.

c) The truth is that this dualism [of class-specific rule] is practical. It doesn't only relate to our theory on democracy. It is a practical procedure to prepare the conditions necessary to sustain and exercise democracy by the vast majority of People to be further enjoyed by all.

(*) The National Democratic Revolution guarantees the exercise of the freedom of religious beliefs, indiscriminately, to the whole population on the basis of these facts:

- The human conceptualization of the self and its integrity and the future of humanity are issues that spring out of contention. No force would be able to impose its determination on a human soul in this regard.

- Apart from agreement or disagreement between religious beliefs, social classes adopt positions in the Social Revolution according to their own interests and whether they keep pace with the movement of history or are backward from it. The social human determines that position, not the religious belief.

- The National Democratic Authority rejects any exploitation of religion for the interests of the reactionary classes in our country that struggle to perpetuate outdated production relations. These reactionary classes abuse religion to exploit people and strip their human dignity. This exploitation is contrary to the interests of society. It antagonizes the best future that humans form with their minds and hands as they move from the level of needs to that of freedom.

- The exploitation of religion in this manner has degraded religion, exploited the struggling workers, and kept them in a miserable condition of ignorance and darkness. In this rotten swamp, the social parasites of sectarianism, lethargy, magic, and sorcery proliferated and supported the colonial powers. They lately supported the semi-feudal bourgeois rule. The evidence for the harm ensuing in the history of the Sudanese political movement is indicated in the process of distorting religion and transforming religious call to a complete program (the Islamic Constitution) in the service of the capitalist path of development and dependency on neo-colonialism.

THE POLITICAL SYSTEM

The National Democratic System of rule will grow out of the democracy that would be penetrating all tissues of the political, social, and economic life of our country. The National Democratic Authority is not separate from the struggling popular masses. It doesn't place itself as an alternative of the activities of these masses, or their creative work.

The authority is part of the masses as it springs out of their creative activity, and it becomes instrumental in the hands of the masses to achieve their interests and the aims of their revolution. With this, a State apparatus that is separate from the masses, specialized in ruling, suppressing the people, and curtailing their initiative, does not represent the National Democratic Authority.

The authority depends in its foundation on the democratic organizations. These are built by the masses as a means of struggling for the establishment of the Democratic Authority first, and secondly for the new organizations that the masses establish while a new modern life is constructed in political, economic, and social terms.

The democratic masses of our nation continue to struggle for the establishment of the New Authority. The masses organized in democratic institutions, for example the workers' unions and the other unions, the Sudanese Youth Union, the Farmers' Union, the Sudanese Women's Union, socialist associations, student democratic front, tribal leagues, the progressive Press, etc. These organizations and the organizational forms that the masses establish would be the democratic basis of the New Authority.

The New Authority would truly be the closest democratic authority [to the People] in accordance with the masses' experience. The thousands, to begin with, followed by millions, who would awake to the significance of [political] organization and the objectives of the Democratic Revolution would be the force to direct the ruling system to achieve the democratic view, i.e., " People rule their own affairs."

The forms of bourgeois democracy that the reactionary systems previously applied in our country distorted democracy and debased its foundation. The public opinion of the masses was not appreciated until lately, after the passage of long years. That occurred in elections that only shackled the vote with heavy social and ideological chains. After elections were over, the affairs of our Homeland would rest in the hands of a few senators and ministers.

When the petty-bourgeois military group seized political power based on the revolutionary struggle of the masses and their sacrifices, it disfigured the slogan of Revolutionary Democracy. It confiscated the democratic institutions that the masses built with sacrificial efforts in a quarter of a century of continuous struggles. It replaced them with hollow institutions devoid of democracy and fully dependent on intelligence work. With these practices, the basis of authority was largely narrowed in the country. It fell down to the bottom of a dictatorial rule that is patronizing the masses and is terrorizing them.

Contrary to this is the Democratic Authority that will not survive without increasing democratic activity among the masses. It only lives through the spread of democratic organizations that explode the energies of creativity and welcome [the participation of] any democratic organization that embodies a section of the People. This is how democratic national unity would be achieved by the organized consciousness of the struggling groups as it provides the solid basis for democracy.

Our country will be liberated from the class-oriented bureaucracy of the Bourgeoisie State. All in all, every union of these organizations, together with the national democratic personalities, will make what is known in the Sudanese political life as the National Democratic Front with the complete independence of these organizations. It is the popular organization of the masses as founded on democracy and is fed with the roots of democracy. Hence, it flourishes in spite of the difficulties of change and construction.

The forces of the National Democratic Front consist of the working class and the farmers' masses with their different strata. The Front includes the intellectuals who maintain honest stands towards the Homeland and who are part of the revolutionary democracy, the middle and small capitalist strata that work in the fields of distribution, industry, and crafts, and the suppressed nationalities that could only be liberated by democracy and socialism.

Within these forces, the alliance between the workers' class and the struggling farmers acts as the heart of the matter because they are the forces capable of building the advanced industrial-agricultural society for the transition to socialism.

The workers' class occupies in this democratic union the front position. It does not impose this position forcibly. It moves to occupy it with high organizational abilities and the role it plays to establish the National Democratic Authority. It is qualified for that role with the sacrifices it always suffered without any selfishness to build the advanced industrial-agricultural society.

The movement of history and the available lessons, up to this point, ascertained that no social class is ever capable of taking a decisive stance in support of the tasks of the National Democratic Revolution other than the workers' class. It is impossible in historical terms to build a socialist society without the leadership of this class, under its own system of rule. Therefore, every step that the Sudanese workers' class takes to step forward in the front line of the revolutionary democratic movement is a guarantee for the victory of the revolution. It is a re-enforcement of the non-capitalist transformation with which our society will adopt socialism.

A class alliance inside our country will be a foundation of our national democratic unity. A class alliance abroad will guarantee our national freedom and the final triumph of the Democratic Revolution towards the transition to socialism. This latter alliance means we have to observe in all our moves that we are part of the revolutionary anti-imperialism international front. Imperialism is the staunch enemy of the aspirations of our People for freedom and progression. We are part of the Front that includes all socialist nations and countries of the National Liberation Movement and the working class movement for the sake of peace and socialism. This is the Front upon which history conferred the task of liquidating capitalism and eradicating all its evil, colonialism and war.

The democratic system of rule was victimized by the State bureaucracy problem of our country. Most of the State employees emphasized their experiences (October, graduates elections, stands against the counter-revolution, and the rule of the petty-bourgeoisie strata). They, however, generally approach the positions of Progression. Notwithstanding, the foundation of State bureaucracy and the legislation that governed it contradict the objectives of disseminating democracy and the installation of the new democratic society.

The movement of the Sudanese Revolution launched several attacks at the State bureaucracy to transform it to a democratic apparatus. The need to purge the administration was raised in the October Revolution 1964 [that overthrew the military rule of 1958-1964] and also when the reactionary rule was overthrown in May 1969. This is not an uprooting solution, however.

The events that erupted after the [Sudanese] October Revolution indicated this result when the State bureaucracy, according to its formation, reproduced once again large bureaucratic forces in connection with the reactionary classes. Corrupted bureaucracy grew in new State apparatuses such as the public censor, custodial agencies, and some institutions of the public sector, etc. Therefore, we believe:

(*) The Democratic Front's institutions must play a prominent role in all production sites to direct the performance of the State bureaucracy on the basis of democracy, popular participation, and supervision.

(*) All civil service laws that protect the State from censorship and criticisms must be reviewed with the aim of systematizing democratic supervision over it. Continuous training must be undertaken to the cadres with respect to technical work and the bondage with popular activities.

(*) Conscious work is required to promote the status of revolutionary democratic forces in the State bureaucracy to be part of the processes of democratic change and a tool of the National Democratic Revolution. In this direction, full utilization of all competent and honest Sudanese technicians and specialists must be ensured. The national democratic system of rule and the democratic revolutionary forces of the State apparatus have the capacity to offer political leadership. They are able to make use of the efforts of these technicians to install the New Society and to train the New Democratic Caliber.

The cause of State bureaucracy figures out in its serious form when we handle the issue of the security forces, the army and the police. Here, the issue is not confined to the democratic construction of our country. It goes beyond that to the whole security of the National Democratic Authority and its survival. This requires implementation of the procedure and processes that would tie up the State with the democratic movement of People, the eradication of the negative factors that perpetuated the bureaucracy and made the State apparatus an instrument of suppressing the popular movement and intimidating it.

(*) Revolutionary Committees of soldiers and non-commissioned officers need to be set-up in all units. The mission of these committees is to disseminate awareness on the aims of the Democratic Revolution and to care for the soldier welfare with cooperatives, trust funds, and life in the Camp. These committees will act as an instrument to improve the living standards of soldiers and the non-commissioned officers. The officers will [only] handle the technical military affairs.

(*) Officer-soldier relations need to be strengthened by joint living arrangements and sharp social distinctions eradicated by means of [intensifying social] interaction in the same club, restaurant, etc.

(*) The laws that humiliate the soldiers and non-commissioned officers and have given rise to the feelings of frustration and bitterness that demoralized the spirit de corps must be changed.

(*) The intelligence departments should be directed to put under close surveillance colonial activities and reactionary conspiracies. The intelligence apparatuses must be placed under permanent supervision by the political leadership and the rule of law. All criminal elements of these agencies must be purged and sanctioned.

(*) The National Democratic State will have constitutional institutions that should be led by the House of Parliamentarians as a national institution. We solemnly believe that the House must truthfully represent the masses as a basis of the democratic socialist rule. All citizens must have the right to elect their representatives. The accomplishment of this goal is consequentially related with the level of production forces and the spontaneous development of the masses.

The masses and the classes aware of the aims of the Democratic Revolution that [further] participate in the struggle for the National Democratic Authority will enjoy the exercise of this right as it starts off. The circle of participation will be enlarged the more that new social forces awake and take part in the movement of social change when it would be liberated from the influence of reaction and backwardness.

The National Democratic Authority will be completed to reach full executive capacity of its goals as the struggling masses organize to exercise with competence the right to representation in a revolutionary national democratic direction.

(*) The New Parliamentary System will be founded with full consideration to the aims of the Democratic Revolution and all major criticisms and protests of the revolutionary democratic forces while they struggle versus the bourgeoisie parliamentary system and the petty-bourgeoisie military dictatorship.

(*) This system of rule in the climax of its triumph over backward production relations, and the growth of the New Democratic Production Relations, will be expressive of the spread of democracy. It will express the political rights of the struggling masses and the strenuous work to promote the State apparatus in a democratic way. It is thence a New Parliamentary System that is expressive of the Sudanese revolutionary democracy.

(*) The New Parliamentary System will place the legislative and executive authorities in the hands of the struggling masses. Through its systematic linkage with the process of spreading democracy in the tissues of the Sudanese life, this system will resolve the contradiction we have always known between the legislative authority and the executive authority. (That contradiction is embodied in the context of the bourgeoisie parliamentary system) when the legislative authority turned into a hollow figure whereas governance rested in the hands of executive groups in the cabinet, State bureaucracy, administration of the economy, etc. The masses will participate in the executive work. They are the only upper authority of the legislature.

(*) The Judiciary of the National Democratic Authority will be founded on these principles:

- The honest and just enforcement of national laws and legislation.
- Enjoyment of impunity within the framework of revolutionary democracy, without any inducement or intimidation.
- The goal-achievement of the Judiciary will aim to maintain democratic revolutionary legitimacy to sustain the rights, freedoms, and tranquility of the working classes and the security of their creative work in the present and future times.
- Unification of the Homeland on the basis of democracy. This will be achieved with the development of the abilities and cultures of the different national groups with freedom, without intimidation or suppression. On the top of these agenda is the problem of the South. The National Democratic Authority will put to task the autonomous rule for the South as called upon by the revolutionary masses.

Evaluating the experiences accumulated since the announcement of the June Declaration (1969), the opportunity to successfully complete this issue will move the working class to put forth the issue of self-determination to national groups in the stage of the socialist installation. We are confident that the success of the National Democratic Rule in accomplishing autonomous rule will lead to the exercise of the right to self-determination by the masses of our national groups, especially in the South, in the framework of socialism and the Sudanese Socialist State.

With the completion of these tasks, a material political and cultural foundation would be prepared to move our country from the stage of the National Democratic Revolution to the stage of Socialist Revolution.

- The standards of production forces will reach the level of a comprehensive installation of the advanced industrial and agricultural society that would allow entry into the stage of prosperity, i.e., the just distribution of the national income in accordance with the labor and production input of every citizen.

- The new production relations will mature as they convert from democratic relations to socialist relations that will not allow any capitalist exploitation. The complete transformation of society will take place on the basis of socialist production relations.

- The workers' class will exercise the leadership role of society with which the new political system, the New Socialist State, will be installed by the alliance of the struggling masses as is led by the workers' class. Society will thus be transformed and installed according to the socialist democracy and its spread over all tissues of the Sudanese society.

- The forms of this alliance, organizational methods, and the forms of socialist democracy depend on the experiences of the stage of the Democratic Revolution. In this concern, the speech by F. I. Lenin that "People build the socialist construction their own way and will contribute with a new form of democracy" will eventually materialize.

- The characteristics of the Sudanese Socialist Society that distinguish it from the other socialist systems are unpredictable at this moment, except for one dimension; that is, the general backwardness of our country and the impact it exerted on the Cause. These characteristics will emerge out of the features of the stage of the National Democratic Revolution and the ability of the

Sudanese revolutionary democracy to apply the scientific method in this period and to discover what is really unique in our Homeland.

- Note: I believe it is important to show in this chapter on socialism its main characteristics as an economic and political system, as well as a cultural and social revolution, etc. Let us concentrate on the need to clarify these features that have been disfigured by the times of distorting socialist slogans. This is an issue that you know, more than I personally do.

(Signed)
'Abd al-Khaliq Mahgoub

NOTES ON THE PROGRAM
M. E. Mahmoud

In June 1971, the Sudanese distinguished writer and socialist thinker 'Abd al-Khaliq Mahgoub, wrote behind the bars of the political detention where the May military junta had been incarcerating him inside the Khartoum's *al-Shigara* military camp, his last and most intriguing document <u>On The Program</u>.

What particularly concern this writer in the translation of this document are these important facts:

(1) 'Abd al-Kahliq Mahgoub addressed himself to his political party, for sure. The ideas he presented, however, were not confined to any partisan or national limits. The context of his ideas is humanitarian. Hence, 'Abd al-Khaliq Mahgoub's ideas are specifically democratic and are universal in essence. This writer further finds 'Abd al-Khaliq's thought most relevant to the contemporary challenges the Sudanese State and society are facing in the present time. This fact further makes his ideas a significant source to handle the escalated crisis of the Sudan today, in light of the ongoing conditions of the terrorist plight the theologian state of the Turabi's party, the National Islamic Front (NIF), brought to the country.

(2) The reference by 'Abd al-Khaliq to a New Sudan, New Society, New Intellectuals, New National Democratic State, etc. in his June 1971's document is much older than the references that emerged in the Sudanese arena in the aftermath. It is therefore an interesting field of research to compare the two sources for authentic knowledge, as well as practical terms, in subsequent research.

(3) <u>On The Program</u> was a progressive projection of the Sudanese Democratic State, the national tasks it is meant to implement, the forces of production the State should mainly support, the economic, cultural, and political policies it must pursue, and many other important issues of State policies and management. His ideas were an organic part of the contemporary literature on the State as a class-instrument that prevailed in the political arena of Third World Countries in the Cold War Era, for example Ghana, Tanzania, Guinea, Algeria, Chile, Egypt, etc.

(4) 'Abd al-Khaliq, however, was a brilliant critic of the experiences of these nations. He made a great effort to utilize the knowledge acquired through these experiences to suggest, and struggle for, the most appropriate reform program to the Sudan, the Homeland he loved most of all. His thought rejected the one party system of the socialist-transformed Egypt, Algeria, and the others. But he strongly supported the anti-colonialism principled stands of these nations and the honest, zealous, and strong commitment to the needs of the poor and the needy their States exercised to free them from economic dependency and foreign domination.

(5) It is oversimplification to imagine that the intellectual origin of 'Abd al-Khaliq's thought is strictly socialist-oriented or only Marxist-Leninist. His thought is complex: it is founded on SCP literature, the long decades accumulating fieldwork contributions by Sudanese workers and peasants' unions, Arab and African ideals, experiences of national independence and socialist transformation, etc. Of all these sources, the component of Sudanese experiences and field research constituted the largest part of 'Abd al-Khaliq's theoretical works and life experiences.

(6) There is a general assumption that the July 1971 Rectification Movement led by Major Hashim al-Atta was influenced by 'Abd al-Khaliq Program. It is true July came to correct the distorted implementation of the May regime's self-announced socialist Economic and Social Reform Program (1969-1970). It is

important, however, to discuss the linkages that could be detected between 'Abd al-Khaliq document (originally prepared to the SCP Fifth Congress) and the Atta Reform Program of the Free Officers' Movement that planned and executed the July 19th Rectification Movement in 1971.

(7) This writer suggests that 'Abd al-Khaliq's ideas were not meant to al-Atta *per se* although some similarities between the Atta Program (July 1971) and the 'Abd al-Khaliq's ideas (June 1971) might be compared. July, for instance, announced that it represented the Authority of the National Democratic Revolution. This referred to the alliance of trades unions, progressive political parties, and armed forces. July aimed to implement the same Reform Program that the May 1969 rulers failed to implement. On The Program laid out a comprehensive configuration of the New State and New Society that included a critical account of the National Democratic Revolution. 'Abd al-Khaliq's document, regardless of the May or July experiences, was and continues to intrigue all those concerned with the structure, performance, and future of the Sudanese Democratic State, its economy, bureaucracy, and culture.

(8) Al-Atta might have been attracted by Mahgoub's ingenious thought. Atta - no doubt - acted as a responsible Sudanese leader who appreciated the value of alliance with the Civil Society, unions and parties. July was decisively planned and executed by the Free Officers Movement (FOM) in the Armed Forces, according to the testimony of Major Dr. Mohamed Mahgoub, a founder member of the FOM, as well as other writers. The Movement did not appoint a cabinet, for it wanted the unions and all the other forces of the National Democratic Revolution to take up that task to be able to exercise the Popular Authority of the July National Democratic Program. Being a change of political power by military action, however, the July Movement collapsed by a counter military action largely encouraged and supported by Egypt and Libya.

(9) The unions supported the July Movement with great sacrifices to regain their own union independence and socio-economic interests that had been harshly curtailed by the May rulers, as Mahgoub Sid Ahmed documented in his memories (1998). The tendency of some circles to blame 'Abd al-Khaliq Mahgoub's thought for the failures of the May or even the July military coup, however, must be directly placed on the coup planners and managers, not on the thought or commitments of 'Abd al-Khaliq Mahgoub. The biggest blame must be placed on the May rulers who, with injustice, extra-judicially executed 'Abd al-Khaliq, the socialist thinker of the Sudan, and his colleagues.

(10) Mahgoub himself never conceived of a military coup or called for it to handle the political economy of the Sudanese State or society. Even when the May coup adopted SCP programs or any part of 'Abd al-Khaliq's thought, in person, 'Abd al-Khaliq was sharply critical of that adoption. He timely hurried to show the coup leaders how to convert their coup to a popular movement, not any partisan interest. The May rulers received his criticisms with hostility; perhaps they never tolerated or grasped the depth and meaningfulness of his critical thinking and objective projection. He and many other opposition leaders were imprisoned, exiled, or extra-judicially killed. This tragic attitude continues to plague the country today under both military rulers and non-democratic politicians. The Sudanese people, however, continue the struggle to put a final stop on this atrocious practice with all levels of popular striving, including public debate.

(11) 'Abd al-Khaliq's thought is direct, clear, and straightforward. He wrote: "The [Sudanese] Revolution will never reach out the horizons of socialist change, through the achievement of the National Democratic Revolution, without democracy. There is no "general" or "absolute" democracy. Democracy has always been class-oriented." Hahim al-Atta and many other progressive leaders

realized 'Abd al-Khaliq's document as inspiring, enlightening, and extraordinarily superb guidance towards the establishment of a powerful State for the working people of Sudan. These are the majority of the Sudanese population, the workers, peasants, and professionals, past, present, and future. It is a Program of Action for a nation that is yearning for progression and social advancement and is eternally most eligible to that honor.

(12) On The Program is composed of four parts: (1) The Cause of the Economic Revolution (Development) as the fundamental issue of which all other issues branch out, (2) The Cultural Democratic Revolution, (3) Democratization as a comprehensive change of life in our country, and (4) The Political System. I will start my commentary on the translated document with the important section of the Cultural Democratic Revolution. 'Abd al-Khaliq's ideas have always been inspiring to all those interested in the current and future concerns of our nation. It is hoped his ideas would be received with the contemplation, discussion, and critique they certainly deserve, especially among the new generations of Sudanese intellectuals as well as the older generations.

Introduction and Commentary on the Democratic Economic Revolution

What amazes this writer in the course of studying and translating 'Abd al-Khaliq's document is the wealth of knowledge, the practical plans of action, and the far-sighted strategies that 'Abd al-Khaliq, himself an academically trained economist, articulated with his thought in this work. Mahgoub completed his study while in detention despite the harsh persecution of the May rulers.

The Economic Revolution and Development Program is the core issue of the Sudanese movement for democracy and social advancement, 'Abd al-Khaliq envisaged in the opening chapter of his intellectual work On The Program.

Most of Mahgoub's terminology in the document, e.g., bourgeoisie, middle-range farmer, etc., are based on the literature of the Sudanese 'revolutionary' democracy. The Economic Program is expressive of the ideas that were diligently pursued by socialist organizations, the workaday factory and field experiences of workers and farmers, in addition to the works of hundreds of union professionals. The ideas are also expressive of an unidentified number of significant contributions by academicians, economists, financiers, and other experts of the businesses of the Sudanese local market and the global market relations in the Cold War Era.

The Economic Revolution of <u>On the Program</u> contained valuable information on the Sudan's agricultural and industrial structures. The analysis 'Abd al-Khaliq presented on the sources of the country's under-development and the projection he eventually offered translates into comprehensive political actions and applicable State policies.

Clearly, the Economic Program presupposes a class-oriented planning and implementation. The Program requires the establishment of the Democratic Authority that acts with the working masses and not simply rules over them. These issues are eloquently handled in a popular program that might possibly apply to the Sudan today although it was succinctly addressed to solve the persistent underdevelopment of the country, thirty years ago. Indeed, the Sudanese State economy, democracy, and society are still lingering in the very state of underdevelopment to which the Program was thoughtfully addressed.

The reader is intrigued with 'Abd al-Khaliq's explanation of the major economic dilemma that continues to cripple the march of the Sudanese nation to the doors of social justice and democracy, the horizon of economic advancement and political modernity up to this moment. This dilemma inhibits the progression of social welfare and economic prosperity. It explains the seasonal exercise of human rights and civil freedoms in the short-lived Sudanese democratic governments. It indicates the absence of a consistent, constitutional, and regular system of democracy and the rule of law. It explains the non-stopping civil war that is still tearing the Sudan, pieces apart.

The dilemma is responsible for the inconsistency of our national sovereignty. Mahgoub recognized the reasons of the dilemma in this strong statement: "The main strategic enemy of our National Democratic Revolution is neo-colonialism and the semi-feudal bourgeoisie alliance at home. The main target of the National Democratic Revolution is to strengthen and develop national sovereignty. [The achievement of this target, however,] is impossible without economic advancement and the installation of an industrial-agricultural society."

Economic dependency and the non-democratic rule have been the major features of the underdevelopment of Sudanese State and society in economic and political terms. The economic and political failures of the 1960s up to the present time testified to the state of underdevelopment and economic dependency that was originally founded by the classical colonial rulers. The State managers who serve in humiliation the neo-colonialism, parasitic investment and ideological domination have further stretched the same state of affairs to the present decades.

Classical colonialism and the new forms of colonial domination are sources of the perpetuation of poverty and deprivation of the majority population of Sudan while a few strata of businesses and State bureaucrats illegitimately, criminally, with no morality, reap the highest portion of the Sudanese national wealth, emphasizes Mahgoub.

'Abd al-Khaliq ascertained that not any State reform would ever be able to resolve this crisis without a clear class-direction: what classes the State serves in the first place. The social structure of Sudan is under-developed because it is a class-stratified structure economically and politically as well as culturally and socially for the benefit of a few semi-feudal lords and parasitic owners of the means of production. It is a society that suffers sharp distinctions in the share of citizens of the national income and production relations by class affiliation. This further reflects the distinction the State "legally" makes with respect to gender relations (male-domination), the chronic geographical uneven regional distribution of wealth and power (civil war and underdevelopment), and the discriminatory categorization of people by ethnicity, language, religious beliefs, etc.

This State-biased structure is only advantageous to the strata of the State-protected investors of the agricultural and commercial sectors. There is change, and new strata obviously have been formed since 'Abd al-Khaliq wrote his Program. Old or new, local or international, the context of underdevelopment is evident and is not yet stopped. 'Abd al-Khaliq's analysis is even more supported by the new formations of the social, economic and political exploitation of the country (civil war, oil investment, NIF privatization projects, unions' control by State authority, backward non-human rights laws, etc.).

The social and economic beneficiaries of the State-protected underdevelopment of Sudan include the heavy exploitation of Sudan Oil by China, Malaysia, Talisman (Canada), Sweden, Qatar, and the other partnerships. These companies reaped huge amounts of money supplying Sudan Government with vital means to suppress the indigenous population in the oil areas with warfare. The unrestricted access of the government to oil returns has mainly benefited the parasitic NIF brokers, the old centuries semi-feudal lords, and the non-productive exploiters of the huge animal wealth of the country.

The path to redress this chronic state of underdevelopment is possible: the principled implementation of people's democracy via the path of development that caters to the needs of the Sudanese working people. True, powerful socialist countries do not exist on earth, as they used to be throughout the 20th century. But the issue is not the existence of international constituency to salvage the Sudanese crisis. The Sudanese people are competent and are capable of solving their own crisis with appropriate external support, ascertained 'Abd al-Khaliq.

Equally true is the fact that 'Abd al-Khaliq never rejected the input of capitalist investment with fair terms of production in Sudan Economic Revolution that definitely requires funding and technology for the infrastructure installations. He argues for the role that should be played by the Sudanese enlightened capitalist class to pursue industry, not to invest only in the services or estate sectors.

The point is that Mahgoub called for the respect of national sovereignty and the need to train Sudanese experts who constitute a vital component of capitalist investment. He called for the realization of the right of the State to act freely for the good of the masses through all avenues of regional and international trade. The State's independent enterprise must be encouraged by the World Bank, the International Monetary Fund, and the Arab funds as well as the other funding agencies to strengthen the national component of development.

Years after 'Abd al-Khaliq Mahgoub was extra-judicially killed (for his peaceful thought and programs) by the May rulers, the World Bank moved a bit (under popular pressure) towards imposing conditional human rights terms on the States receiving WB funds. Equally, the IMF austerity measures were strongly criticized by millions of workers and farmers all over the world, which brought them to a small stop.

In the strongest industrial nations that are still largely capitalistic, like the US and Japan, more opening was allowed for social welfare programs and poverty alleviation endeavors by the State. These changes testify further to the correct direction of 'Abd al-Khaliq Program that is much needed to eradicate the prevailing underdevelopment of the Sudan.

The issue for Sudanese thinkers is to be able to provide people with factual action-oriented analysis of the economic and political development of the country. This issue must equally discuss the righteous handling of the crisis elements that are most related to Sudanese State and society. This is exactly what 'Abd al-Khaliq Mahgoub creatively provided in his well-thought Economic Program.

Commentary on 'Abd al-Khaliq's Statement on Religion

On the issue of Religion and Religious Beliefs, Mahgoub wrote: "The National Democratic Revolution guarantees the exercise of the freedom of religious beliefs indiscriminately to the whole population. The human conceptualization of the self and its integrity and the future of humanity are issues that spring out of contention. No force would be able to impose its determination on a human in this regard. Apart from agreement or disagreement between religious beliefs, social classes adopt positions in the Social Revolution according to their own interests and whether they keep pace with the movement of history or are backward from it. The social human determines that position, not the religious belief."

Mahgoub made the point that, " The National Democratic Authority rejects any exploitation of religion for the interests of the reactionary classes in our country that struggle to perpetuate outdated production relations. These reactionary classes abuse religion to exploit people and strip their human dignity. This exploitation is contrary to the interests of society. It antagonizes the best future that humans form with their minds and hands as they move from the level of needs to that of freedom."

Mahgoub believed that, "The exploitation of religion in this manner has degraded religion, exploited the struggling workers, and kept them in a miserable condition of ignorance and darkness. In this rotten swamp, the social parasites of sectarianism, lethargy, magic, and sorcery proliferated and supported the colonial powers. They lately supported the semi-feudal bourgeois rule. The evidence for the harm ensuing in the history of the Sudanese political movement is indicated in the process of distorting religion and transforming religious call to a complete program (the Islamic Constitution) in the service of the capitalist path of development and the dependency on neo-colonialism."

'Abd al-Khaliq Mahgoub was very committed to the dignity, values, and struggles of the Sudanese for democracy, peace, and social progression. He was highly aware of the influence of religion in the life of the Sudanese, the diversity of religious beliefs, and the need to respect the right of every single human in the whole country to exercise freely the right to religious beliefs. His party further required this commitment by the party ordinance that committed all members or even supporters to respect the right to religious beliefs and avoid sarcasm, insult, or offending the peoples' religious beliefs.

This requirement did not prohibit scientific or critical thinking about religious issues. Nor did it inhibit the legitimate struggle to stop the abuse of religious beliefs by the social groups that economically and politically exploit the population. On the contrary, progressive thought has consistently encouraged constructive critique of all individuals or groups that wrongfully control society for cheap material gain with the sinful falsification of religion. That distorts the true ethos of religion: morality, individual and collective creativity, respect of the human dignity, and spiritual integrity.

'Abd al-Khaliq was an intellectual free of hatred or prejudices towards religious believers. He was a progressive thinker whose struggle to reform and advance

Sudanese State and society was firmly based on the good understanding and appreciation of the social values of Sudan, and the deep respect of Sudanese entities, cultures, and heritage. Based on this deep understanding of the Sudanese social life, he maintained important relations with many religious believers all over the country. He praised the emphasis of Islam on rational thinking and spoke highly of the Prophet of Islam and his Companions.

Mahgoub emphasized the right to exercise spiritual practices for all individuals and groups. He did not discriminate between the right to believe in Islam, Christianity, or African indigenous religions. He clearly criticized, however, all aspects of religious behavior that contradicted in his opinion the right to reflect and act thoughtfully, question, reason, and argue for a better utilization of the good values. These values should effectively strengthen the needs of a modern, free, and healthy State and society for all Sudanese. For him, the State would be a National Democratic State, the final product of the democratic, social, economic, and political movement by the social classes beneficiaries of the National Democratic Revolution.

'Abd al-Khaliq's peaceful attitude towards religious believers, which emphasized his strong commitment to democratic thought and socialist manners, influenced many citizens. One significant result showed out in the national election of the Parliament in 1960s when he won the Omdurman al-Janoubia Constituency. That constituency was almost controlled by the ruling party of Ismail al-Azhari, the renowned Sudanese leader and the first elected Prime Minister of Sudan. Sufi sects, many *Ansar* and *Khatmiya* supporters positively gave their vote to 'Abd al-Khaliq Mahgoub. This attitude was only surprising to his competitors from the other non-democratic parties.

This experience indicated that the way to win the popular vote in democratic elections would be successful only when voters trust the perseverance and commitment of a candidate to the popular interests. That candidate was Mahgoub – the Sudanese leader who never insulted the values or religious beliefs of his people. He was a Sudanese thinker who bravely, thoughtfully, and scientifically insisted that the exercise of religious beliefs by believers of all religions must not linger behind the Sudanese popular movement, or handicap the striving for freedom, democratic rights, and human dignity.

Commentary on 'Abd al-Khaliq's Democratic Revolution

What Democracy does the Sudan most need nowadays?

The next sections of 'Abd al-Khaliq Program on the Sudanese Revolution, the New Production Relations, the New State, and the New Society are some of the most intriguing contributions by Sudanese thinkers in contemporary political thought.

Here Mahgoub, with a straightforward, principled and brave approach spoke his mind on behalf of millions of the Sudanese urban working classes (workers and professionals) and the rural poor (farmers and Bedouins).

Mahgoub analyzed in the sections of the Economic Revolution the internal structure of this advanced popular movement, the forces and means of production relations, besides the ideological and cognitive categories it has. He drew heavily upon the logical needs of this structure and the functions it presupposes.

There is no compromise here. There are no twisting phrases or shaky statements. Sudan has no option but to move - for good – "out of the rotten swamp of economic underdevelopment and its unabated political, cultural, and social forms: the formalized, ritualistic democracy, party corruption or disorganization, and the dehumanizing backward thought of manipulating religion for sex and ethnicity inequalities."

These forms of underdevelopment have been embodied in the existing State of the Sudan because of colonialism (classical military conquest and occupation) and the neo-colonialism (the financial, economic, cultural, and technological domination by funding nations) that repressed the spontaneous progression of the country. Ruling coalitions of the semi-feudal alliance (military or civilian) have consistently reflected the national means, forces, and relations of production that perpetuated the same forms of underdevelopment.

This backward alliance included "the non-progressive coalition governments" that existed before the May regime of Nimeiri and the Nimeiri's Sudan Socialist Union (SSU) "petty-bourgeoisie one party system," according to Mahgoub. Using the power of the State, the anti-progressive governments and tyrannous regimes accumulated additional experiences against the democratic movement. More difficulties continue, "to barricade the march of the masses," in his words.

Along with this internal crisis, regional and international conspiracies continue to put the pressure on the Sudanese Revolution. These foreign intrusions deny the role that must be played by Sudan's progressive groups. They deliberately neglect the huge potential of the pauperized, suppressed, and marginalized masses of the urban and rural parts of the country to participate in national decision-making. They underestimate the unions and obviously discourage them in spite of the clear principles of international law and labor rights, which guarantee union rights.

Mahgoub's observations on the evolution, growth, and development of Sudanese classes, consciousness, and struggles for social change and the "New Life" are evident in the Sudan today. "Modern Forces" specifically comprise "the revolutionary democratic forces," the "New Production Forces": workers, professionals (civil or military), farmers, enlightened capitalist, soldiers, etc. These are the working classes and struggling masses that are economically impoverished and are politically repressed with no enjoyment of civil freedoms or human rights, especially the women, students, children, and low-income worker classes.

Without changing the production relations inherited from the classical colonial rule that have been further developed by State/neo-colonialism relations, the Sudanese modern forces will not play the role it is destined to play, affirms Mahgoub. The only solution is to install the "Popular Form of Democracy" that coincides with the advanced, conscious, and *well-prepared working classes' alliance with the enlightened Sudanese capitalists* to install the New Sudan, the New Society, and the New State.

What 'Abd al-Khaliq projected in the 1970s is quite relevant to the lively changes of our world today. The corrupted semi-feudal petty-bourgeoisie alliance with anti-progression groups will never change the poverty or the ongoing state of underdevelopment in the Sudan. It has only added unprecedented suffering, repression, and State corruption to the situation. And yet, a conscious alliance of the working class and enlightened capitalists will possibly develop the nation.

Under these devastating economic and political conditions, the vast majority of the Sudanese citizens will never enjoy the wealth of their bountiful Homeland. Current reports on Sudan Oil and other minerals only testify to this fact. The horrific and frightening performance of the economy under the NIF Triple Program (1989/1992), the escalated State spending on the armed forces and State Security, civil war, heavy anti-workers taxation, etc, testify to the correct reading of 'Abd al-Khaliq about the non-productive "semi-feudal-petty-bourgeoisie governance and economic relations."

Democracy is class-specific, taught Mahgoub. He strongly held that the false, hypocritical and failing concept of some politicians that democracy is "the rule of an elected majority to maintain the interests of the electoral majority" would desperately blur the shining analysis of his class-dialectical model. In his opinion, democracy "is class-specific." The class specific authority of the State should straighten out the disenfranchisement of the majority poor. Also, economy "is class-specific." It has to be directed in the service of the Sudanese majority working classes (rural and urban), not the old feudal lords, military generals, parasitic businesses, or the greedy foreign oil investors. These include China, Canadian Talisman, Malaysia, European companies, and Qatar whose oil investments escalated the government's warfare against the innocent people of South Sudan and the other regions.

Mahgoub affirmed that the "New Democracy" is not a compromising system of rule. Democracy must be based on direct, strict, and uncompromising constitutional principles to guarantee the full enjoyment of human rights and civil freedoms to the worker classes, the real majority of the nation's population, to stop any exploitation or unfair treatment of the masses. This is not an exclusionary form of rule to the other small strata (semi-feudal lords, parasitic non-productive capitalists) if they comply with the principles of the non-exploitation, non-suppression, equalitarian, class-oriented New State, which would be the people's state and the new society according to Mahgoub.

The production forces must be empowered by the constitution and policies of the New State to enjoy the energy they daily exert to produce with adequate wages, healthy services, and respectful status. A state established by these forces for their sake is a precondition to carry on that role. A democracy guaranteeing the stability of the production forces and the rights they deserve certainly follows.

This eloquent statement explains Mahgoub's revolutionary doctrine: "The conscious implementation of democracy in production centers requires the establishment of production councils with legislation, participation of the working masses in the administration of economic and administrative units, etc. Effective participation must be run in accordance with the free democratic desire of the working masses and their class organizations (unions, associations, revolutionary committees, cooperatives, etc.)."

"This is an investment for raising the rate of productivity and increasing the Gross National Product. It involves training and practice of the working masses to establish the material foundation of the People's Authority, and to help the masses march in the path of integrity and vigilance (prohibiting estrangement). It prevents the growth of the bureaucracy that separates the executive productive instrument from the masses."

The NDA and 'Abd al-Khaliq's Program:
Concluding Remarks

Earlier in the opening words of his contribution, 'Abd al-Khaliq explained: "We conceptualize our aims for the stage of the National Democratic Revolution at a time the concepts and aims of this stage are laid out by the petty-bourgeoisie strata. Some of these conceptions and aims in question are wrongful and false. Therefore, our Program will be presented in a high level of both ideological and practical context."

What is irrelevant in 'Abd al-Khaliq Mahgoub's thought (1971) to our life today?

To deal with this question, let us first summarize relevant aspects of 'Abd al-Khaliq's thought in light of the prevailing economic, political, and cultural facts of the Sudanese State and society today.

I. Relevance of 'Abd al-Khaliq's Thought to the Sudanese Market Relations

The general conditions of Sudan, the non-productive mode of production, the sharp distinction between the semi-feudal-petty-bourgeoisie classes (military or civilian) and the vast majority of the Sudanese worker classes (urban or rural, including technicians and professionals) have not changed in any way different from 'Abd al-Khaliq's configuration 30 years ago.

The major crisis of the country (political and economic, social or cultural) continues to grow and to spread within the same rules of the Sudanese political economy that 'Abd al-Khaliq objectively analyzed. The emergence of new "modern" parasitic strata of the non-productive parasitic capitalists is not surprising. Indeed, 'Abd al-Khaliq predicted that Sudan would continue to suffer the non-productive path of development and economic dependency until the Economic Revolution would be consistently implemented.

The one form of capitalism that is desperately needed to move Sudan out of the swamp of underdevelopment has not yet played its significant role to advance the industrial and agricultural development of the country. The NIF (1989 to the present) policies in this matter have only legalized the corruption of the Sudanese State and national wealth by the Turabi/Bashir *Shura* businesses that are fully controlled by the NIF and its allies, the Muslim Brotherhood groups.

There is not a single development indicator to support the growth of the Sudanese middle class, prosperity of the working class, or increase in the purchase power of the poor. All indicators on the contrary show that the only beneficiary of the NIF financial policies were the tiny stratum of NIF businesses, the Chinese and other arms' exporters and oil investors, and the other war-mongering national and international brokers.

The tax policy most recently announced by the Bashir regime is nothing but a new wave of State brokering in the interest of the semi-feudal petty bourgeoisie alliance. The exploitative under-developed production relations that Mahgoub competently analyzed and correctly cautioned about in 1971 "should be eradicated and replaced by the worker classes/enlightened capitalist production relations in a democratic system of rule."

The Sudanese farmers, for example, will not be benefited from the *tax relief* since the Gezira Scheme (the largest in Sudan) was already transformed to a non-State financial venture. Even the older State tenant administration partnership that guaranteed a few advantages to small farmers was mercilessly crushed. Not a single guarantee, tractor service or irrigation services have been offered to the poor farmers that massively migrated to work in the oil-producing Gulf States, as cheap labor, decades ago.

Similarly, the most exploited wage earners of the Sudanese agricultural seasonal workers will not be advantaged by the new tax system. They had already abandoned the long-standing cheap labor relations and non-union protection, and have been joining the small farmers in massive emigration to Libya, the Gulf States, Egypt, and the West. Dismissed in the thousands by the NIF coup leader Omer Bashir and his mentor Hassan al-Turabi, the bulk of skilled workers and technicians of the State bureaucracy and private sector were forced to leave the country to sustain their lives.

The necessary investor in the establishment and development of the advanced industrial and agricultural infrastructure without which no possible transformation would come about is *the Sudanese enlightened capitalist.* This is certainly not the NIF businesspeople that abused the economic and political powers of the State *by coup* to evacuate the Sudanese markets of all competitors, contractors, and the middle-class national capitalist or the indigenous businesses in the rural side of the country.

The promising form of capitalist production that 'Abd al-Khaliq talks about is based on the capitalist who endeavors to invest in the industrial and agricultural sectors, not simply the services and estate sectors. This is the capitalist that would respect the unions' rights, observe the industrial safety of workers, and pay fairly to the seasonal workers. This is the capitalist who is committed to the People's State, not to a terrorist government or a corrupted regime.

The conditions for such investment are both objective and subjective: The objective conditions pertain to the conditional establishment of the People's State, the democratic authority of the production classes. The role of the People's State is to eradicate the old production relations, the existing NIF petty-bourgeoisie alliance with the semi-feudal lords and the other military or civilian State managers, including the notorious *Shura* groups of the NIF repressive rule.

The subjective conditions include the organized, conscious, and committed popular movement, which is well expressed by the worker, professional, and farmer unions besides the Bedouin associations in alliance with the enlightened capitalist. These comprise the productive groups of investors with whom the People's State should realize fair economic and political relations.

II.   Relevance of 'Abd al-Khaliq's Thought to the International Arena

Many changes occurred in the international arena. In the present time, the Cold War Era (CWE) was almost brought to an end, save for the new espionage and other CWE symptoms that cover media screens from time to time. The international human rights norms, specifically democratic rights and civil freedoms that 'Abd al-Khaliq struggled for decades to have recognized and realized all over the country, are now widely known even in the remote rural side of the country.

The State did not accomplish this achievement, however. The Sudanese civil society groups, political parties, and trades unions did. The voluntary human rights movement has certainly contributed to this national awareness. The relatively easy access to international media and the impact of the information revolution contributed largely to this awareness. And yet, these rights will never be fully practiced, Mahgoub earlier insisted in his Program, "without the active pursuit of the working classes movement on the basis of daily struggle to disseminate this popular awareness, to stretch it to its highest point – the Popular Democratic Revolution."

Here is where the National Democratic Alliance (NDA) popular movement is in need of 'Abd al-Khaliq Mahgoub's Program, especially in planning and action, structure and functioning, strategy and tactics. There are major differences, however, between the two sources of planning or action. The major cause for this difference lies in the fact that Mahgoub offers a program that projects "the socialist democracy horizon," which is the only substitute of the perpetuated semi-feudal petty-bourgeoisie alliance in Sudan.

The NDA's political alliance is composed of the political strata in question. Together with a few enlightened capitalists, the NDA's forces include political parties, trades unions, professional associations, and armed groups whose class affiliation is organically enmeshed with the poor farmers, workers, and the nomads of the Sudan.

The NDA political integrity has thus far been maintained in a reasonable stature. And yet, the nature of the NDA's contradictory class-composition has repeatedly revealed non-conformity of the class affiliations and interests of the NDA partners. The contradictions appeared clearly in the issues of women's participation, the financial support for advanced information programs, etc. The NDA class-differential might hence continue to pull the NDA into class conflicting stands the more that the popular movement advances and asks for more progressive action.

'Abd al-Khaliq's Program is founded on a deep ideological orientation. The NDA has no ideological commitment of any sort because it seeks only to maintain a common bondage amongst its different groups for a minimum standard commitment to a broad national program of reform. Mahgoub's Program anticipates national, regional, and international cooperation towards the establishment, support, and strengthening of the People's State. The NDA mainly struggles to correct the performance of the existing State on the would-be overthrow of the NIF rule, including, whenever necessary, the re-establishment of State institutions in the center and the regions. In spite of these fundamental differences, the NDA Comprehensive Political Solution (CPS) to the crisis of Sudan is worthy of credit.

A minimum standard program attempting to move Sudan away from the hole of terrorism and backwardness, President Moi's most recent Proposals, IGAD Principles, the Egyptian-Libyan Initiative, and the American successful peace agreements in the Nuba Mountains are all short of the required conditions to stop the NIF Bashir/Turabi crisis of Sudan. The NDA's Comprehensive Political Solution appears the best deal since it solemnly respects the Sudanese minimum standards for peace, democracy, and the rule of law based on the NDA national agreements to solve the Sudan's crisis.

III. Between 'Abd al-Khaliq's Thought and the NDA Resolutions

In his insightful work, 'Abd al-Khaliq Mahgoub writes: "In the world today and in the less-developed nations there is no way available to increase development rates such that the masses would be saved the suffering of poverty and pauperization. There is no way without facing the issues of social, political, and economic change (social structure), and also dealing directly with the super-structure of this society."

This writer will draw heavily from this eloquent idea to contrast 'Abd al-Khaliq's Program with the NDA Comprehensive Political Solution to the crisis of Sudan in the present time. Reference is made to an urgent message by this writer, dated July 1999, to Farouq Abu Eissa, the NDA Spokesperson Member of the NDA Committee of Five, copied to Dr. Shafi' Khider Saeed, Chair of the NDA's Committee of Masses Mobilization.

In that message, this writer mentioned that the Sudanese democratic popular movement happily received the NDA Resolutions and Recommendations of Asmara (7-14 July 1999). The resolutions clearly expressed the clarity, integrity, and will power of the People of Sudan to pursue the fundamental issues of the nation at this particular time. "1) Liquidate the dictatorial rule existing in Sudan since June 30, 1989, up to this moment. 2) Stop civil war by a permanent and just peace. 3) Establish a democratically oriented transitional rule to solve the economic, administrative, and cultural problems of Sudan; and 4) Honor all provisions of the NDA Charter and Resolutions."

Sudanese masses abroad and the NDA supporters at home endorsed the NDA Resolutions concerning the Peaceful Political Solution with reference to (a) Resolutions of the Asmara Conference on Fundamental Issues (1995), (b) Declaration of the IGAD Principles (1994), (c) The NDA Resolutions on Political Solution (March 1998), and (d) The two Memorandums of the NDA inside dated June 10th, 1996, and December 29th, 1998.)

The Sudanese noticed with satisfaction the NDA Resolutions on suitable machinery for the Political Solution, namely: (a) Agreement shall be reached between the parts of the conflict through mediators on a suitable machinery and place outside of The Sudan for holding a meeting under regional and international monitoring. (b) NDA affirms confidence in the IGAD Initiative and the role of the IGAD Partners. (c) NDA welcomes the fraternal initiatives of Egypt and Libya for looking at the ways of solving the Sudanese crisis. (d) NDA welcomes all regional and international initiatives that seriously aim to make peace, stability, and democracy in The Sudan.

In July 1999, the NDA pledged to "approach [all these initiatives] together." It was unclear from the NDA performance in the period following the July Meeting of Asmara whether or not the NDA would actually implement the July Resolutions by approaching all IGAD, Egyptian-Libyan, and American initiatives as they "seriously aim to make peace, stability, and democracy in The Sudan."

The attitude of some NDA partners, however, was not fully supportive of a principled implementation of these plans. For example, a number of NDA leaders sent various, contradictory, and ambiguous messages to the Press. Many of these messages rejected the IGAD, supported without reservation the Egyptian-Libyan initiative, and almost "reprimanded" American statements supportive of the IGAD. In so acting, the NDA did hurt itself at least in diplomatic terms at that particular time.

With such reactions by NDA partners, the NDA's July Resolutions were not consistently applied. There was confusion, and there was frustration. That was dangerous to the image of the NDA in and outside Sudan. NDA needs to be seriously handled and straightened. The Sudanese masses expect the NDA to speak with a united letter. They require the NDA to lead the diplomatic battle with consistency of thought and action.

The Sadiq al-Mahdi/Hassan al-Turabi and al-Mahdi/Bashir political agreements to reconcile their differences in the late 1990s undermined the NDA's integrity. The most recent SPLM/Turabi faction letter of understanding strengthened the NDA enemy (i.e., Turabi and his ruling group) when the time was ripe to isolate the NIF dictatorship for good. The NDA must stop unilateral statements by any of its partners at this sensitive stage for the cause of Sudan's people and nation.

The NDA announced in July 1999 "it will be responsible of dealing with the issue of the political solution and reaching decisions provided that a committee prepares a working paper on NDA position and vision of the political solution to be approved by the NDA Leadership Council next meeting." Sudanese Masses were wondering: Did the NDALC prepare the working paper as decided by the July Meeting? If the paper was ready, why not share it with Sudanese Masses?

The NDA decided "to prepare a conducive atmosphere for political solution, the Khartoum regime must take these necessary measures: (a) Freeze all articles of the 1998 constitution that restrict public freedoms, according to the remarks reported by the UN Special Reporter on Human Rights in The Sudan as presented to the 55th Session of the UN Human Rights Committee in Geneva (b) Cancellation of the second constitutional decree."

The NDA equally requires the NIF regime to: "(c) Cancellation of the Emergency Law (d) Cancellation of all exceptional powers of the Public Security Law (arrest, inspection, detention, abduction, inspection without judicial warrant, etc. (e) Cancellation of the "*Tawali*" Political Law and any patronage over political and unions' activities (f) Cancellation of police and courts of the Public Order (g) Guarantee the right to free movement, expression, and organization, and abrogate all laws banning public freedoms (h) Release all political prisoners and drop all sentences issued against political prisoners; and (i) Return all confiscated properties."

344

IV. NDA Needs to Consider Mahgoub's Program for Popular Support

The Khartoum NIF regime has not moved in any meaningful direction to apply a single measure of the NDA necessary agenda. Instead, the Khartoum regime moved in the worst direction a dictatorial regime ever could. The head of the regime, Omer Bashir, insulted the NDA and started building up a special security brigade to "massacre, crush, and skin political opponents.

The regime continues to kill and displace the innocent citizens in the oil regions in South Sudan and to torture professionals and unionists without remorse. In 2001, the NIF regime further arrested the NDA leaders at home and put them under trial for meeting with the American Cultural Attaché in Khartoum.

Even if the NDA rejected all this negative performance of the NIF ruling regime, the NDA media and information activities failed to reflect the NDA position in a strong way to rally support of the international community to the NDA's legitimate cause of national liberation, peace, and democracy. The NDA information and media represented a weak voice of the NDA. Where is Al-Ittihadi al-Dawliya Journal, for example, which until recently voiced the principled opposition of the Sudanese in the Diaspora?

What is the NDA plan to force the Khartoum regime to comply with democracy, peace, and economic development? Are the concerned foreign powers putting the pressure on the Khartoum regime to comply with the NDA necessary requirements for the Political Solution? Was it wise to silence the Al-Ittihadi al-Dawliya outspoken criticisms of the regime to favor the Tripoli/Cairo initiative? Did the Khartoum regime and its leader respond positively to the NDA Peaceful Solution for the NDA to silence its opposition propaganda?

The NDA is not sufficiently putting pressure on the NIF tyranny. The NDA must issue a clear statement to the masses evaluating the current state of affairs and enlightening them with the facts of the situation, where the NDA stands and to what extent it is progressing. This is the least that an opposition leadership must do to maintain a strong link with its own masses. The key to gain masses support is this linkage, 'Abd al-Khaliq correctly taught. The core of Mahgoub's Program is that, democratic leaderships must promote the closest relations possible with the popular movement.

The NDA is not doing enough in this respect. Appreciative of the external initiatives to help the Sudanese liquidate State repression, the Sudanese want the NDA, the Sudanese Leadership of the democracy struggle, to lead the ongoing round of diplomatic negotiations, as was firmly decided by the NDA's July Resolutions. In this direction, the NDA is advised to assign diplomatic missions to the caliber of democratic diplomats who, led by the former ambassador Nuraddin Manan, have been contributing a great deal in the Diaspora to boost the NDA image in the regional and international arenas.

The NDA decided in July 1999 to "increase necessary contributions from Sudanese in Diaspora and other donors" to activate the program of the Masses Mobilization and Organization Committee "to execute the tasks designated by the transitional program." The Sudanese masses have been willing to support serious national efforts to strengthen democracy and human rights at home. It is expedient that the NDA convenes an all-Sudanese Constitutional Conference in the Diaspora to boost the NDA financial campaign and to consolidate the NDA Resolutions.

In theoretical terms, these NDA decisions are comparable to the 'Abd al-Khaliq's strategic thought. The future of implementing these important decisions, however, would best materialize in actual reality when the other elements of the Mahgoub Program would be fully implemented for the New State, the New Society, Economic Revolution, and the Democratic Revolution.

That is when the striving for peace with massive popular activities and the effective, well experimented, and organized peaceful striving of the Sudanese National Democratic Alliance will hopefully proceed with no stoppage to the advanced industrial and agricultural development - towards the socialist horizon, the Sudanese masses' ultimate goal-achievement.

In practical terms, 'Abd al-Khaliq's Program provides a comprehensive well-thought solution to the underdevelopment crisis of the Sudan. The unrelenting military actions, city attacks, and the other violent actions between government and the warring opposition groups will continue to sink the country – nowadays under direct responsibility of the NIF Bashir/Turabi factions - deeper into the swamps of misery, disaster, and increased backwardness.

The Machekos Peace Protocol (Kenya, August: 2002) that the Sudan Government signed with the Sudanese people's Liberation Movement and Army (SPLM/SPLA) is a significant step to insure peace of the country. The Protocol, however, will only succeed if the negotiation process would fully accommodate the NDA and the Sudanese civil society groups to make of the bilateral talks a national constitutional conference.

To conclude, Sudan desperately needs 'Abd al-Khaliq's thought for popular discussion and for popular action. Sudanese are brave, open, and outgoing people, especially when it comes to their beloved people and nation of Sudan. *Rahima Allah* 'Abd al-Khaliq Mahgoub! (May God have mercy on his soul). His thought is alive. His people, the Sudanese, and his country, The Sudan, certainly miss his lovely presence.

REFERENCES

u Salim, Mohamed Ibrahim (1989): Al-Haraka al-Fikriya fi al-Mahdiya (Intellectual vement in the Mahdiya), University of Khartoum.

u Shiqqa, 'Abd al Halim Mohamed Ahmed (1987): Al-Maraa Papers of the Fourth ernational Meetings of the International Institute of Islamic Thought, Washington, DC, and chology Department, University of Khartoum.

u Zaid, Mohamed Ibrahim (1990): Tanzim al-Igra'at al-Jizaiya fi al-Tashri'at al-Arabiya ganization of Criminal Procedure in Arab legislation), Part One, Arab Center for Security dies and Training, Riyaadh.

ned, Jamal Mohamed (1960): Al-Usul al-Fikriya lil Wataniya al-Masriya (Intellectual gins of Egyptian Nationalism), Oxford. Translated by Mahgoub El-Tigani Mahmoud, ional Committee for the Commemoration of Jamal Mohamed Ahmed (1996).

i, A. Yusuf (1983): The Holy Qur'an Text, Translation and Commentary, Amana Corp., twood, Maryland.

Na'im, 'Abdullahi A. (1992): "Application of Shari'a (Islamic law) and Human Rights lations in the Sudan," in: Religion and Human Rights – The Case of Sudan, proceedings of conference convened by the Sudan Human Rights Organization, London.

Na'im, 'Abdullahi. A. (1990): Towards an Islamic Reformation – civil liberties, human ts, and international law, Syracuse U. Press, New York.

ad, Mohamed Mohyi al-Deen (1991): Badayil al-Jiza'at al-Jinaiya fi al-Mujtama' al-Islami ernatives of Criminal Penalties in Islamic Society), Arab Center for Security and Training, dh.

ri, Haja Kashif (Undated): Al-Haraka al-Nisaiya fi al-Sudan (Women's Movement in The an), Khartoum.

sese, Antonie (1991): Human Rights in A Challenging World, Polity Press, Cambridge.

k, Ramsey (1993): "A Working Paper for Peace," in: NORD – SUD XXI – Droits de omme, Liberte', No. 2, Geneva.

De Waart, Paul (et al) (1988): International law and Development, Martinus Nijhoff Publishe Dordrecht, Boston.

Egeland, Jan (1988): Impotent Supporters – Potent Small State, Norwegian U. Press, printed England by Page Bros (Norwich) Ltd.

al-Fa'ar, Hamza (1990): "Al-Madkhal li Dirasat al-Shar' al-Islami (Introduction to the Study Islamic Shar'ia) in: Al-Tashri' al-Jinayi' al-Islami (Islamic Criminal Law), Arab Center Security and Training, Riyadh.

al-Fadil, Mohamed Daif-Allah Ibn Mohamed al-Ja'ali (Undated): Kitab al-Tabaqat fi Khosos Awliya wa al-Saliheen wa al-'Ulama fi al-Sudan, (The Book of the Tabaqat on the Saints, Go Ones, and Scholars of The Sudan) Beirut.

Fluehr-Lobban, Carolyn (1987): Islamic Law and Society in The Sudan, Frank Cass, London.

al-Gaddal, Mohamed Saeed (1981): Al-Siyasa al-Iqtisadiya lil Dawla al-Mahdiya, (Econom Policy of the Mahdist State), Khartoum University Press, 1st edition.

Hassan, Riffat (1982): "On Human Rights and the Qur'anic Perspectives," in: Journal Ecumenical Studies, No. 19.

Hill, Richard (1970): 'Ala Tukhum al-'Alam al-Islmai, Hikba min Tarikh al-Sudan. On tl Frontiers of Islam: Two manuscripts Concerning The Sudan under Turco-Egyptian Rule, 182 1845, Oxford, England, Clarendon Press, 1970). Translated by 'Abd al-Azim Mohamed Ahm 'Akasha, Al-Matbo'at al-Arabiya, Khartroum, 1st edition, 1987.

Ibn Kathir, Al-Hafiz 'Imad al-Deen (1979): Mukhtasar Tafseer ibn Kathir, (Summary of the Il Kathir's Interpretation [of the Qur'an]) Volume II, abridged and revised by Mohamed 'Ali a Sabooni. Dar Al-Qur'an Al-Karim, Beirut, 7th edition.

Ibrahim, Fatima Ahmed (Undated): Hassadona fi Ishreen 'Ama.

Ibrahim, Mohamed al-Mekki (1976): Al-Fikr al-Sudani, Usulu wa Tataworu, (Sudanes Thought, Origins and Development), Department of Culture, Khartoum, 1st edition.

Khair, al-Haj Hamad Mohamed (1982): Medieval Eastern Sudan and the Arabs: A Study on tl Evolution of Economic Relations (640-1400 AD), PhD., University of Khartoum.

al-Kordofani, Ismail 'Abd al-Gadir (1972): Saa'dat al-Mustahdi bi Seerat al-Imam al-Mahd (Ed.) by Mohamed Ibrahim abu-Salim, Khartoum, 1st print.

Lawson, Edward (1991): Encyclopedia of Human Rights, Taylor & Francis Inc., New York.

bban, Jr., Richard, Robert S. Kramer, and Carolyn Fluehr-Lobban (2002): Historical ctionary of The Sudan, The Scarecrow Press, Inc., Lanham.

ding, Francis Deng (1987): The Search for Peace and Unity in The Sudan, Brooks Institute, ashington, D.C.

Mahdi, Sadiq (1985): Al-Islam wa Masa'lat Janoob al-Sudan, (Islam and the Question of uth Sudan)

----------------(1984): Al-Nizam al-Sudani wa Tajribatohu al-Islamiya, (The Sudanese Regime d its Islamic Experience)

----------------(1981): Al-Sahwa al-Islamiya wa Mustaqbal al-Da'wa, (Islamic Vigilance and ure of The Islamic Call).

----------------(Undated): Jihad fi Sabil al-Istiqlal, (Struggle for The Sake of Sudan), Umma blications.
----------------(Undated): Al-'Uqobat al-Shar'iya wa Mawqi'a min al-Nizam al-Ijtim'ai al-mi, (The Position of Shari'a Penalties in The Islamic Social Order), Umma Publications.

hgoub, 'Abd al-Khaliq (1967): Afkar hawla Falsafat al-Ikhwan al-Muslimoon. (Thoughts on Philosophy of Muslim Brotherhood), Omdurman.

hmoud, Mahgoub El-Tigani (1992): "Al-Sujoon baina al-Kharaj wa al-Qanun al-Dawli" sons between The Al-Kharaj and International Law), in: Majalat al-Amn (The Journal of urity), Riyadh.

hmoud, Mahgoub El-Tigani (1984): Tatawur al-Jarima wa al-Iqab fi al-Sudan. (The 'elopment of Crime and Punishment in The Sudan), Omdurman, 1st edition.

Maqrizi, al-Imam Tariq al-Deen Ahmed (845H): Al-Khitat al-Maqriziya: al-Mawaiz wa al-ar bi Zikr al-Khitat wa al-Athar, (The Maqrizian History, Lessons from History and haeology), Maktabat al-Adab, Cairo, 1996.

thews, Robert D. (1980): "National Security: Propaganda or Legitimate Concerns," in: blems of Contemporary Militarism, edited by Asbjorn Eide & Marek Thee, Croom Helm, don.

ver, Ann Elizabeth (1988): "The Dilemmas of Islamic Identity," in: Human Rights and The ld's Religions, edited by Leroy S. Rouner, University of Notre Dam Press, Notre Dam.

Mubarak, Khalid (1992): in: Religion and Human Rights – The Case of Sudan, op. Cit.

al-Nawawi, Mohi al-Deen Abu-Zakariya al Shafi'e (undated): Riyadh al-Saliheen min Kal; Sayed al-Mursaleen. (The Garden of Hadith by The Master of the Messengers [of God]), edition, Al-Shamarli, Cairo.

Nickel, James W. (1987): Making Sense of Human Rights - Philosophical Reflections on Universal Declaration of Human Rights, U. of California, Berkeley.

Nugud, Mohamed Ibrahim (1992): fi Hiwar hawla al-Naz'at al-Falsafiya al-Arabiya al-Islami (A Dialogue on Materialist Tendencies of the Arab Islamic Philosophy), Dar al-Farabi, Beirut.

Pasha, Slatin (1987): Al-Saif wa al-Nar fi al-Sudan. (Sword and Fire in The Sudan), Al-Matbc al-'Arabiya, Khartoum.

Qasim, Own Al-Sharif, Osman Sid Ahmed et al. (1984): Al-Islam fi al-Sudan: Dirasa fi Takwe al-Shakhsiya al-Sudaniya. (Islam in The Sudan – A Study on the Formation of the Sudane personality). Papers of the International Conference on the Application of Islamic Shari'a Law the Sudan, Khartoum.

al-Saboni, Mohamed 'Ali (1981): Mukhtasar Tafsir ibn Kathir, (Summary of the Ibn Kathi; Interpretation [of the Qur'an]), Volume I, Dar Al-Qur'an Al-Karim, Beirut, 7th print.

Satti, Zakiya Awad (1984): Al-Usra fi Al-Islam, (The Family in Islam), Papers of the International Conference on the Publication of Shari'a, op.cit.

Shestack, Jerome J. (1989): "The Jurisprudence of Human Rights," in: Human Rights International Law – Legal and Policy Issues, edited by Theodore Meron, Clarendon Pres Oxford.

Sid Ahmed, Mahgoub (1997): Muzakirat Mahgoub Sid Ahmed fi al-Haraka al-'Umaliya ; Sudaniya, (The Memories of Mahgoub Sid Ahmed on the Sudanese Labor Movement), Sud; Human Rights Organization Cairo Branch (SHRO-Cairo), Cairo.

Sinaceur, Allal Mohamed (1986): "Islamic tradition and human rights," in: Philosophic Foundations of Human Rights, Unesco, Mayenne, France, pp. 193-225.

Sivanandan A. (1991): "A Black Perspective on The War," in: Race and Class, Volume 32, N 4, April-June, London.

Sudan Communist Party (Undated): Al-Marxiya wa Qadaya al-Thawra al-Sudaniya, (Marxis; and the Issues of Sudanese Revolution), Dar al-Wasilya, Khartoum.

Taha, Mahmoud Mohamed (1974): Al-Deen wa al-Tanmiya al-Ijtima'iya, (Religion and Soci; Development), 1st edition.

-----------------------------(1973): Al-Marxiya fi al-Mizan, (Marxism in a Balance), 1st edition.

-----------------------------(1973): Rasayil wa Maqalat, (Messages and Essays), 1st edition,
y.

-----------------------------(1972): Al-Thawra al-Thaqafiya, (The Cultural Revolution).

-----------------------------(1971): Tatweer Shari'at al-Ahwal al-Shakhsiya, (Developing the
ri'a Personal Status Law).

.............................(1964): Al-Risala al-Thaniya lil Islam (The Second Message of
m), Omdurman.

-------------------------------(Undated): Tariq Muhammad, (The Path of Muhammad),
durman, 1st edition.

e, Marek (1991): "The Post-Gulf War Technological Armaments: Spiral-transcending
tary technology and its conversion for human needs." Paper prepared for the East Workshop
Conversion Research, Berlin. April 9-13, 1991, Norwegian Institute for Human Rights, Oslo.

International institute of Islamic Thought (19860: Islamiyat al-Ma'rifa, al-Mabadi al-'Ama,
at al-'Amal, al-Ingazat, (Islamic Knowledge, General Principles, Plans of Action, and
ievements), Washington, DC, in collaboration with Al-Dar al-Sudaniya lil Kotob, Khartoum.

urabi, Hassan (1984): Al-Islam wa Nizam al-Hukm fi al-Sudan, (Islam and The System of
in Islam), Papers of the 1st International Conference, op. cit.

-----------------(1984): Khitab al-Umma al-Sudaniya li Qul al-Milal al-Ukhra, (Address by the
anese Nation to All Other Sects), Khartoum University Press.

-----------------(1980): Tagdid Usul al-Fiqh al-Islami, (Renewing The Fundamental
ciples of Islamic Jurisprudence), Matboat al-Fikr, Khartoum, 1st edition.

ed Nations (1992): "An agenda for peace, preventive diplomacy, peace-making, and peace-
ing," Report of the Secretary General pursuant to the settlement adopted by the Summit
ting of the Security Council on 31 January 1992." In: African Journal of International &
parative Law, October 1992, Vol. 4 pt 3, p. 754.

INDEX OF SUBJECTS

A

'Abdallab Dynasty, 6

Africa, African, xiv, 24, 66, 71, 145, 241, 316, 326, South Africa, 66

Ahmediya, Ahmedism, 48, 97, 103, 123

Algeria, 316

American, peace initiative, 336, 338, 340

Ansar, 12, 18, 19, 58, 120, 326, *Ansar al-Sunna*, 252

Arabs, 2, 26, 241

Awliya, 9, *Awliya al-Umur*, 47

al-Azhar University, x, 22, 23

B

*Baqt (*agreement), 230

Baghdad, 6

Bait al-Mal, 19

Beja, 2, 71, 72

Britain, xiv, 18, 19

Brotherhood, Muslim, xi, v, 55, 57, 127, 144, 149, 177, 252, 265, 266, 267, 332, National Islamic Front (NIF), i, vii, xiii, 29, 161, 251, 254, military coup, 315, 322, 329, 332, 333, 334, 336, dictatorship (see Bashir, Turabi), 339, 340, 342, *Ansar Sunna*, 252, Republican, v, 88, 90 (see Taha)

C

Cairo, 15, 71

Caliph, 48, 55, 62, 63, Caliphate, 'Abbasite, 23

Capitalism, capitalist, 187, 270, 271, 272, 273, 276, 277, 278, 279, 283, 284, 285, 287, 288, 295, 297, 303, 306, 307, 312

Christianity, Christian, 21, 61, 71, 114, 196, 207, 211, 230, 240, 241, 242, 250, 257, 259, 326, kingdoms, 5, Copts, 230

Communism, communist, xv, 61, 71, 72, 79, 88, 89, 113, 114, 163, 255, 269, 293, 298, 299, 301

Cultural democratic renaissance (see Mahgoub, Sudan), 291, 294

D

Da'wa, iii, 3, 31,33, 58

DarFur, 179

Dhikhr, xii

diversity, 2, 122

E

Egypt, Egyptian, 15, 18, 19, 21, 22, 23, 25, 26, 41, 42, 48, 55, 71, 72, 113, 194, 198, 201, 226, 229, 230, 236, 316, 317, 333, 336, 338, Egyptian-Libyan Initiative, 338

Europe, European, xv, 42, 128, 136, 145, 242, 243

F

fatwaa, fatawi, 7, 47, 82

Feminism (see women's rights), 262, 264, 265, 266

al-Fiqh, 6, 30, 125

47, 50, 51, 53, 55, 56, 58, 59, 60, 61, 63, 65, 67, 70, 71, 72, 73, 76, 81, 82, 85, 87, 91, 93, 94, 98, 102, 104, 109, 116, 118, 136, 139, 141, 142, 147, 153, 189, 192, 193, 194, 195, 197, 198, 200, 206, 217, 225, 226, 231, 237, 238, Jurist (Grand), 93, (see *imam*)

K

Karari, 18

Khartoum, xvi, 48, 247, 339, 340, University of Khartoum, 57, 74, 139, 151, 173

Khatmiya, 12, 326

Khedive, 15, Mohamed Ali Viceroy of Egypt, 22

King Umberto of Italy, xiv, Sultan Decain of the Funj, 10, 26, John of Abyssinia, 12, Ottoman Sultanate, 7, 22

L

Libya, 316

M

Madzhab, Madzahib, 44, 59, 93, 118, 137, 171

Mahdist, ii, 14, 15, 20, 51, *Mahdiya,* 12, 14, 15, 17, 18, 19, 20, 26, 170, 171, 179

al-Maghrib, *6*

Maglis al-Shura, 16

Malamatiya, 9

Manjuluk, 6

al-Maraa, Sawt, ix, 139, 151

marisa, 251

Marxian, *Marxiya,* (see Marx), ii, v, 52, 75, 76, 77, 78, 79, 80, 87, 88, 89, 119, 122, 123, 128, 129, 184, 185, 186, 187, 188, 189, 190, 192, 203, 237

Mecca, *Meccan,* viii, 43, 125, 186, 188, 189, 191, 192, 199, 200, 203, 204, 211, 212, 216, 234

Meddina, 45, 49, 183, 185, 186, 188, 189, 190, 191, 192, 199, 200, 203, 204, 211, 212, 234

Mi'raj, 30, 78, 96, 101, 102, 103, 124

Mo'tazila, 23

Morocco, 226

Mua'malat, 93

Muhammadiya, Muhammedism (see Muhammad), 78, 97, 103, 123

Mujtahid, Mujtahideen, 59, 137

N

National Democratic Alliance (NDA), democratic opposition, 258, 331, 335, 336, committee of masses' mobilization, 337, national memorandums, resolutions, 338, 339, 340, 341, 342

National Democratic Front (see Mahgoub), 306

Nasserism, (see Nasser), 163, 177

Nilotics, 2

Nubians, 2, 230

O

Omdurman, 143, 150, 180, 247, *Suq al-Tawaqi* (see women), 247

Oriental life, 23

AFRICAN STUDIES